Before becoming a professional entertainer, songwriter, verse writer and singer in 1988, Jim Haynes taught writing, literature, history and drama in schools and universities from outback New South Wales to Britain and back again. While teaching he gained two masters degrees in literature, from New England University and the University of Wales (UK). Jim is the author of many great Australian titles including books on railways, the trucking industry, sea exploration, aviation and horse racing. He is one of our most successful and prolific Australiana authors.

THE BEST AUSTRALIAN BUSH STORIES

JIM HAYNES

ALLEN&UNWIN

SYDNEY·MELBOURNE·AUCKLAND·LONDON

THIS BOOK IS FOR FRANK 'JOE' DANIEL

Published by Allen & Unwin in 2013

Allen & Unwin
83 Alexander Street
Crows Nest NSW 2065
Australia
Phone: (61 2) 8425 0100
Fax: (61 2) 9906 2218
Email: info@allenandunwin.com
Web: www.allenandunwin.com

Cataloguing-in-Publication details are available
from the National Library of Australia
www.trove.nla.gov.au

ISBN 978 1 74331 439 5

Set in 12/15 pt Minion Pro by Bookhouse, Sydney
Printed and bound in Australia by Griffin Press

10 9 8

CONTENTS

PART 4   THERE'S A PATRON SAINT OF DRUNKS

PART 5   TO THE CITY

PART 6   BENEFIT OF CLERGY

ACKNOWLEDGMENTS

Thanks to Foong Ling Kong, Laura Mitchell, Katri Hilden and all at Allen and Unwin—and to Jackie Kent for guiding me to certain authors.

Thanks also to Frank Daniel, Manfred Vijars and the families of the late Grahame Fredrikson and Wilbur Howcroft.

INTRODUCTION

Australia's national character and spirit have always been defined, rightly or wrongly, by 'the bush'.

'The bush' can mean just about anything 'non-urban' in Australia—the remote outback, a cattle station, a wheat farm, a small selection, or a rural town of any size. Our iconic characters are invariably found living in, taking refuge in, or exploring, 'the bush'. The Aborigine, explorer, squatter, free selector, bushranger, pioneer and the tall bronzed laconic stockman—along with the country bumpkin out of place when away from 'the bush'—are the raw material for much of the popular literature of Australia from colonial times to the present.

Some of the stories in this collection were written over a century and a quarter ago, and some were written quite recently. The bulk of the stories, however, come from the period between 1890 and 1960, when the short story was a very popular form of writing.

A few of the stories in this collection are true 'short stories' in the 'literary' sense, while most are 'stories' in a more general sense. The majority represent the more common journalistic style favoured by *The Bulletin*—what the Europeans would call 'sketches' and the Americans 'pieces'. These were far more commonly found in *The Bulletin* than true short stories.

Lawson's more serious 'stories' are mostly sketches—vignettes and character sketches—while his humorous stories would be classed as 'pieces' in the more journalistic, American sense of the term.

Several of Edward Dyson's stories come close to the classic short story form, but perhaps the best examples are the stories by D'Arcy Niland and Ethel Mills.

During the era from which the majority of these stories come, 1890 to 1960, bush towns were prosperous little communities with a self-contained social structure. They were places where people worked, played sport, ran community organisations and shopped locally. Those were also the days before technology and the motor car changed small towns forever, leaving many of them almost deserted and others, nearer to larger centres, as mere dormitory towns. The workforce on farms and in small towns was reduced dramatically by technology and centralisation after World War II, and the 'good old days' of small town prosperity were gone by the 1960s.

Those seven or eight decades also happened to be the years in which *The Bulletin* was proudly carrying popular Australian writing to a huge readership.

The Bulletin was established by J.F. Archibald and John Haynes in 1880. Known as the 'Bushman's Bible', it introduced almost every Australian author of note to the reading public. It was hugely popular in the bush, as well as in the cities of Australia, and was widely read in all the colonies.

The Bulletin was an odd magazine. It was radical, racist, xenophobic, iconoclastic, anti-British and at times vehemently conservative. Although its editorial stance varied over its 128-year history, it can be best described, I think, in the same way that one of its greatest discoveries, Joseph Furphy, described himself— 'offensively Australian'.

I believe that *The Bulletin* actually played a major role in establishing our nation. Australia was a continent housing six British colonies beset by rivalry and self-interest when *The Bulletin* was founded in 1880. By 1900 the population had voted 400,000 to 160,000 to federate. I believe *The Bulletin*, and the works of the authors it had discovered and let loose on the Australian colonial public, gave the population a sense of being 'Australian' rather than just being citizens of various British colonies.

The importance of *The Bulletin* to our literary heritage simply cannot be overestimated. Its founder and editor, J.F. Archibald, and A.G. Stephens, the magazine's literary editor from 1894 to 1906, virtually established the Australian literary 'scene' by finding, publishing and encouraging writers like Banjo Paterson, Henry Lawson, Joseph Furphy, Mary Gilmore, Miles Franklin, Steele Rudd, Edward Dyson, Charles Souter, Victor Daley, C.J. Dennis, Vance Palmer, Will Ogilvie, Harry 'Breaker' Morant, 'John O'Brien' and Gavin Casey.

Stephens established the famous 'Red Page' of literary reviews, news and gossip in 1896, and eventually the poet and essayist Douglas Stewart edited that section of the bulletin from 1940 until 1961.

It would be easier to list the authors and poets represented in this collection who were *never* published in *The Bulletin* than to list those who were. For the record, however, those who were '*Bulletin* writers', apart from those listed above, include Ernest Favenc, 'Ah Chee', Henry Fletcher, Ethel Mills, J.J. Poynton, Alexander Allen, D'Arcy Niland, Brian James, E.O. Schlunke, Jack Sorensen, Adam McCay, 'Jim Grahame' and Frank Dalby Davison, who also published his short stories in a magazine, the *Australian*, which was owned by his father.

Of course, not all the authors represented here were *Bulletin* writers. Ethel ('Henry Handel') Richardson established her literary career while living in Germany and Britain, and Mark Twain was probably the world's best-known author when he visited Australia in 1890.

None of Kenneth Cook's stories ever appeared in *The Bulletin*, which had changed its focus by the time he was writing. Some of his stories first appeared in *People* magazine, but many of them were published for the first time in the three volumes of collected stories edited by his second wife, Jacqueline Kent.

The Bulletin had long ceased to be a magazine that solicited short stories when ABC Books published my first collection of stories in 1999, while Frank Daniel's stories and yarns have previously only appeared in amongst his verse in several self-published collections.

The nine parts in this collection really evolved from the stories themselves as I read and re-read them. Once I had a few ideas about which stories would sit well together, the stories sorted themselves into the various sections.

I am fascinated by the different attitudes and angles authors take to various subjects, and the same subjects kept cropping up, which made it easy to sort the stories into sections and to establish what it is about 'the bush' that has always fascinated Australian writers.

Jim Haynes
2013

Part 1

DELIGHTS OF
THE BUSH

Written with tongue firmly placed in cheek, 'The Delights of the Bush', by that mysterious *Bulletin* writer of the 1890s 'Ah Chee', sets the tone for this collection of humorous tales about the vagaries, annoyances, struggles and indignities of bush life.

The vitriol is always sugar-coated with humour—to varying degrees. Mark Twain could find the comic element in most situations and in any character. In his yarn about a young cleric's verbal attack on the Maryborough Hotel, he was able to craft a conversation in a train into a humorous character study.

Frank Daniel takes a simple childhood memory and creates a story which verges on Keystone Cops slapstick in 'The Tallagandra Turkey', while Kenneth Cook takes situation comedy and exaggeration to another level in 'The Killer Koala' and 'The Drunken Kangaroo'.

Kenneth Cook had a gift for writing brilliantly about encounters with various creatures, and always managed to capture the sense of fear many of us feel when we find ourselves 'one on one' with another species.

It takes the zany word play of Lennie Lower, however, to push the boundaries of prose into sheer, and hilarious, nonsense. A writer way ahead of his time, Lennie Lower also, sadly, died before his time, at the age of just 44, in 1947.

'MALLEE MORNING'

WILBUR HOWCROFT

Bright early in the mornin',
The dawn a-showin' red,
I levers up me eyelids
An' blunders outa bed.

I lights me up a gasper
Then moseys out ter see
What palpitatin' prospects
Fate has in store fer me.

There's maggots in the meat safe,
The rain tank's sprung a leak
An' damn me if the cart horse
Ain't bogged down in the creek.

Me old dog's got the staggers
An' whimpers as in pain,
The wheat crop's slowly dyin'
Through want o' ruddy rain.

The crows are at the chickens,
A water pipe 'as bust
While headin' hell fer leather
I spots a wall o' dust.

The sheep are in the haystack,
The milkin' cow is dead—
I shoves aside the missus
An' climbs back inter bed.

THE KILLER KOALA

KENNETH COOK

I DO NOT LIKE koalas. They are nasty, cross, stupid creatures without a friendly bone in their bodies. Their social habits are appalling—the males are always beating their fellows up and stealing their females. They have disgusting defensive mechanisms. Lice infest their fur. They snore. Their resemblance to cuddly toys is a base deceit. There is nothing to commend them.

On top of all that, a koala once tried to do me a very nasty mischief.

A small island named Kudulana about ten kilometres off the coast of Tasmania used to maintain a large population of koalas. Then somebody introduced sheep to the island, cleared too many trees, and suddenly there weren't enough of the right sort of gum leaves and the koalas were in danger of dying out.

A National Parks and Wildlife field officer named Mary Anne Locher was appointed to the task of rounding up the koalas and shipping them to greener pastures on the mainland. She invited me to help her, and on the grounds that there is a story in everything, I accepted.

Mary Anne Locher was rather like a koala herself in appearance. She was short, fat and round and had fluffy brown hair which she wore quite short, and her ears stuck out through it. I suppose she was about fifty at the time, a little older than I.

She always wore brown overalls and these, aided by the effect of her button nose and bright brown eyes, increased her similarity to a koala. Her voice was soft and slightly sibilant and she gave the impression that if you poked her tummy she would squeak. Unlike a koala, she was very pleasant and gentle.

At that stage I was not as corpulent as I am now, but nevertheless I was a well-fleshed man. That is to say, I could tie up my own shoelaces without much difficulty, but I was not athletic.

The unkind might have thought that Mary Anne and I were a slightly comical-looking pair as we left the ferry at Kudulana, one tall and round and bearded, the other short and round and fluffy-haired, each carrying a large, long-handled net and wearing identical brown overalls, for I had borrowed a departmental pair to wear on the job. As the ferry driver unloaded the wooden-slatted cages that were to hold our catch, he went so far as to suggest that our task would be made easy because the koalas would fall out of the trees laughing.

To catch a koala, all you do is startle it so that it jumps or falls off its branch, and then you entrap it in your net. At any rate that's what Mary Anne told me. She didn't mention that it only works with cooperative koalas.

We stacked our gear, camping equipment, medical kit and the cages near the wharf and went koala hunting.

The trees on Kudulana are all very small and spindly and we had no trouble locating the koalas. There were only twelve, and they were in a grove of eucalypts around a large deep pool surrounded by ferns. They were all nestled in forked branches at the tops of the trees. But the trees were only three or four metres high, so the koalas were well within reach of our long-handled nets.

All Mary Anne and I had to do was get them loose, catch them in our nets, then transfer them to the wooden-slatted cages. In theory.

The koalas, furry balls with their heads tucked into their stomachs, didn't seem remotely interested in our presence.

'OK, we'll try that fellow first,' said Mary Anne briskly, pointing to a largish koala nestling in a fork not much higher than I could reach. 'You frighten him and I'll catch him.'

She raised her net so that the mouth was just under the koala and stood poised, waiting to see which way the koala would jump. I held my net ready as a backup.

The koala seemed to be asleep, and I wondered for the first time just how one went about startling such a lethargic creature.

'Should I poke it with my net?' I asked Mary Anne.

'No, that'll just make it hang on. Shout.'

I had no idea in what terms one shouted at koalas, but I did my best.

'Boo!' I cried.

The koala didn't stir.

'Boo! Boo!' I shouted, as loudly as I could.

The koala opened one eye. Surprisingly, it was bloodshot. It looked at me for a long level moment, then wearily closed its eye again.

'It doesn't startle easily,' I said.

'No,' said Mary Anne. 'Try shaking the tree.'

I laid down my net, grasped the tree which was very slender, no more than a sapling, really—and shook it violently.

The koala opened both its red-rimmed eyes and looked down on me malevolently. Then it applied a defensive device common to most arboreal marsupials. My hair, beard, face and shoulders were drenched with foully acrid fluid.

'Oh, sorry,' said Mary Anne, 'I should have warned you about that.'

I did my best with a handkerchief while the koala, apparently satisfied with its work, closed its eyes and went back to sleep.

'Why don't we push the bloody thing off the branch with our nets and catch it on the ground?' I said when I was more or less dry, but still smelling vile.

'You can't dislodge a koala once it's got a hold on something. They've got a grip of iron.'

'Well, what are we going to do? Nothing short of a bomb is going to startle that creature.'

Mary Anne thought. 'Could you climb that tree?'

I looked at the tree. It wasn't very big, but it would hold my weight and the koala wasn't far up.

'Yes,' I said, 'I think so.'

'Then go up and shout in its ear. Don't touch it. It'll probably jump when you get near.'

With considerable effort I hauled myself to the base of the branch in which the koala was snuggling. I wasn't much more than my own height above the ground, and I could have reached out and touched the koala, which was not far from my head. I kept my head carefully away from the little beast.

'Boo!' I shouted.

The koala took no notice. I edged closer along the branch.

The branch broke. Branch, koala and I dropped abruptly into the thick ferns below.

The koala landed on its back. I landed spread-eagled on the koala. The koala was out of sight beneath my considerable bulk, but I knew it was there because it was growling and snorting and trying to dig its way to freedom through my yielding flesh.

It was an extraordinary experience down in those ferns, winded, able to see nothing but fern fronds, half-stunned so that I couldn't coordinate myself, with that hard-muscled, surprisingly large fur-covered length of malevolence trying to disembowel me.

Where the hell was Mary Anne?

In fact she was running around to the other side of the patch of ferns to catch the koala when it came out.

Now, koalas have another protective device, apart from the one they use on you from a great height. They cling to the belly of their oppressor and simply hang on with tooth and claw. It's a mechanism probably designed to work on dingoes. Once the koala is clinging to the dog's underside, the dog can't get at it with its jaws. I gather that in these circumstances the koala is quite prepared to hang on until the dingo collapses.

I didn't know this at the time. It wouldn't have helped if I had.

The koala evidently gave up all hope of escape and decided on the anti-dingo defence. It was upside down in relation to me and its back claws grasped my chest and dug in. Its front claws grasped my thighs and dug in. Its head went between my legs and its teeth dug into my crotch.

Fortunately a koala's mouth isn't very big. But it's big enough.

I screamed.

'What's happened?' called Mary Anne, out of sight.

'It's got me!' I bellowed, rolling over on my back and clawing at the koala with both hands. It rolled with me and clamped its hold tighter—all its holds.

I screamed again and started pummelling the brute with my fists. It was like pummelling fur-covered wood and made as much impression. The thing had muscles fashioned from some substance far harder than any animal tissue ought to be.

Again I screamed and I could hear Mary Anne crashing through the ferns towards me.

The koala, presumably thinking I had reinforcements coming, gripped harder still at all points.

It was growling like something demented, which it was, of course, and its backside was almost in my face—even my peril in no way diminished the frightful stench of the creature.

Mary Anne's head came in sight over the ferns. I was thrashing and clawing in a tangle of fern fronds and she couldn't see exactly what was going on beyond the fact that I had the koala and the koala had me.

'Careful you don't hurt it,' she called. I would have laughed in different circumstances.

'Get it off!' I gasped.

'Never get him off now,' she said vexedly, 'I'll have to sedate him.' And the bloody woman trotted off to the wharf to get her medical kit.

'Won't be a minute,' I heard her call as she disappeared through the ferns. 'Just lie still—don't worry, he won't let go now.'

That wasn't my worry at all. 'Mary Anne!' I roared, 'The brute has got me by the . . .' but she didn't hear me.

There was no way I could lie there until she came back, with that creature vigorously trying to desex me.

I struggled to my feet complete with koala and tried to run after her.

Ever tried to run with a koala's claws in your chest and thighs and its teeth in your crotch? It's not possible.

I was very close to tears of rage, pain and frustration. I floundered through the ferns and tried barging into a tree, koala first.

All I did was drive tooth and claw further in. I tried falling on the damned thing. I winded myself.

On all fours now and near collapse, my disintegrating mind suddenly grasped the fact that I was on the edge of a pool in the centre of the koala-haunted grove of trees.

With a manic cry of hope I scuttled forward, took a deep breath and flung myself in, complete with koala.

The water was blessedly deep and we went down like stones.

I didn't know how long a koala could hold its breath but as far as I was concerned we were both staying down until the koala let go or we both drowned.

Unfortunately, it seems that koalas can hold their breath indefinitely.

The koala was a dead weight holding me down and we stayed in those brown dark depths for what seemed like half an eternity. The pain in my bursting lungs began to equal my other pains.

Eventually, I realised that there was no need for me to have my head under water. It may seem I was slow in reaching an obvious conclusion but if you've never been submerged in a bush pool in the clutches of a furious koala, you can't appreciate how difficult it is to think clearly in the circumstances.

I struck for the surface, got my head out, breathed deeply and gratefully and set about trying to throttle the koala.

Koalas are very hard to throttle, particularly when they have the sort of grip on you this one had on me. But I tried hard, completely disregarding the fact that it was a member of a protected species.

The koala seemed determined to die under water with my fingers around its neck. That was all right by me, as long as it died quickly.

Then, even through my pain, I had the terrible worry that a dead koala might not loosen its grip. Would I need surgery to detach me from this malign beast?

Then the beast gave up—a good twenty minutes, I swear, after it was first submerged, although Mary Anne has claimed she was away less than a minute. Time is, of course, relative.

The koala let go and surfaced near my face. Its toy features were expressionless, but it coughed and growled viciously and I backed away fearfully.

A gleam of contempt seemed to appear in its bloodshot eyes and it turned and swam expertly to the edge of the pool, clambered out, trundled across to a tree, climbed it, looked down at me bleakly, and went to sleep, dripping water.

I climbed out of the pool.

Mary Anne came back and expressed surprise that the koala had let go and asked why I was all wet.

I said I would explain later and went off into the bush to examine my person.

The overalls I was wearing were of very thick cloth and no serious damage had been done. No thanks to the koala.

Mary Anne and I eventually caught all the koalas on the island and set them free on the mainland, but I didn't carry out the task with good grace. I'll never go to the aid of the brutes again.

I do not like koalas.

THE DELIGHTS OF
THE BUSH

'AH CHEE'

AMONG A CERTAIN CLASS of fatuous writers there has always existed a custom of sending forth gushes of gladsome song, and warbling, in more or less tuneful warbs, about the pleasures of country life.

The miserable wretch who is condemned by hard fate to live in the city, with all its inconveniences (such as postal deliveries, newspapers, shops and trams), is held up to the gaze of public sympathy; while all are requested to envy the lucky individual whose habitation is in the backwoods, about 387 miles from nowhere in particular, who lives in a humpy made of several sheets of stringybark, with three big rocks on top to hold on the roof, and who has to walk seven miles for his mail.

When he does walk the seven miles he usually finds there is no mail, as the mailman couldn't cross the Buggabulla 'crick'. Or has lost his horse, or is drunk, or something.

It is time that some hard-fisted resident of the back country formed himself into a Royal Commission to inquire into the best mode of inflicting capital punishment, diversified with floggings, on the perjurers who so wantonly trifle with the immortal truth.

If a ton or two of these miscreants were placed in the hands of a conscientious forwarding agent, and dumped down in judiciously chosen spots in the back-blocks where they would have to chop wood, and cook damper, and boil junk, and 'graft' hard all day, and walk to the township for provisions, and do without society

12

and clean shirts and socks, the amount of imbecile verse on the glorious lot of the bush dweller would be reduced by several cubic yards.

I know it—I have lived in the bush till the light of my once beauteous hazel eyes has become dimmed with suffering, and the noble chestnut curls that once adorned my commanding brow have vanished into thin hair.

And when something does occur that momentarily lifts a man from the black gulf of despondency into which he has sunk, it is morally certain that something else will occur which has the effect of making him feel much the same as ever.

Here is an illustration.

One of the many afflictions which I bear (with as large a quantity of fortitude as is possible for one who, after all, is but human) is the nightly visitation of numerous bovines of inquiring character and assorted sexes.

My hut is not fenced in; indeed it would make little difference if it were, for, when the average bush cow means business, such a trifle as a fence does not daunt her. So, about the time I am snugly settled in my bunk, and have knocked the ashes out of my last pipe, some robust young steer begins to paw up the dirt outside with sickening thuds, preparatory to organising a party to prospect for soap, or towels, or shirts, or similar delicacies.

Pretty soon his comrades, and the milky mothers of the herd, and the little cowlets, and eleven of eight working bullocks, chip in. They eat up any soap that is left about, also saddlecloths and undershirts and pyjamas and socks. Then they 'moo'. Singly at first, then as a number of duettists, afterwards in trios, and eventually their fresh young voices ring out in the frosty atmosphere as a full orchestral symphony.

Sometimes they go away after this, but mostly they stay till daylight.

One night I arose in my wrath, and a brief nightshirt, and hunted them all away, through a very irritating wattle scrub, for about two miles and a distance. When I returned, covered with splinters and perspiration, I found that I had overlooked two brindled steers and their ma. They were inside the hut chewing my blankets.

What is the use of a man forming a resolution not to swear?

The exertion of pursuit and the subsequent wrath did not agree with me. I took a chill and later contracted inflammation of the lungs, combined with two large abscesses on the liver and a rupture of the bicuspid artery.

I also stubbed my big toe while pursuing the oxen.

Prompt remedial measures were necessary, so I made a warm mustard-plaster and applied it to the ailing parts. Next day I threw it out. It seemed to excite some interest among the leading members of the herd which visited me at sundown. A meditative, matronly-looking old cow elbowed one of her daughters out of the way and tackled the poultice in a sort of *nil admirari* manner. She got a good grip and laid it well back on her tongue. Then the poultice began to get its work in.

The female ox laid it down, sighed deeply, and went away to look for sour grass.

The next candidate was a red steer that I had once helped to pull out of a shaft. On that occasion he had put down his head and charged his rescuers as soon as he emerged. He opened the poultice out before sampling it, and then got about seven ounces of the mustard well under his tongue before his suspicions were aroused. Then he retired to the creek, breathing hard.

I thought I had hit on a splendid idea. Visions of taking out a patent for the invention, and getting about £10,000 royalty from the Agricultural Bureau, flashed through my mind. I was positively exhilarated! For the first time in thirteen months I smiled! The thought that I had at last got level with those piratical beeves had a truly wonderful effect on my sorrow-laden bosom.

For five minutes I was ecstatically happy.

Then one of my most constant interviewers came along. His name is Strawberry, and he is a working bullock. 'Working' is a courtesy title, given to Strawberry because he is yoked up with the team, but it has no real significance, for Strawberry has long abandoned any idea of actually pulling. He is a gaunt male beast, and is scored with ancient whip marks, so that he looks like a railway map. His favourite food is gunny bags, but he will also eat tarpaulins and bridles.

Strawberry ambled up, with a modest confidence oozing out of every square inch of his hide. He swallowed the poultice without a tear. In fact, he lingered over it as if he loved it, and I saw him chewing the cud of that mustard-plaster three weeks afterwards.

When I get over this spree, I will try the effect on Strawberry of arsenious acid spread on dynamite.

THE TALLAGANDRA TURKEY

FRANK DANIEL

WE WERE VISITING UNCLE Roy's farm at Tallagandra, near Gundaroo. It was sometime around 1951.

As was usual in those days, the folks went inside the big old house and left us kids outside with the standard message, which was 'don't get into any mischief'.

I had already seen plenty of opportunities for mischief that I could get into.

Uncle's farm always had so many extra things on offer in the way of 'entertainment value'. Horse-drawn vehicles and farm equipment scattered about the farm and in the sheds offered plenty of scope for 'imagining'.

The last warning given us as we watched and waited for the folk to go inside, however, was from Uncle himself.

He said, 'Stay away from that flaming gobbler or I'll give youse a kick in the pants!'

Gobbler!

What gobbler? Where's the gobbler?

Quick, let's find the gobbler! What could be wrong, or right, or interesting or dangerous, for that matter, with an ordinary old gobbler?

Colin, our cousin, was about our age, and was used to doing what he was told. He knew what a kick in the pants from Uncle

Roy was and was not as eager as Jim and I were to find the turkey that was supposed to be worth a good kick in the pants.

'What's wrong with him?' we asked our cousin.

'What does he do?'

'Is he cranky?'

'Is he mean?'

'Why can't we go near him?'

'Because he'll chase ya! He hates kids!' said Colin.

'Good! Let's find him and have a look!'

'Where is he?' asked Jim.

'He's locked in the back garden so he can't get us,' warned Colin.

Behind the old Tallagandra Homestead was an orderly vegetable garden set out in neat rows and paths.

There was no sign of the gobbler as we walked along outside the garden fence.

It was deemed necessary by Jim and me, although it was against our cousin's wishes, to climb the fence and make a more positive search.

What harm could a gobbler do? Besides, there were three of us and only one of him. He wouldn't stand a chance.

The garden stretched out across the yard behind the house. There were a number of fruit trees along one side and the back verandah of the house was on the other side. There was a large pepper tree at one end and a dairy at the opposite end.

The dairy was a concrete building, square in shape and fairly tall with a pair of galvanised iron water tanks on top. The water was pumped into the tanks from an underground tank and a nearby well. This was the water supply for the house.

The lower part of the dairy was in fact two rooms. One room, known as the 'meat house', was where the carcasses of beef and hogget were hung, after being slaughtered on the property. The other room was the separating room, where the milk from each morning's milking was separated and the cream was churned into butter. For some unknown reason it was serviced by two doors on opposing walls, each leading to and from the garden. It was the coldest room on the farm.

Once inside the yard, it was no trouble to find the turkey. He was in the shade beneath the peppercorn tree, his back towards us. His head was turned back over his shoulder, giving us the eye.

'There's nothing wrong with him!' said Jim. 'What's wrong with him? What does he do?'

'He chases ya,' said Colin.

'Well what makes him chase ya?' asked Jim.

'Flick a rock at him! You'll see!'

So Jim, the hero, picked up a white quartz pebble from the garden path and in true marbles fashion, fudged it in the direction of the gobbler. No results. He tried a couple more times.

'He won't hurt ya!' gloated Jim.

We each gathered up some white quartz stones, 'cemetery stones' we used to call them, and we all flicked and fudged and fumbled stones in the direction of the turkey.

As brave as we were we didn't get too close, so our 'marbles' shots were none too accurate.

The big bird only stared and waited.

Jim turned his back on the target and announced that it was a waste of time and that we should find something else to do. We agreed and turned to go.

It was at that very moment that we heard a very loud and frightening hiss from the gobbler!

We hardly had time to look back.

'He's coming!' cried Colin. 'Let's get out of here!'

Three pairs of skinny legs went bolting up the garden path before he'd finished speaking.

The three of us bolted in the direction of the dairy, Jim and Colin out front and me not very far behind.

A quick look over my shoulder, as a measure of safety, revealed the gobbler in pursuit, his wings outstretched downwards towards the ground making a sound like heavy boards dragging on the gravel path. His body was fully stretched out with his breast low to the ground and he looked enormous. He was hissing and was making a lot of noise, really going crook.

I didn't get a look at his eyes in that frightening fleeting moment, but I could tell that he meant business.

'Go round the dairy!' shouted Colin, 'Go round the dairy!'

Around the dairy we went full pelt. Then we turned back towards the peppercorn tree as fast as we could.

Fright now gave my old blucher boots a new turn of speed and racing up between the house and the rows of cabbages I managed to overtake my cousin. Jim made a right-hand turn at the spinach and we followed. Up to the apricot tree and round to the right again we raced in procession—Jim, me, Colin and the turkey.

'Go through the dairy!' shouted Colin. 'Go through the dairy!'

We did. At a hundred miles an hour! In one door and out the other! The crazy gobbler was still running fourth but was not too far behind.

Again we followed the same path around behind the house. Once again we turned right at the spinach and made another right turn at the apricot tree. We were fairly blowing by this time and Colin was still shouting advice.

'Go through the dairy—go through the dairy.'

It must have been in all our minds that we were travelling too fast to risk scaling the fence. Any slip was death! So, it was do as we were told, and back through the dairy we went.

As Jim and I entered the first door of the building, our cousin, who was now some yards further behind, shouted further advice.

'Out the other side and shut the door . . . shut the door . . . shut the door!'

He sounded like he was getting further behind.

Always ones to heed good advice in a tight situation, we shut the door, and locked Colin inside with the turkey.

There was a terrible commotion.

Uncle Roy quickly arrived on the scene and smartly rescued his youngster.

What a row it was that followed.

I'm not too sure exactly *what* happened after that, however, as I was too far from the house. All I could hear was them calling after me.

It was a long hot day sitting on the strainer post at the front gate from where I could keep an eye on our car 'til my folks were ready to go home.

Perhaps they could see me too, but nobody bothered to come and get me for dinner.

I missed out on my favourite too, baked dinner; and watermelon, of which Jim had two slices.

Maybe it would have been worth a good kick in the pants.

Fancy missing out on two slices of watermelon!

THE HOTEL IN MARYBOROUGH

MARK TWAIN
(EXCERPT FROM *FOLLOWING THE EQUATOR*)

SOMEWHERE ON THE WAY to Maryborough I changed for a while to a smoking-carriage. There were two gentlemen there; both riding backward, one at each end of the compartment. They were acquaintances of each other. I sat down facing the one that sat at the starboard window. He had a good face, and a friendly look, and I judged from his dress that he was a dissenting minister. He was along toward fifty. Of his own motion he struck a match, and shaded it with his hand for me to light my cigar. I take the rest from my diary:

In order to start conversation I asked him something about Maryborough. He said, in a most pleasant—even musical voice, but with quiet and cultured decision:

'It's a charming town, with a hell of a hotel.'

I was astonished. It seemed so odd to hear a minister swear out loud. He went placidly on:

'It's the worst hotel in Australia. Well, one may go further, and say in Australasia.'

'Bad beds?'

'No, none at all. Just sand-bags.'

'The pillows, too?'

'Yes, the pillows, too. Just sand. And not a good quality of sand. It packs too hard, and has never been screened. There is too much gravel in it. It is like sleeping on nuts.'

'Isn't there any good sand?'

'Plenty of it. There is as good bed-sand in this region as the world can furnish. Aerated sand—and loose; but they won't buy it. They want something that will pack solid, and petrify.'

'How are the rooms?'

'Eight feet square; and a sheet of iced oil-cloth to step on in the morning when you get out of the sand-quarry.'

'As to lights?'

'Coal-oil lamp.'

'A good one?'

'No. It's the kind that sheds a gloom.'

'I like a lamp that burns all night.'

'This one won't. You must blow it out early.'

'That is bad. One might want it again in the night. Can't find it in the dark.'

'There's no trouble; you can find it by the stench.'

'Wardrobe?'

'Two nails on the door to hang seven suits of clothes on if you've got them.'

'Bells?'

'There aren't any.'

'What do you do when you want service?'

'Shout. But it won't fetch anybody.'

'Suppose you want the chambermaid to empty the slop-jar?'

'There isn't any slop-jar. The hotels don't keep them. That is, outside of Sydney and Melbourne.'

'Yes, I knew that. I was only talking. It's the oddest thing in Australia. Another thing: I've got to get up in the dark, in the morning, to take the five o'clock train. Now if the boots—'

'There isn't any.'

'Well, the porter.'

'There isn't any.'

'But who will call me?'

'Nobody. You'll call yourself. And you'll light yourself, too. There'll not be a light burning in the halls or anywhere. And if you don't carry a light, you'll break your neck.'

'But who will help me down with my baggage?'

'Nobody. However, I will tell you what to do. In Maryborough there's an American who has lived there half a lifetime; a fine man, and prosperous and popular. He will be on the lookout for you; you won't have any trouble. Sleep in peace; he will rout you out, and you will make your train. Where is your manager?'

'I left him at Ballarat, studying the language. And besides, he had to go to Melbourne and get us ready for New Zealand. I've not tried to pilot myself before, and it doesn't look easy.'

'Easy! You've selected the very most difficult piece of railroad in Australia for your experiment. There are twelve miles of this road which no man without good executive ability can ever hope—tell me, have you good executive ability? First-rate executive ability?'

'I—well, I think so, but—'

'That settles it. The tone of—oh, you wouldn't ever make it in the world. However, that American will point you right, and you'll go. You've got tickets?'

'Yes—round trip; all the way to Sydney.'

'Ah, there it is, you see! You are going in the five o'clock by Castlemaine—twelve miles—instead of the seven-fifteen by Ballarat—in order to save two hours of fooling along the way. Now then, don't interrupt—let me have the floor. You're going to save the government a deal of hauling, but that's nothing; your ticket is by Ballarat, and it isn't good over that twelve miles, and so—'

'But why should the government care which way I go?'

'Goodness knows! Ask of the winds that far away with fragments strewed the sea, as the boy that stood on the burning deck used to say. The government chooses to do its railway business in its own way, and it doesn't know as much about it as the French. In the beginning they tried idiots; then they imported the French—which was going backwards, you see; now it runs the railways itself—which is going backwards again, you see. Why, do you know, in order to curry favour with the voters, the government puts down a track wherever anybody wants it, anybody that owns two sheep and a dog; and by consequence we've got, in the colony of Victoria, 800 railway stations, and the business done at eighty of them doesn't foot up twenty shillings a week.'

'Five dollars? Oh, come!'

'It's true. It's the absolute truth.'

'Why, there are three or four men on wages at every station.'

'I know it. And the station-business doesn't pay for the sheep-dip to sanctify their coffee with. It's just as I say. And accommodating? Why, if you shake a rag the train will stop in the midst of the wilderness to pick you up. All that kind of politics costs, you see. And then, besides, any town that has a good many votes and wants a fine station, gets it.

'Don't you overlook that Maryborough station, if you take an interest in governmental curiosities. Why, you can put the whole population of Maryborough into it, and give them a sofa apiece, and have room for more. You haven't fifteen stations in America that are as big, and you probably haven't five that are half as fine. Why, it's perfectly elegant. And the clock! Everybody will show you the clock. There isn't a station in Europe that's got such a clock. It doesn't strike—and that's one mercy. It hasn't any bell; and as you'll have cause to remember, if you keep your reason, all Australia is simply bedamned with bells.

'On every quarter-hour, night and day, they jingle a tiresome chime of half a dozen notes—all the clocks in town at once, all the clocks in Australasia at once, and all the very same notes; first, downward scale: mi, re, do, sol—then upward scale: sol, si, re, do—down again: mi, re, do, sol—up again: sol, si, re, do. Then the clock—say at midnight clang–clang–clang–clang–clang–clang– clang–clang–clang–clang—and, by that time you're . . . hello, what's all this excitement about?

'Oh I see, a runaway, scared by the train; why, you wouldn't think this train could scare anything. Well, of course, when they build and run eighty stations at a loss and a lot of palace-stations and clocks like Maryborough's at another loss, the government has got to economise somewhere hasn't it?

'Very well, look at the rolling stock. That's where they save the money. Why, that train from Maryborough will consist of eighteen freight-cars and two passenger-kennels; cheap, poor, shabby, slovenly; no drinking water, no sanitary arrangements, every imaginable inconvenience; and slow? Oh, the gait of cold molasses; no air-brake, no springs, and they'll jolt your head off every time they start or stop.

'That's where they make their little economies, you see. They spend tons of money to house you palatially while you wait fifteen minutes for a train, then degrade you to six hours' convict-transportation to get the foolish outlay back. What a rational man really needs is discomfort while he's waiting, then his journey in a nice train would be a grateful change. But no, that would be common sense—and out of place in a government. And then, besides, they save in that other little detail, you know—repudiate their own tickets, and collect a poor little illegitimate extra shilling out of you for that twelve miles, and . . .'

'Well, in any case . . .'

'Wait, there's more. Leave that American out of the account and see what would happen. There's nobody on hand to examine your ticket when you arrive. But the conductor will come and examine it when the train is ready to start. It is too late to buy your extra ticket now; the train can't wait, and won't. You must climb out.'

'But can't I pay the conductor?'

'No, he is not authorised to receive the money, and he won't. You must climb out. There's no other way. I tell you, the railway management is about the only thoroughly European thing here. Continentally European I mean, not English. It's the continental business in perfection; down fine. Oh, yes, even to the peanut-commerce of weighing baggage.'

The train slowed up at his place. As he stepped out he said:

'Yes, you'll like Maryborough. Plenty of intelligence there. It's a charming place, with a hell of a hotel.'

Then he was gone. I turned to the other gentleman:

'Is your friend in the ministry?'

'No—studying for it.'

DOWN AMONG THE WOMBATS

LENNIE LOWER

PEOPLE WHO THINK THERE are no more thrills to be had in our wide-open spaces have not heard anything. Why, only the other day a man was attacked by a six-foot kangaroo in the bush near Corinda, and fought with it for ten minutes.

I have had similar experiences with wombats. Not dingbats—wombats!

While camped on the edge of a small nullah-nullah or waterhole I was startled by a loud roar. With true bushman's instinct I fell into the waterhole, and, on looking around, observed a huge wombat devouring one of my dogs. From tip to tip its antlers were about eight feet across.

My rifle was on the bank, and I had broken my sheath-knife off at the hilt trying to cut a damper I had made. I knew I was safe so long as I stayed up to my neck in the water. Unfortunately I had not foreseen the cunning of this wombat.

Stamping its feet with rage, it approached the edge of the waterhole and commenced to drink. Rapidly the water level went down, from my neck to my armpits, then down to my waist.

Every now and then it would pause and glare at me with its little red eyes. This gave me an idea. Next time it glared at me I glared back at it. This seemed to disconcert the beast and it looked away and hiccuped.

It resumed drinking after a while but without any great enthusiasm.

The water was down to my ankles when the wombat gave me one last pitiful, frustrated look and rolled over on its side—full.

I splashed towards it. 'Come on now,' I said, 'pull yourself together. I'll get you a taxi. Where do you live?'

(This, of course, was sheer force of habit.)

'Brr-hup! Groo,' he answered.

'Don't give in to it,' I said. 'Do you think you can walk? Lean against me. That's the way.'

Well, it was just the sort of thing you would do for anybody, but you wouldn't believe how grateful that wombat was when next I met it. Of course, things don't always work out that way. I could never get on with goannas—or iguanas, as you city folk say. They have a nasty habit of turning up at the wrong time. This would not be so bad if it were not for their penchant for climbing up trees.

I recall the time I was leaning against a gum tree talking to the squatter's daughter. We were getting along famously, and I had even got to the point of shyly asking her what she thought about the price of fat lambs at the saleyards.

I could see the faint glow in her cheeks, her dewy, downcast eyes and tremulous lips as she replied, 'You really want to know? You are not one of those . . . those men who, oh you wouldn't understand.'

It was then that the goanna missed his footing and fell down the back of my shirt. If I had been wearing a belt all might have been well, but as I was wearing braces the thing went right down my left trouser leg. Its beady eyes looked out from just above my left boot and its tail waved frantically about the back of my neck.

'Are you in the habit of indulging in this horseplay?' she asked in icy tones. All the spirit of her ancestors—both of them—was in that steely glance.

I tried to explain. 'You see,' I said. 'I'm wearing braces . . .'

'I see,' she said haughtily, 'you usually keep your trousers up by sheer willpower, I suppose?'

I wanted to tell her that if I had been wearing a belt the goanna wouldn't have gone all the way down. But she spurned me. She wheeled her horse with a look of utter loathing and gave it a slash with the whip. Surprised and indignant, the horse leapt in the air and the squatter's daughter landed on a hard portion of one of her father's many acres of grazing property.

'Serves you right,' I said.

Chivalry did not permit me to laugh out loud, so I contented myself with a quiet smile.

'Are you in the habit of indulging in this sort of horseplay?' I drawled.

Then we walked away—me and the goanna.

But for that goanna I might now have been the squatter's son-in-law, pushing sheep about the place and picking the flies out of my ears, with a trip to the city once a year when the Show was on.

No, one doesn't have to go abroad for thrills. In one day on an outback station I was—

a)   Kicked by a horse.
b)   Chased by a bull.
c)   Savaged by a dog.
d)   Lacerated on a barbed-wire fence.

Also, in some mysterious fashion, I managed to put the lighting plant out of action.

You can't tell me anything about bush life. I am fully qualified to put an advertisement on the 'positions wanted' column containing the words, 'Do anything. Go anywhere.'

Address all communications to 'Lantana W. (Wallaby) Lower'.

I am equally good as a horse-breaker, tutor, or native companion.

THE DRUNKEN KANGAROO

KENNETH COOK

My DEEP FEAR OF all Australian animals probably stems from my childhood association with an alcoholic kangaroo.

My father was a policeman and for a time was stationed at Walgett in northern New South Wales. He, my mother and I found ourselves living next door to an old man who kept as a pet a huge red kangaroo.

The old man's name was Benny and he called his kangaroo Les after a famous boxer. Benny was a fuzzy-haired, sparrow-like man with a sweet disposition. Les was almost two metres of muscle and malice. I never saw why Benny was so fond of him.

Les lived in Benny's backyard. It was surrounded by a tall paling fence which he simply hopped over when he wanted to get out. He wanted to get out at least six times a day, and poor old Benny spent most of his life trying to persuade Les to come home. Benny used to get badly bruised in these encounters because the roo had a habit of hitting him with his forepaws, kicking him with his hind legs or whacking him with his tail when Benny tried to catch him.

Sometimes Benny tried to take Les for walks on a lead, and it was a sad sight to see that nice man being dragged through the main street of Walgett by a massive marsupial given to punching, kicking or whacking him with great frequency.

People often advised Benny to turn Les loose, or, better still, to convert him into dog's meat, but Benny would protest that he loved the animal and, contrary to all the evidence, the animal loved him.

At that stage, Les was no problem to anybody else in Walgett and if Benny wanted to maintain an unusual association with a kangaroo, that was his business. Nobody interfered.

My father and I became quite friendly with Benny and often used to help him catch Les and bring him home. It was an exciting business, and I used to enjoy it, particularly as Les never punched, kicked or whacked anybody but Benny.

*   *   *

But then Les took to drink and became a public menace.

There was a brewery in Walgett in those days, and every Wednesday the hops mash was strained off the brew and dumped at the rear of the premises in a large pond.

Les discovered this on one of his jaunts, tasted it and found he loved the beery, sloppy mess. He ate and ate until he fell down in an alcoholic stupor.

Benny learned of this when a messenger from the brewery called to tell him that his bloody kangaroo had dropped dead in the rear of the brewery premises and would he please get the corpse out of there immediately.

Poor old Benny was distraught, and enlisted my father and me to help him. The three of us trooped down to the brewery and found Les not dead, but very, very unconscious.

'He's mortal bad,' keened Benny in his squeaky old voice.

'No, he's not,' said my father, eyeing the great pool of hops mash and noting that the same stuff was liberally splattered over the kangaroo's brutish face. 'He's rotten drunk.'

Benny pleaded with us to help get Les home. My father was a big man, and strong, and I wasn't bad for my age. Benny wasn't much use. The three of us grabbed Les by the tail and tried to drag him home. But half a tonne of comatose kangaroo is hard to drag and we finally had to go and get a draught horse to do the job. We rolled Les onto a gate and the draught horse dragged him the half kilometre or so to Benny's backyard.

We left Benny covering Les with a blanket and pressing wet towels to his forehead, if kangaroos can be said to have foreheads.

I was there the next morning when Les finally woke up. Benny was squatting next to him, holding his right paw, as he had apparently been doing all night. Les opened one eye with extreme care. It was very bloodshot. He shut it quickly. There was a long pause, during which Benny clucked and tutted sympathetically, and then the kangaroo opened both bloodshot eyes. I swear he winced.

My memory may be playing me false, but I am convinced that at this point Les very slowly and clumsily scrambled to his feet and leaned against the paling fence, holding both front paws to his head. He groaned. Kangaroos do groan.

Benny went rushing off to get a bucket of water and Les drank the lot without pausing for breath, which is normally a very difficult thing for a kangaroo to do.

The water seemed to help him a lot. He stood looking reflectively into the empty bucket. Then suddenly he leaped straight over the paling fence and went bolting down the street towards the brewery.

'After him!' squeaked Benny, flung open the gate and went hobbling after the kangaroo as fast as a man of eighty or so can hobble, which is not very fast.

I ran ahead of him and managed to keep Les in sight. He made straight for the brewery, leaped the two-strand wire fence around the rear of the building, flung himself into the hops mash and began sucking the stuff up as though his life depended on it. He probably felt that it did.

I stood helplessly at the edge of the pond, watching the huge kangaroo, waist-deep in hops mash, plunging his head again and again into the yeasty mess, eating, imbibing, inhaling the whole highly alcoholic mixture. I later realised that I was witnessing a classic case of instant alcoholic addiction.

Benny came panting up and nearly burst into tears when he saw what was happening.

'Come out of it, Les, you naughty kangaroo,' he cried, 'you'll make yourself sick as a dog.' Les took no notice whatsoever.

'Go and get your father, boy,' squeaked Benny. I shot back home and told my father what was happening. A kindly man, he stroked his beard and thought for a moment.

'He's actually in the pond this time?'

'Yes.'

'So if he takes in enough of the stuff, he'll probably pass out and drown?'

'Yes, I suppose so.'

'Might be the best possible solution,' said my father.

But I was young and fond of Benny. I pleaded with my father to come to the rescue. He eventually collected a rope and the draught horse and we returned to the brewery.

Quite a crowd had gathered by then. Old Benny was literally in tears as he pleaded with Les to pull himself together and give up the drink. Les determinedly continued to try and absorb enough of the hops mash to render himself insensible.

My father made a lasso out of the rope, threw it over Les's chest and tied the other end around the neck of the draught horse. Les was hauled from the pond kicking and grunting and desperately trying to swallow a few more mouthfuls.

As soon as he was on dry land, dripping hops mash, he turned ugly. This was no comatose, alcohol-sodden marsupial: this was a fighting-drunk kangaroo. He leaped at my father, grunting angrily, and knocked him down with one mighty kick. Then he turned on the crowd, who ran away shrieking. Les went after them but was brought up short by the rope around his chest. He turned and went for the draught horse. The draught horse looked at him sourly and kicked him in the stomach. Les stood for a moment, gasping, and Benny rushed in and threw his arms around the beast. Les drew back his left paw, struck and knocked Benny flat on his back.

My father had recovered a little by then but was still obviously dazed. He drew his revolver and advanced on Les, shouting, 'Surrender in the name of the king!'

Les just stood there, grunting furiously.

'Surrender in the king's name,' repeated my father, pointing his revolver, 'or I'll blow your bloody head off!'

Benny was on his feet now and he flung himself between my father and Les. The conversation became inconsequential.

'You can't shoot a kangaroo,' said Benny.

'Yes, I can,' said my father. 'I have, often.'

'But this is a civilised kangaroo,' said Benny. 'You can't shoot a civilised kangaroo without a charge.'

'The charge is being drunk and disorderly,' roared my father.

'But you don't shoot people for being drunk and disorderly,' pleaded Benny.

'Kangaroos aren't people,' said my father, who could never resist an argument.

'There you are,' said Benny triumphantly. 'That's exactly what I mean.'

'Eh?' said my father.

Les, meanwhile, on a slack rope, had slipped back into the pond and was absorbing hops mash again.

'You wouldn't shoot my old mate, would you, man?' asked Benny piteously.

My father, whose head seemed to be clearing, began to see the funny side of the situation. He slipped his revolver back into its holster.

'All right,' he said, 'I'll tell you what we'll do. Let him guzzle on for a while. He'll get dopey, then we'll drag him out and toss him in the lockup until he's sober.'

So that's what we did. Les went on tucking into the hops for about half an hour, then he started to sway, went cross-eyed and was about to collapse when my father began to lead away the draught horse, to which Les was still attached.

'What are you doing with my kangaroo?' squeaked Benny.

'I told you,' said my father. 'I'm going to gaol him until he sobers up.' He pulled out his handcuffs, preparatory to handcuffing Les's legs together, if you can handcuff legs.

'How long are you going to lock him up for?' asked Benny.

'Until I'm satisfied that he's no longer a public danger,' said my father.

'But you can't do that without charging him,' said Benny. 'I'll have habeas corpus on you.'

'Then I'll charge him,' said my father desperately.

'With what?'

'Disturbing the peace, being drunk and disorderly, assault, resisting arrest, causing a public disturbance—I've got enough on your bloody kangaroo to keep him in gaol for life. Now stop making a fuss, or I'll shoot him dead for trying to escape.'

'But he's not trying to escape,' said Benny plaintively.

'What's that got to do with it?' asked my father.

'I'm going to get a lawyer,' cried Benny and hobbled away purposefully.

While all this legal argument was going on, Les unobtrusively slipped out of the noose and went bounding drunkenly up the main street. He was far from being comatose; he was in an advanced state of delirium tremens.

The street was packed with horses and sulkies, drays, motor cars, shoppers, old ladies and small children.

Les was bounding higher and more wildly than any sober kangaroo possibly could. Emitting loud explosive grunts, he went over the head of a horse harnessed to a cart and kicked it on the nose as he passed. The horse whinnied, reared and bolted. Les blundered into a shop window and smashed it. Two old ladies had hysterics.

My father, revolver drawn again, went racing after the kangaroo, but his shooting was restricted by fear of killing too many innocent civilians. Les stunned an old gentleman with his tail, then did shocking damage to an expensive motor car with his rear claws.

My father got close enough for a safe shot, but missed (he was a rotten marksman) and blew out another shop window. Les leaped over four fat middle-aged ladies, three of whom fainted. My father tripped over one of them and accidentally shot the tyre of a motor bus. All the passengers started to scream. The main street of Walgett, for the first and probably last time, was like a Marx Brothers movie.

Finally Les stopped in front of a pub, as though instinctively looking for more drink. My father caught up with him and loosed off four shots at point-blank range. They all missed and the pub window suffered irreparable damage. But Les's booze-soaked mind finally grasped the fact that he was in real danger. He turned and bolted out of town.

My father commandeered a car and went after him, still shooting, but soon lost him when Les turned off the road and went into the scrub.

Benny was disconsolate. 'I loved that kangaroo,' he told my father reproachfully, 'and now you've frightened him right out of my life.'

Privately my father thought he had done Benny a favour, but he was a soft-hearted policeman and he caught a young wallaby and gave it to the old man as a pet. 'But for God's sake, keep it off the grog,' he warned.

'Well, thank you,' said Benny, wrapping his arms around the wallaby, 'but it's a terrible thing to know I'll never see Les again.'

This wasn't true. Les came into town every Wednesday night, after the new hops mash had been poured into the pond, got disgustingly drunk and cleared out before dawn.

Lots of people saw him, but he didn't do any more harm so nobody bothered about him.

He went on doing this for five years. Then the brewery closed down, there was no hops mash, and nothing more was seen of Les.

But even to this day I cannot go out to the bush without worrying that I might blunder into the clutches of a huge, red, drink-crazed kangaroo who may well be bearing a grudge against me.

'THE DROVER'S LAMENT'

ANON

There's the red kangaroo and the mad cockatoo,
That nests in the old gum tree,
And there's all those rabbits with engaging habits,
And they've all got a mate but me!
The emu on the flat, the little bush rat,
The wedgetail flying free,
Goanna lying still, wallaby on the hill—
They've all got a mate but me!

Part 2
BUSH JUSTICE

The bush is a great leveller. Pretention, cleverness, education and snobbery are often defeated by the simple ways and wisdom of the bush folk. A sense of bush justice which is all about giving credit where it is due, whether the protagonist be a decent citizen or not, is seen in 'Marks's Cutter', where the strong Lutheran morals of the farmer are tempered by a sense of fairness which leads him to work in subtle ways against the 'letter of the law' to give a ne'er-do-well back his livelihood.

In other stories, like 'Bush Justice', the happy outcomes are achieved by a more deliberate conniving. Here the hero is the simple, good-hearted, hard-working bushman or respected local identity who finds the means to see 'bush justice' achieved in spite of officialdom or the superior knowledge of the city slicker.

Lawson's final twist in 'The Ironbark Chip' turns the whole idea on its head and leaves the hero laughing at himself, along with the reader.

'THE SIX-STITCHER'

FRANK DANIEL

A brand new six-stitcher, shiny, red and hard.
Dad saw us playing with it as he walked across the yard.
'Where'd ya get that, fellas?' was his curious remark.
'It's alright Dad, we found it in the long grass at the park.'
'You sure that it was lost?' he asked, his voice was turning sour.
'Bloody oath!' my brother said, 'They were searching for an hour!'

BUSH JUSTICE

BANJO PATERSON

THE TOWN OF KILEY's Crossing was not exactly a happy hunting ground for lawyers. The surrounding country was rugged and mountainous, the soil was poor, and the inhabitants of the district had plenty of ways of getting rid of their money without spending it in court.

Thus it came that for many years old Considine was the sole representative of his profession in the town. Like most country attorneys, he had forgotten what little law he ever knew, and, as his brand of law dated back to the very early days, he recognised that it would be a hopeless struggle to try and catch up with all the modern improvements. He just plodded along the best way that he could with the aid of a library consisting of a copy of the *Crown Lands Acts*, the *Miner's Handbook* and an aged mouse-eaten volume called *Ram on Facts* that he had picked up cheap at a sale on one of his visits to Sydney.

He was an honourable old fellow, and people trusted him implicitly, and if he did now and then overlook a defect in the title to a piece of land, well, no one ever discovered it, as on the next dealing the title always came back to him again, and was, of course, duly investigated and accepted. But it was in court that he shone particularly.

He always appeared before the police magistrate who visited Kiley's once a month. This magistrate had originally been a country storekeeper, and had been given this judicial position as a reward for political services. He knew less law than old Considine, but he was a fine, big, fat man, with a lot of dignity, and the simple country folk considered him a perfect champion of a magistrate.

The fact was that he and old Considine knew every man, woman, and child in the district; they knew who could be relied on to tell the truth and whose ways were crooked and devious, and between them they dispensed a very fair brand of rough justice. If anyone came forward with an unjust claim, old Considine had one great case that he was supposed to have discovered in *Ram on Facts*, and which was dragged in to settle all sorts of points. This, as quoted by old Considine, was 'the great case of Dunn v. Dockerty, the 'orse outside the 'ouse'.

What the 'orse did to the 'ouse or vice versa no one ever knew; doubts have been freely expressed whether there ever was such a case at all, and certainly, if it covered all the ground that old Considine stretched it over, it was a wonderful decision.

However, genuine or not, whenever a swindle seemed likely to succeed, old Considine would rise to his feet and urbanely inform the bench that under the 'well-known case of Dunn v. Dockerty, case that Your Worship of course knows, case of the 'orse outside the 'ouse', this claim must fail; and fail it accordingly did, to the promotion of justice and honesty.

This satisfactory state of things had gone on for years, and might be going on yet only for the arrival at Kiley's of a young lawyer from Sydney, a terrible fellow, full of legal lore; he slept with digests and law reports; he openly ridiculed old Considine's opinions; he promoted discord and quarrels, with the result that on the first court day after his arrival, there was quite a little crop of cases, with a lawyer on each side, an unprecedented thing in the annals of Kiley's Crossing.

In olden days one side or the other had gone to old Considine, and if he found that the man who came to him was in the wrong, he made him settle the case. If he was in the right, he promised to secure him the verdict, which he always did, with the assistance of *Ram on Facts* and 'the 'orse outside the 'ouse'.

Now, however, all was changed. The new man struggled into court with an armful of books that simply struck terror to the heart of the P.M. as he took his seat on the bench. All the idle men of the district came into court to see how the old man would hold his own with the new arrival.

It should be explained that the bush people look on a law case as a mere trial of wits between the lawyers and the witnesses and the bench; and the lawyer who can insult his opponent most in a given time is always the best in their eyes. They never take much notice of who wins the case, as that is supposed to rest on the decision of that foul fiend the law, whose vagaries no man may control nor understand. So, when the young lawyer got up and said he appeared for the plaintiff in the first case, and old Considine appeared a verdict for the defendant, there was a pleased sigh in court, and the audience sat back contentedly on their hard benches to view the forensic battle.

The case was simple enough. A calf belonging to the widow O'Brien had strayed into Mrs Rafferty's backyard and eaten a lot of washing off the line. There was ample proof. The calf had been seen by several people to run out of the yard with a half-swallowed shirt hanging out of its mouth. There was absolutely no defence, and in the old days the case would have been settled by payment of a few shillings, but here the young lawyer claimed damages for *trespass to realty, damages for trover and conversion of personalty, damages for detinue*, and a lot of other terrible things that no one had ever heard of.

He had law books to back it all up, too. He opened the case in style, stating his authorities and defying his learned friend to contradict him, while the old P.M. shuffled uneasily on the bench, and the reputation of old Considine in Kiley's Crossing hung trembling in the balance.

When the old man rose to speak he played a bold stroke. He said, patronisingly, that his youthful friend had, no doubt, stated the law correctly, but he seemed to have overlooked one little thing. When he was more experienced he would no doubt be more wary. (Sensation in court.) He relied upon a plea that his young friend had no doubt overlooked, that was that plea of *cause to show*. 'I rely upon that plea,' he said, 'and of course Your Worship knows the effect of that plea.'

Then he sat down amid the ill-suppressed admiration of the audience. The young lawyer, confronted with this extraordinary manoeuvre, simply raged furiously. He asserted (which is quite true) that there is no such plea known to the law of this or any other country as an absolute defence to claim for a calf eating washing off a line, or to any other claim for that matter.

He was proceeding to expound the law relating to trespass when the older man interrupted him. 'My learned friend says that he never heard of such a defence,' he said, pityingly. 'I think that I need hardly remind Your Worship that that very plea was successfully raised as a defence in the well-known case of Dunn v. Dockerty, the case of 'the 'orse outside the 'ouse.'

'Yes,' said the bench, anxious to display his legal knowledge, 'that case . . . er . . . is reported in *Ram on Facts*, isn't it?'

'Well, it is mentioned there, Your Worship,' said the old man, 'and I don't think that even my young friend's assurance will lead him so far as to question so old and well-affirmed a decision!'

But his young friend's assurance did lead him that far, in fact, a good deal further. He quoted decisions by the score on every conceivable point, but after at least half an hour of spirited talk, the bench pityingly informed him that he had not quoted any cases bearing on the plea of *cause to show*, and found a verdict for the defendant.

The young man gave notice of appeal and of prohibitions and so forth, but his prestige was gone in Kiley's. The audience filed out of court, freely expressing the opinion that he was a 'regular fool of a bloke; old Considine stood him on his head proper with that plea of *cause to show*, and so help me goodness, he'd never even heard of it!'

THE IRONBARK CHIP

HENRY LAWSON

Dave Regan and party—bush-fencers, tank-sinkers, rough carpenters, etc.—were finishing the third and last culvert of their contract on the last section of the new railway line, and had already sent in their vouchers for the completed contract, so that there might be no excuse for extra delay in connection with the cheque.

Now it had been expressly stipulated in the plans and specifications that the timber for certain beams and girders was to be ironbark and no other, and Government inspectors were authorised to order the removal from the ground of any timber or material they might deem inferior, or not in accordance with the stipulations.

The railway contractor's foreman and inspector of sub-contractors was a practical man and a bushman, but he had been a timber-getter himself; his sympathies were bushy, and he was on winking terms with Dave Regan. Besides, extended time was expiring, and the contractors were in a hurry to complete the line. But the Government inspector was a reserved man who poked round on his independent own and appeared in lonely spots at unexpected times, with apparently no definite object in life, like a grey kangaroo bothered by a new wire fence, but unsuspicious of the presence of humans. He wore a grey suit, rode, or mostly led, an ashen-grey horse; the grass was long and grey, so he was seldom spotted until he was well within the horizon and bearing leisurely down on a party of sub-contractors, leading his horse.

Now ironbark was scarce and distant on those ridges, and another timber, similar in appearance, but much inferior in grain

44

and 'standing' quality, was plentiful and close at hand. Dave and party were 'about full of' the job and place, and wanted to get their cheque and be gone to another 'spec' they had in view. So they came to reckon they'd get the last girder from a handy tree, and have it squared, in place, and carefully and conscientiously tarred before the inspector happened along, if he did.

But they didn't.

They got it squared, and ready to be lifted into its place; the kindly darkness of tar was ready to cover a fraud that took four strong men with crowbars and levers to shift; and now (such is the regular cussedness of things) as the fraudulent piece of timber lay its last hour on the ground, looking and smelling, to their guilty imaginations like anything but ironbark, they were aware of the Government inspector drifting down upon them obliquely, with something of the atmosphere of a casual Bill or Jim who had dropped out of his easy-going track to see how they were getting on, and borrow a match.

They had more than half hoped that, as he had visited them pretty frequently during the progress of the work, and knew how near it was to completion, he wouldn't bother coming anymore. But it's the way with the Government. You might move heaven and earth in vain endeavour to get the 'Guvermunt' to flutter an eyelash over something of the most momentous importance to yourself and mates and the district, even to the country; but just when you are leaving authority severely alone, and have strong reasons for not wanting to worry or interrupt it, and not desiring it to worry about you, it will take a fancy into its head to come along and bother.

'It's always the way!' muttered Dave to his mates. 'I knew the beggar would turn up! . . . And the only cronk log we've had, too!' he added, in an injured tone. 'If this had'a been the only blessed ironbark in the whole contract, it would have been all right . . . Good-day, sir!' (to the inspector). 'It's hot?'

The inspector nodded. He was not of an impulsive nature. He got down from his horse and looked at the girder in an abstracted way; and presently there came into his eyes a dreamy, far-away, sad sort of expression, as if there had been a very sad and painful occurrence in his family, way back in the past, and that piece of timber in some way reminded him of it and brought the old sorrow home to him. He blinked three times, and asked, in a subdued tone:

'Is that ironbark?'

Jack Bentley, the fluent liar of the party, caught his breath with a jerk and coughed, to cover the gasp and gain time. 'I . . . ironbark? Of course it is! I thought you would know ironbark, mister.'

Mister was silent.

'What else d'yer think it is?'

The dreamy, abstracted expression was back. The inspector, by the way, didn't know much about timber, but he had a great deal of instinct, and went by it when in doubt.

'L . . . look here, mister!' put in Dave Regan, in a tone of innocent puzzlement and with a blank bucolic face. 'B . . . but don't the plans and specifications say ironbark? Ours does, anyway. I . . . I'll git the papers from the tent and show yer, if yer like.'

It was not necessary. The inspector admitted the fact slowly. He stooped, and with an absent air picked up a chip. He looked at it abstractedly for a moment, blinked his threefold blink; then, seeming to recollect an appointment, he woke up suddenly and asked briskly:

'Did this chip come off that girder?'

Blank silence. The inspector blinked six times, divided in threes, rapidly, mounted his horse, said 'Day,' and rode off.

Regan and party stared at each other.

'Wha . . . what did he do that for?' asked Andy Page, the third in the party.

'Do what for, you fool?' enquired Dave.

'Ta . . . take that chip for?'

'He's taking it to the office!' snarled Jack Bentley.

'What . . . what for? What does he want to do that for?'

'To get it blanky well analysed! You ass! Now are yer satisfied?' And Jack sat down hard on the timber, jerked out his pipe, and said to Dave, in a sharp, toothache tone:

'Gimmiamatch!'

'We . . . well! What are we to do now?' enquired Andy, who was the hardest grafter, but altogether helpless, hopeless, and useless in a crisis like this.

'Grain and varnish the bloomin' culvert!' snapped Bentley.

But Dave's eyes, that had been ruefully following the inspector, suddenly dilated. The inspector had ridden a short distance along the line, dismounted, thrown the bridle over a post, laid the chip (which was too big to go in his pocket) on top of it, got through the fence, and was now walking back at an angle across the line in the direction of the fencing party, who had worked up on the other side, a little more than opposite the culvert.

Dave took in the lay of the country at a glance and thought rapidly.

'Gimme an ironbark chip!' he said suddenly.

Bentley, who was quick-witted when the track was shown him, as is a kangaroo dog (Jack ran by sight, not scent), glanced in the line of Dave's eyes, jumped up, and got a chip about the same size as that which the inspector had taken.

Now the 'lay of the country' sloped generally to the line from both sides, and the angle between the inspector's horse, the fencing party, and the culvert was well within a clear concave space; but a couple of hundred yards back from the line and parallel to it (on the side on which Dave's party worked their timber) a fringe of scrub ran to within a few yards of a point which would be about in line with a single tree on the cleared slope, the horse, and the fencing party.

Dave took the ironbark chip, ran along the bed of the watercourse into the scrub, raced up the siding behind the bushes, got safely, though without breathing, across the exposed space, and brought the tree into line between him and the inspector, who was talking to the fencers. Then he began to work quickly down the slope towards the tree (which was a thin one), keeping it in line, his arms close to his sides, and working, as it were, down the trunk of the tree, as if the fencing party were kangaroos and Dave was trying to get a shot at them.

The inspector, by the by, had a habit of glancing now and then in the direction of his horse, as though under the impression that it was flighty and restless and inclined to bolt on opportunity. It was an anxious moment for all parties concerned—except the inspector. They didn't want *him* to be perturbed. And, just as Dave reached the foot of the tree, the inspector finished what he had to say to the fencers, turned, and started to walk briskly back to his horse. There was a thunderstorm coming. Now was the critical moment, there were certain prearranged signals between Dave's party and the fencers which might have interested the inspector, but none to meet a case like this.

Jack Bentley gasped, and started forward with an idea of intercepting the inspector and holding him for a few minutes in bogus conversation. Inspirations come to one at a critical moment, and it flashed on Jack's mind to send Andy instead. Andy looked as innocent and guileless as he was, but was uncomfortable in the vicinity of 'funny business', and must have an honest excuse.

'Not that that mattered,' commented Jack afterwards; 'it would have taken the inspector ten minutes to get at what Andy was driving at, whatever it was.'

'Run, Andy! Tell him there's a heavy thunderstorm coming and he'd better stay in our humpy till it's over. Run! Don't stand staring like a blanky fool. He'll be gone!'

Andy started. But just then, as luck would have it, one of the fencers started after the inspector, hailing him as 'Hi, mister!' He wanted to be set right about the survey or something, or to pretend to want to be set right, from motives of policy which I haven't time to explain here.

That fencer explained afterwards to Dave's party that he 'seen what you coves was up to', and that's why he called the inspector back. But he told them that after they had told their yarn, which was a mistake.

'Come back, Andy!' cried Jack Bentley.

Dave Regan slipped round the tree, down on his hands and knees, and made quick time through the grass which, luckily, grew pretty tall on the thirty or forty yards of slope between the tree and the horse. Close to the horse, a thought struck Dave that pulled him up, and sent a shiver along his spine and a hungry feeling under it. The horse would break away and bolt! But the case was desperate. Dave ventured an interrogatory 'Cope, cope, cope?' The horse turned its head wearily and regarded him with a mild eye, as if he'd expected him to come, and come on all fours, and wondered what had kept him so long; then he went on thinking.

Dave reached the foot of the post; the horse obligingly leaning over on the other leg. Dave reared head and shoulders cautiously behind the post, like a snake; his hand went up twice, swiftly. The first time he grabbed the inspector's chip, and the second time he put the ironbark one in its place. He drew down and back, and scuttled off for the tree like a gigantic tailless goanna.

A few minutes later he walked up to the culvert from along the creek, smoking hard to settle his nerves.

The sky seemed to darken suddenly; the first great drops of the thunderstorm came pelting down. The inspector hurried to his horse, and cantered off along the line in the direction of the fettlers' camp.

He had forgotten all about the chip, and left it on top of the post!

Dave Regan sat down on the beam in the rain and swore comprehensively.

HERE COMES THE BRIDE

FRANK DALBY DAVISON

CLOUDS LIKE A BIG bruise had risen above the ranges, towering like the wrath of God, thunderously growling, spreading like coils of sulphurous smoke, casting an unearthly light upon the distant scene, and wafting a scent of rain on the gusts of wind that were driven from their lower darkness. Now they were rolling low above the treetops.

With his axe, straining fork and a couple of loops of wire over his shoulder, Pa Pettingel, who had been mending a fence at the back of his selection, was stumping home through the drenching storm. He plodded through a rain-striped gloom where wet tree trunks glistened darkly. From his sodden old hat the water trickled down his face carrying the taste of sweat to his lips. Water squelched and bubbled from the lace-holes of his boots at every step. His shirt and trousers clung to him like a half-sloughed skin.

But Pa's heart was light. The thrash of the rain on the earth was like music to him. He welcomed the beat of it against his body as it swept past. The cool clean smell of it and of wet soil and leaf were scent to get drunk on. He felt as if the tensions of a spring, long coiled with aching tightness, had been loosened within him. His thoughts were fixed in happy anticipation on the moment of his arrival at the homestead.

Times had gone rather hard with Pa of late. It had begun when he handed his wife what amounted practically to an open cheque for Rose's wedding expenses. The district was in the middle of a prolonged dry spell, but he didn't know that—how could he? He

50

had been moved by the recollection of the weddings of his other daughters, living in Gippsland. Violet and Myrtle had each been given a spanking send-off; trousseaux lacking nothing, generous presents, wedding parties that were still talked of in the district.

Rose and her mother, in view of it being only the second year of their occupation of the western Queensland selection, had been a little diffident about drawing too heavily on his resources; but here another factor had entered into the matter. His optimism in persuading them to up-sticks and leave their old home among the green hills of Gippsland had not yet been fully vindicated. He had a thought, as well, of the mob of yearlings he had recently bought on spec from one of his neighbours. To hedge on wedding expenses after the expansive attitude shown on that outlay would indicate a poor spirit.

'Rose can have the same as her sisters,' he said.

His wife had made no comment but had glanced at him as much as to say, 'That's very handsome of you, Pa!' Rose, emotional, though usually chary of display, had rubbed the side of his head with her cheek when she caught him sitting alone.

So Pa was launched upon a sea of troubles that were not to end until he had experienced, for the first time in his life, dragging bogged and drought-stricken beasts from a shrunken waterhole, and skinning a ten-pound cow to salvage a ten-shilling hide.

Preparations for the wedding developed apace. Rose and her mother sent to Brisbane for mail order catalogues and spent hours licking their thumbs over them. Occasionally they called Pa into consultation.

'Look, Pa. Do you think this . . . ?'

Pa, pleased at having his opinion asked, assisted to the best of his ability, and joined in the fun if his judgment was provocative of mirth. His was the honour and privilege of paying. He remembered how the cheques he had had to sign for the other weddings had made him wince a little; but somehow the wince had been the gauge of his importance and pleasure. Now, when his views were sought, he intimated, by opinions into which considerations of price had obviously not entered very much, that he was standing by the promise he had given on Rose's account. He was rewarded by his womenfolk with small flatteries indicative of vast approval.

His first intimation that things were not well with him came one morning when he went out to the road to intercept Snooker Hall, driving past on his way to the railhead. He wanted Snooker to buy him some roofing nails at the store. By this time, brown paper packages had begun arriving from the city for the Pettingels, and the chief sounds indoors, in the intervals of routine housework, were the silvery snip of scissors and the purr of the sewing machine.

Pa had not yet had time to subdivide and it happened that his cattle were all gathered grazing near the front fence, opposite where he had stopped Snooker. They were a goodly band. It was September and they had come through the winter well. Pa noticed Snooker running his eye over them as they exchanged a little talk and, although he pointedly ignored them himself, he had them pridefully in mind. He was a little taken aback when Snooker said:

'A bit over-stocked for this time of the year, aren't you, Pettingel?'

Snooker was one of those men who always have a sharp eye toward other people's business and, disturbing factor, he had an authoritative air which implied that he had mostly found himself right in his conjectures.

'There's a good stand of feed at the back of the paddock,' answered Pa, off-handedly.

Snooker nodded without taking his eyes off the stock, as much as to say, 'I knew you'd say that!' His protracted survey of the cattle was pointed, and said as plainly as words, 'You've been over-reaching yourself, old man!'

The incident troubled Pa during the course of the day and in late afternoon, when he rode old Spring to the back of the selection to bring in the milkers, he took careful note of the amount of feed remaining. His paddock didn't look very much different from those adjoining. The tall grass, dry and yellow, from last growing season, still stretched away under the box and ironbark trees like a paddock of thin wheat. He noticed that the soft under-feed was well bitten away but still . . .

It was hard to feel pessimistic, sitting comfortably in the saddle after a heavy but satisfactory day, with the sun slanting serenely down through the ragged boughs and the cattle trailing contentedly home in front of him.

'One day you think you've got some feed left, and a couple of days later it's all gone!' That was the voice of an old hand with whom he had discussed the character of the country. The words came back to him ominously; but Pa had a heart not readily given to dread. He looked at the fine condition of his stock, at the feed still standing; he thought of the advantageous price at which he had bought that mob of yearlings, and thrust misgiving into the back of his mind.

That night Rose's husband-to-be came on his twice-a-week visit. His selection was three miles across country, at the back of the Pettingels'. He'd have come oftener only that since he had proposed and been accepted, he had dropped temporarily into second place. It was the wedding that held the centre of the stage. Pa remembered that it had been like that when Ma—Lucy—had been in the throes of wedding preparations. Bart had to do his love-making when Rose went with him as far as the creek crossing on his way home; a proceeding, incidentally, that usually took as long as it would have taken Bart, alone, to go home and back a couple of times.

This night the women were stitching. Bart sat on the other side of the lamp from Pa, taking his part in the general yarning, being polite to Pa and Ma, and taking a frequent eyeful of Rose. There was a certain undercurrent of regret at the thought of parting with the last daughter, but she was getting a fine steady chap and on the whole the arrangement was a desirable one. Pa, full willing, was caught up in the mood of the occasion. He, too, looked forward to the wedding. With his stockinged feet stretched before him he even rehearsed in his mind a little of the wedding speech that had gone down so well on previous occasions: 'Ladies and gentlemen, it gives me and my wife very great pleasure to see the faces of so many good friends and neighbours . . .'

That night, in bed, while Rose was still down at the creek crossing saying goodnight to Bart, Pa was given additional reason for seeing her well started. Ma spoke of how strange the house would seem with only the two of them. She called him Jim, a name she had rarely used since the children were little. Ma, too, felt that Rose's going drew attention to the sands steadily running.

October passed and brought no rain with it. Pa spent the month putting up a fence to make a night paddock for the milkers, around the homestead. He was anxious now. From where he worked he could see into one of the neighbours' paddocks, the one from whom he had bought the yearlings. You could see the difference; in his the under-feed was used up, and the cattle were starting on the top-feed. The stalky tufts were bitten off here and there, square, like brushes, and as appetite became less discriminating the stock would bite lower and lower. Freshness, too, was noticeably departing from the earth. Except at early morning and late afternoon there was a searching glare, as if the year was withering away.

'You generally get rain when the weather warms up?' That was Pa talking to one of the old hands, seeking verification of his observations of the previous season.

'Yes, if it happens to be a good year.'

'And what if it happens to be only a middling year?'

'Well, we mostly get rain here in western Queensland—general rains that is—some time after Christmas. We might get a thunderstorm or two before then—if you're lucky and happen to be in the track of it.'

The casualness of the old hands, as against his fast increasing need, brought stabs of panic to Pa as he went about his work.

He said nothing of his anxiety to his womenfolk. Going indoors, he would see a newly opened parcel, the paper still hanging loosely about it. 'What's that?' he would ask.

'That's towelling—or sheeting—Pa,' he would be told. 'Look, Pa! Only two, eleven, three a yard. Special discount for brides!'

Pa wondered where all the contents of the brown paper parcels disappeared to. When Violet and Myrtle married there had been dressmaker's bills to pay, but this time—he had been told—out of consideration for their being on a new selection, it had been decided to save money by doing all the needlework at home. It seemed to him, however, that economies effected by home manufacture were more than made up for by liberal purchases of material. Still, he let no sign be seen. He had given his word. Also, his prestige abroad as well as at home was involved. Word of the forthcoming fine wedding was passing around among the neighbours.

He was glad when the new fence was finished. The cows would soon bite it to the dust, and the sight of bare earth around the homestead would be a commonplace. That would be just the night paddock; in the big paddock, extending to the back of the selection, peace and plenty would still presumably reign.

The milch cows were going off in their yield; a fact that could not but be noticed by Rose, who helped with the milking. However, nothing else but a fall in the yield could be expected, according to Pa. They had been milking a long time now on dry feed. He remarked—with some truth—that everybody was complaining of the same thing.

It was about this time that Pa relieved Rose of her customary job of taking the cream to the railway in the sulky. It would give her more time for getting ready for the wedding, he said. His real reason was that he was aware of Snooker Hall's discerning eye directed at his selection every time he passed by, and he wanted to come between Rose and whatever neighbourhood gossip might be circulating on train days. To bluff even the stationmaster, he paid full freight on a half-empty cream can—and put it in the van himself, lest some too-obliging neighbour, helping load the van, should stumble on an interesting fact. Pa, by nature, didn't like resorting to subterfuge, but things were closing in on him.

The women gave Pa no rest. To keep his mind off his anxieties he was building a new pig-pen, of straight brigalow logs, to replace the cockatoo structure he had thrown together the first year. Rose came to him while he was notching the logs. She had evidently awaited an opportunity to speak with him, daughter to father. 'Pa, do you think we ought to get a good suite for the parlour while we're at it? There's one at fourteen pounds ten and another at eighteen pounds ten.' Pa recalled, with a sinking of his stomach, that his wedding present to Violet and Myrtle had been to furnish their parlours—where they could entertain in bang-up style. He hadn't counted on it this time, somehow; but Bart, he recalled, had been building his house; he had put everything else aside; no doubt on Rose's suggestion. Rose would want to have a good tale to tell in her letters to her sisters.

Pa examined the log under his hands for a long while before looking up to meet his daughter's eyes. 'I think it would be best to get the good one,' he said. 'Better to have something that will last.'

While pleased that he should have so decided, Rose was evidently not surprised. She thanked him, and dutifully asked if she could be of any help. He thanked her and assured her that he could manage. She stood awhile and admired the new pig-pen before going back, with quickening steps, to the house.

After she had gone Pa's hands fell idle for a time. He was wondering what was in store for him, if he could get through summoning his strength of spirit to face unknown ends. Rose was evidently out for all there was in it—but that was only natural. As against a momentary flash of resentment at the way women lost themselves in a wedding, he recalled that Rose had been very good in the early camping days on the selection, shovelling dirt out of the post-holes when they were fencing, while he was wielding the spud-bar; bending in the hot sun, paying out from the coil when he was running the wires through the posts; handing up planks, tools and sheet iron when he was building; interested, rarely complaining, making light of grimed and scarred hands. Pa blew a deep sigh and turned again to his work.

Bart brought cheering news, one night. 'I hear they've had storms down the line, Mr Pettingel. Nogganilla copped three inches!'

This was indeed heartening. In imagination Pa saw one of these beneficent storms sweep across his selection.

'You'll be all right, Pa?' This from Ma, looking up from matching buttons, referring to his affairs in general. This was very nice of

Ma; perfunctory, of course, for her mind was on other things, but well intended.

'Yes, I can't complain,' from Pa. At the same time he caught a look in Bart's eye, and he knew what he had suspected for some time; that Bart fully realised the parlous state of his affairs. In coming visiting Bart crossed a back corner of Pettingel's selection; he came at night admittedly, but these bush-bred lads had eyes in their feet.

It was humiliating for Pa that Bart should know his position, because that position was entirely Pa's own fault; he shouldn't have bought that mob of yearlings; forty youngsters, busy eating and growing, had made the difference between security and desperation. That was why Bart had made no comment, but had been eager with hopeful news. Bart was not over-stocked. Pa had a feeling that he had only to say the word and Bart would relieve him by taking some of his cattle. But was he, the man with a lifetime's experience, to make a start by falling on the shoulders of his future son-in-law? No, by the Hokey Pokey! The look he returned Bart revealed nothing.

'Funny how stock make a dead set on an ironbark ridge,' said Pa. 'They must find 'em sweet.' He was giving the conversation a tactical twist. It was an ironbark ridge over which Bart came.

Only dry storms—those subject fiends of Demon Drought— came to Pettingel's selection. Twice Pa was driven by them to seek shelter. Overpowering heat, a smell of rain somewhere about, a clouding up, thunder rolling, darkness, a rushing of wind, a wild thrashing of boughs, a scattering of large ineffectual raindrops, like florins, pitting the dust; then dispersal, and the sun again, hotter than ever, mocking the aching earth, and seeming to jeer: 'Did you think it was going to rain, Pettingel?' At such times Pa's heart nearly broke.

Cementing the cow bails—a job he set himself to as a sort of a penance—Pa had a brief nostalgia for the snug little property he had left in the Gippsland Ranges. Green maize ten feet high on the tiny creek flat, cocksfoot and clover like a green mantle on the spurs; water gurgling under musky leafage down every gully.

He was led from his consideration of his present plight to wonder why he had uprooted himself and come north. Bigger acreage. Change. A stirring in the blood. A wave of optimism similar to that which had carried him into buying those yearlings. A belief, vaguely founded, that by leaving the old stand he could outwit nature—shake off the gathering weight of years. In some measure he had. Here on the new settlement he had shared in the days of beginnings. He had held his own, too, in hard work, stepped into the job with younger men and kept up with them, pace for pace, stroke for stroke—but he wished he hadn't bought those yearlings!

While he was toiling through the hot hours to escape his thoughts, Alec Lavresen, from whom he had bought them, was probably making a long midday of it, his back against the shady side of his house, reading the paper, his family around him, easy of mind. Alec was only half his age, but a western Queenslander, an old hand in regard to the country.

'Once the stock start to die they go quicker and quicker. It's one today, two or three more by the end of the week, five or six next week, ten or a dozen the following week.' The grim old hands were talking again!

Pa hurriedly finished smoothing off the cement in the bail where he was at work. Then he flung down his tools and went for old Spring. He was going to have a thorough good look at his land, ride right over it, see how much longer the feed would last.

He saw little to comfort him, riding over the hill, flat and gully. The best country—the ironbark ridges—was completely eaten out, black and bare. On the box sidings the tufts were bitten back to about three inches, right back to the hard wood, and the stock were still at it, except a few that he noticed making an experimental attack on a clump of wilga bushes. It was pretty much the same on the best of the flats. There was one small stretch, swampy in wet weather, covered with long tough blady and wire grass. Stock wouldn't look at it ordinarily, but a lot of them were in it now, nosing after a bite at the bottom. Pa sat his horse, watching disconsolately.

How long could he last? He hadn't the money to buy agistment; that had gone into Rose's wedding. He couldn't raise money; he had borrowed to build—Ma needed a proper house at her age. Could he last until after the wedding? Another fortnight? He might be compelled to fall back on Bart. That thought galled him. And then there was the thought that perhaps the district was in for a real drought. What right had he to ask the younger man to shoulder some of his risks in the face of that possibility?

He rode home heavily. His stock would be on their feet for two or three weeks yet, but after that they would go down like scrub falling; that was one of the penalties of having almost all good country—and over-stocking. The thought of the wedding turned his insides to lead. The guests would know. The story had got around. He had a neighbour on each side and one at the back, as well as Hall, going by. At the railway he had met Tom Sturges, from over on Bluey Creek, ten miles away. Tom had asked how he was getting on, and on being told that he was doing fine, had expressed surprise. 'Oh, I'm glad to hear that. I heard you were in deep water!' Pa could imagine the swarm of guests, jovial, friendly, congratulatory—and silently critical, quietly observant of the shameful difference between his ostentatious board and his hungry paddocks. That ate into Pa; he had always—at least when not tempted to over-optimism—paid respect to sound and careful husbandry.

Dinner, on the day the rain came, had been a scratch meal eaten in an atmosphere of dress manufacture. There was the uncovered sewing machine, loose heaps of material piled on chairs—and smelling like a draper's shop—snippings on the floor, and Rose with her hair tousled from dragging things on and off over her head.

The women were talking of the wedding. Pa was thinking about his cattle. During the week he had had to pull three beasts out of the bog at the top end of the waterhole in the creek. He had had the satisfaction of seeing them go tottering off on their muddied legs, but one of them had died, a cow. He had spent the morning skinning her. Pa wasn't accustomed to skinning. He had made a laborious and bloody job of it. He had washed the blood off his hands and arms at the waterhole and flung the hide over a log to avoid bringing it home. That was the first of them! Before Pa's inner eye was the image of that obscene carcass lying in the gully, and in his ears the ca-a-a-rk, ca-a-a-a-a-rk, of gathering crows. Although a stock-keeper, Pa was humane, and was troubled by a sense of moral guilt as well as of financial loss.

He wished they would stop talking of the wedding. Rose and her mother everlastingly yabber-yabbering about it, their heads together over this and that; feet and hands flying at the machine. 'Do you mind, Pa, if we just have left-overs for dinner today?' And always cocking an eye on him to see if they were reaching the danger limit of expenses. Today they were discussing the actual wedding. It was only a week off. How to seat all those people? They hadn't realised how many there would be! Plank tables under the verandah would be best. How many cases of fruit would they need? How many dozen soft drink? Or would they have a keg of beer? Or both? Perhaps they had better have both!

Pa's clenched fist crashed down on the table in a way that made the cups leap in their saucers and the two women turn to him with the arched eyebrows of consternation. 'My God, woman,' be shouted at his wife, 'have a little mercy on me!'

This happened only in Pa's imagination. What really took place was that he choked back his feelings and rose, a little white of face, and quietly left the room. It was a minute or two before the others noticed his absence, so deep were they in discussion, then Ma remarked, 'Your Pa went out very quietly.' She got up and went to the window. She saw Pa, with the axe and straining fork and loops of wire over his shoulder, plodding off through the timber—just a man going about his work, moving a little slowly on account of the heat. 'It looks hot out there,' she murmured; then, in quickening accents, 'Rose, do you think that pink georgette will look well with . . . ?'

There were puddles ankle-deep and fifty yards long on the flat when Pa emerged from the timber. He didn't care. He sloshed right through them! The rain was coming straight down now; a steady beat; it looked like general rains, all over the state. He couldn't see to the front fence through the downpour.

'The stock don't move in western Queensland once the rains come.' The old hands were talking again, this time with grinning faces. 'They just stand in one place and bite the grass off as it jumps up!' Pa flung his tools into the cart shed—its earthen floor miraculously dusty as against the lovely sodden world without—and headed for the homestead. He'd do well out of those yearlings now! Within a week or ten days the grass would be knee-high.

As he climbed the steps he could hear, above the splash of the overflowing tank and the roar of the rain on the iron roof, another sound; a long purr and a pause, a long purr and a pause. Ma was still on the sewing machine. Well, they could have their wedding now and welcome. He was looking forward to it himself!

Forgetting that they who had been shielded from sharing his anxieties could hardly be expected to understand the measure of his relief, Pa stepped to the threshold. With a hand on each side of the door, and standing back so as not to drip water on the lino, he looked into the room, soaked but beaming. Ma had dragged the machine over to the window for better light, and was bent above it, her feet on the flying treadle. Rose, near the door, bare-armed, her mouth full of pins, was making adjustments to the hem of a slip she was trying on.

'Hey, Ma,' Pa shouted. 'It's rainin'!'

Ma, startled at the sound of his voice, looked round. It was a moment before she took in his words properly, then she smiled and nodded vigorously, a pleasant and dutiful spouse. She glanced out the window, up at the resounding roof and back to Pa. 'Yes, we've been looking at it,' she screamed. 'Very nice, isn't it?' She nodded again and then turned back to the machine.

Rose took the pins out of her mouth and spared him a few words of daughterly advice, kindly intended. 'Hadn't you better get your wet things off, Pa?'

HIS BAD LUCK

EDWARD DYSON

THE LOVERS WERE NOT animated by any romantic appreciation of the picturesque in selecting the western slope of Magpie Hill for their meeting place. The trysting spot possessed one advantage—it was secluded.

Since the Macdougals had given up their search for the gold reef, believed to exist in the locality, as a bad job, they were never led in that direction by inclination, and rarely by duty. The coarse grass growing sparingly in the hard, hungry soil seldom enticed the cattle from the flats near the river. On the hillside the gums grew straggling and strangely contorted, and only a few clumps of drooping, stunted saplings relieved the dull brown expanse of surface with a touch of bright green, and offered anything like shelter from the penetrating rays of the fierce summer sun now glinting upon the motionless leaves and weaving an ebullient mirage far down in the dry bed of Spooner's Creek.

Harry Grey waited at the foot of the hill, evidently in no very gracious humour; with his hands thrust deeply into his pockets, and his back set against a tree, he gazed gloomily at his feet, propped out before him, seeking a satisfactory solution of the difficulty he had in hand, and which for the last nineteen hours, sleeping and waking, had defied his not particularly ingenious mind. His boots suggested nothing, and time was pressing. The girl might come at any moment, and his diplomacy was equal to no better line of action than the bald and brutal truth.

Any fool can tell the simple truth. What the young man wanted was a lie that would 'fill the bill' and at the same time save him the indignity of a confession of his own weakness. Open confession is good for the soul, but when one's confessor is a pretty young woman, with a reserve of native dignity, to whom a fellow has sworn eternal constancy a thousand times, and undying devotion as often again, and the confession is a cruel renunciation of her affection and her fealty, one is so far lost to the teachings of his youth as to be willing to give all his moral copybook maxims for a really serviceable deceit.

Harry groaned dismally, and vented his feelings on his horse, but Eaglehawk, accustomed to these impassioned addresses, and stung out of all patience by the voracious flies, continued to paw up the dirt and lash out viciously with his heels, regardless of his owner's ill-humour and his objurgations.

When the young man heard the rattle of a horse's hoofs above on the ridge he abandoned all thoughts of subterfuge, and resolved to make a virtue of necessity. He would be candid. He would give a plain statement of the case. They must separate and endeavour to forget each other; family reasons, etc., rendered it imperative.

An air of melancholy, tempered with firmness, was necessary to the explanation. Harry assumed such an air, and awaited the ordeal, but as the sound of the hoofbeats drew nearer his firmness melted into trepidation and his melancholy dwindled into a pitiful shamefacedness, for beneath the veneer of sophistry with which he had tried to delude his better self there was a consciousness of the paltry nature of the part he was playing, and a still small voice told him that selfishness and not filial affection prompted his action. Comet came over the hill at a rattling gallop, clearing the logs and stumps and clumps of scrub in his long, swinging stride, and his mistress sat him with the ease of a bush-bred girl, to whom a good horse is one of the necessities of life, and with a grace rarely seen in bush or town.

'Whoa, boy!'

Vic brought the nag up standing within a few feet of her lover, and dropped lightly to the ground before he could offer assistance.

No wonder the young man shrank from the idea of offending Victoria Macdougal. The distressing nature of his task came home to him with an increase of bitterness as she stood there, smiling coyly, and curtseying with mock dignity. She looked prettier than ever today; her cheeks glowed like newly blown brier roses after rain, and her beautiful hair clung in exquisite little curls about her white brow and her dainty pink ears.

He noted, with a great regret at his heart, the elegance of her slim figure in the light, well-fitting habit she wore. Her lips were even more tempting than usual, too, and he thought, sighing, that her fine eyes had assumed a brighter blue, but were gentler withal. She was sweet and inviting, but he did not kiss her. He leaned against the tree more determinedly, and ruefully congratulated himself upon his strength of mind.

Victoria missed the customary salutation, and noted Harry's reticence, and her manner changed at once. She also could be cold and careless.

'Good afternoon, Mister Grey.'

They might have met for the first time at the show ball last week.

'Good afternoon, Vic.'

Harry felt supremely uncomfortable, and tugged at Eaglehawk's rein and bullied the horse in a poor endeavour to hide his discomposure, and to avoid looking into her beautiful, inquisitive eyes.

Harry is a tall, strong fellow, spoken of by most of his male friends as a good fellow (usually with a superfluous adjective, be it regretfully recorded) with an ordinarily well-developed sense of honour, but lacking the moral stamina to act up to it in all cases. He is the first son of old Jock Grey, of Wombat. Grey, of Wombat, is a successful farmer and breeder in so large a way as almost to merit the dignity of being included amongst Victoria's 'squatocracy.'

Vic is the daughter of George Macdougal, a farmer in a smaller way, and not a good farmer at that. He and his big athletic sons are imbued with the digger's passion, and devote more time to prospecting up and down the creek and trenching for the reef than to the prosaic work of cutting scrub, ring-barking, fencing, and putting down crops. A Jew from the city has been seen wandering over their land, and there is much talk amongst the widely scattered neighbours of mortgages and liens on stock.

After kicking at a tuft of grass, with a brave show of unconcern, for a few awkward moments, and trying hard to control his nerves and his ideas, Harry became desperate.

'Vic,' he blurted, 'I'm going to make you hate me!'

'Hate you, Harry?'

There is much concern in her face now.

'You frighten me. You look serious enough to have all the mounted police in the colony on your track,' she continued, with a pathetic assumption of raillery. 'Have you been bank-breaking or cattle-stealing? Well, sir, don't you see how impatient I am?'

He hung Eaglehawk up to the tree, and, pointing to a log by a clump of saplings, said: 'Hadn't you better sit in the shade?'

He made this arrangement cunningly, that he might stand behind her whilst telling his story. He was afraid of the sudden unveiling of that deeper light in her eyes, which had flashed forth at times to his great discomfort.

Vic turned to obey him, and, sitting upon the log, with a stick she had picked from the ground she played nervously amongst the stony soil at her feet, and Harry Grey stood behind her and faltered through his explanation.

'Vic, I have to give you up. We must meet no more, but just forget all this . . . this foolishness that has been between us.

'You know that our fathers are bad friends. Dad expects me to marry Mary Lalor up at Gumleaf, and he has heard of my meetings with you. Sandy Martin dropped to it and reported it to the boss, who tackled me about it yesterday, and I up and told him we were sweethearts, and that I had asked you to marry me.

'Then dad tore round and went on like a dingo in a snap-trap; said I must drop fooling, or go and punch cattle for my tucker for the rest of my days. He swore that if I did not cut this . . . this . . . you know, I could give up all thoughts of working in with him, or of ever owning a shilling of his or an acre of Wombat land. And he means it.

'I didn't reckon on the old man cutting up rusty about it, but he is real mad, and as he's got the whip-hand of me I had to cry small, and promise him I'd ride across for the last time today and square matters up like. We must part for good and all, Vic.'

The young woman's face paled, and her head bent lower, but she did not speak; she still played nervously amongst the dead leaves and stones with her stick, and struggled bravely to stifle the sobs that rose in her throat.

'It isn't that dad has any objection to you, Vic . . . Miss Macdougal,' added the young man, clumsily, 'or doesn't think you good enough for me, or anything like that; but Wombat needs more cash than he can command to work it properly, and your people are too poor, you know.'

The girl started as the last words fell from his lips, but gave no answer for a minute or more. Drawing the dirt and dead leaves back over the small hole she had made in the ground, she dropped the stick, and then, turning her white face towards him, repeated, 'Too poor?'

Harry flushed a deeper red, and looked fixedly from the eyes that turned upon him full of bitter reproach.

'Yes,' he muttered, 'too poor. I hope you won't feel cut up, and that you'll soon forget.'

'I may not soon forget, but I shall not feel our parting much. I never knew you till now, Harry.'

He was going on to explain or excuse his conduct in a feeble way, but she gave him no attention. Comet, who, throughout the interview, had been fighting the flies at a little distance, came in answer to the call of his mistress, and she sprang lightly to the saddle from the log, disdaining Harry's proffered assistance.

'Have you nothing to say?' he asked miserably, as she gathered up the reins.

'What need I say? Your father has settled the matter.'

The young man winced, and he gazed gloomily after her as she put her horse at the brush fence, and rode at a dangerous pace along the foot of the hill, till her figure was lost to his view beyond the bend. Then he mounted Eaglehawk, and that game little animal broke his record for seven miles in the run to Wombat.

Miss Victoria did not ride straight home; she pulled up and dismounted by a patch of young wattles, about a mile and a half from the trysting place, and in a familiar shaded nook indulged in a long reverie, ending in tears, and then took herself severely to task, and scolded herself into a proper state of dignity and self-respect.

Two days later the whole of the district was in a fever of excitement over the intelligence that the Macdougals had struck a golden lode at the foot of Magpie Hill, on their sister's selection. The news reached Wombat, and Harry and his father rode across to inspect 'the find'.

Intelligence of gold discoveries travels through mysterious agencies, and flies to every point of the compass as if a staff of aerial Mercuries were always in waiting to carry the electrifying news from ear to ear. When the Greys reached the paddock there was a great crowd about the cutting in which the Macdougals, father and sons, were at work. Miners and prospectors had gathered from miles around, and scores of envious agriculturists swelled the excited throng. One glance at the cap of the reef convinced all with the slightest knowledge of mining that the Macdougals had struck it rich and were 'in for a big thing'.

The outcrop showed almost as much gold as stone, and the pure yellow metal shone with dazzling lustre in the bright rays of the midday sun. The men had already laid bare a great quantity of the quartz, showing that the reef 'widened as she dipped', and to the astonished onlookers it seemed that there must be a fortune now in sight.

Harry Grey stood, speechless, staring at the reef. He had some little knowledge of quartz mining, and had seen golden stone before, but never anything like this. Yet it was not the gold alone that amazed him; he remembered how, only a few hours before, he had stood upon this very spot, within a foot or two of the great treasure glowing before his eyes, telling Victoria Macdougal that she was too poor ever to be the wife of the son of Grey of Wombat.

The young man plucked at his father's sleeve, and backed out of the crowd. His eyes danced with excitement, and the hand on his father's arm shook like that of an old man.

'Great Scott!' he gasped, when beyond earshot of the people standing about. 'Dad, listen. I stood on top of that golden pile when I broke with Vic on Monday. My boots must have touched the gold. She sat upon that log which they have been forced to roll aside to get at the reef, while I babbled about her poverty like an inspired jackass!'

Mr Grey held his chin, and seemed to pull his naturally long visage down to an extraordinary length as he heard this, and a ludicrous expression of intense solicitude grew in his pawky face.

'Couldna ye mack it up again, boy?'

'Good-day, Mr Grey. How do you do, Master Harry?'

It was Vic who had obtruded into their conversation. She looked at Harry with a peculiar little smile that made him flush to the eyes. She wore the dove-coloured riding-dress he had so often admired, and her abundant bright hair rippled from under her hat. The young man noticed with selfish satisfaction that her face was unusually pale, and, despite the faint smile upon her lips, she did not look as happy and radiant as might have been expected of one who had experienced great and sudden good fortune.

'They have struck it at last, Vic,' said the young man, indicating the cutting with a toss of his hand.

'I have struck it,' she answered with emphasis. 'At about nine minutes past two on Monday afternoon I was sitting on a log over the spot where my brothers are working, playing amongst the dirt with a stick and listening to your story. You'll remember, Harry, when I turned up this golden key to wealth.'

She held out for their inspection a fine nugget, on which a quaint pattern was wrought in white quartz.

'You see,' she said, 'it is almost the shape of a broken anchor.'

She turned away, but paused after walking a few yards, and looking back, said, with an artfully ingenuous air: 'By the way, Mr Grey, have you heard of my brother Dick's engagement to

Mary Lalor, of Gumleaf? They have been in love with each other for some time, it appears, but said nothing about it till yesterday.'

When she had gone father and son stood in thoughtful attitudes for a few moments, and then turned, and each looked into the other's blank face and breathed a great sigh.

'Just my infernal bad luck!' muttered Harry, cutting fiercely at a dandelion with his riding whip.

SHOOTING STARS

C.W. PECK

THERE WAS ONCE A very great tribal leader who lived somewhere in the belt of basalt country where the waratah does not grow. The hard rocks of this country had once been subjected to terrific heat. In fact, they are born of fire, and this the people knew very well.

For a long time he had been a very good leader, doing all he could for the people he led. He had all the prowess that a chief should have. His spear he could hurl furthest and straightest. His nullah struck hardest, and his boomerang always sailed in its twirling rings and pretty curves out further into the air and returned to sit poised and still twirling above the players and himself before striking the ground at his feet. His killing boomerang never failed to bring down game.

But when he was growing old he developed the whim to roam the bush alone. He lost the desire to remain a leader. All he did for the tribe was search out the best bits of fallen stone so that they might grind them into tomahawk blades, axe heads, or spear points.

One day a thick mist fell amongst the rugged hills and he lost his way. He had travelled over the valley between two rounded peaks, and descended into a ravine on the other side. He went on and ascended other peaks and went down into other gullies until he grew tired and then he tried to return to the camp. But he was not sure that he had negotiated as many ridges and tramped through so many gullies, for they were all so much alike that it was very difficult for anyone to know one from another.

When he realised that he was lost—had failed to remember in what direction he had come—he simply sat down to wait until the mist cleared away. But rain set in and he grew very cold. Then night fell, and, as everything was wet, he could not make a fire.

He remembered quite well the feel of the steep fall of ground on the side of the first peak he had crossed when the fog came and tried to find it again, though it was still dark. He walked as much to make himself warm as to find the way. He crossed over high ground and went into other deep places, and at last he felt that he was going down a steep enough place to be where he had started to climb, and there he rested until the day broke.

The mist lightened and he could see that he was not at the place where he wished to be and where he was when the fog first shut out the scene. There the trees were the white-barked tea-tree and the underscrub was wire grass and small rushes. But here were gums and wattles, and the undergrowth was Macrozamia and Chorizema and Wild Fuschia and Clematis and Sarsaparilla Vine. And it was much deeper. He knew all the plants that grew in his part of the country. He, of course, had his own names for them. The Acacia glaucescens, with its long yellow rolls of pollen he called 'Karrawan', and the beautiful little Dillwynia ericifolia he called 'Wannara'; the white-flowering Bloodwood he called 'Mannen', and the pretty Wonga Vine he knew as 'Telaaraweera'.

What was he to do now? His hand had lost its cunning. His mind was not so alert. Unless he could find the tribe soon, he must die of cold and hunger. So he turned and endeavoured to go back. He climbed again the steep mountainside and on top he was amongst many boulders, and the tussocked grasses and the burrawangs were such as he had never seen before. He blundered on. In his anxiety he became uncertain of foot and often he faltered and almost fell. The rain came on again and the mist—the clouds that fell to earth—rested once more about him.

He coo-eed, but no answering coo-ee came to him. Several days went by and it still rained and was still cold and misty, and it gave no promise of clearing. He had found roots in plenty but he lacked animal food, especially its fat, which was his most nourishing article of diet. He lived, though he grew weaker.

At last he found a track. He knew it to be the well-beaten track of the brush wallaby, and he reckoned that if he waited patiently that night beside the path and hid, he would intercept the animal, and meat and fat would be his. During the night the rain ceased, and a wind sprang up that shook the water from the leaves and blew away the clouds.

He hid beside the wallaby track and he had not long to wait. Thud, thud, crash, crash, thud, thud—the wallaby was coming down from the ledges above to browse on the succulent grasses of the level and clear country.

The man was patience itself. He grasped his nullah more firmly, and with one hand parting the leaves before him he decided just when to strike the blow.

(It is strange that no white man can hunt a wild animal so. Wild things see him or smell him; and, besides, he cannot wait.)

The marsupial hopped unsuspectingly on, stopping every little while to nibble at some young shoots that overhung or infringed upon the track. Then, like lightning, the nullah sprang into being and it shot out straight to the wallaby's ear. The wallaby made a feeble defence with his clawed feet but he went down and his life went out with the trickle of blood that wandered slowly and brokenly down from the place where it had been struck.

Next day the man ate and was filled, and then he slept—a sounder sleep than he had had since he left his tribe. The wind that had been but a slight breeze sprang into life. It grew stronger and stronger, and increased until it roared through the great gum trees like a mighty torrent of water. The huge branches were tossed, and they swayed and crashed amongst one another and were twisted apart and fell. The small twigs snapped and were whirled about and strewed the ground like thick moss. The huge bark trunks leaned and strained and groaned and split and often cracked and thundered down. Giant masses of cloud swept overhead. A bird now and then attempted flight and was whirled and dashed to death. Wallabies and native rats and dingoes grew afraid, and, leaping from the safety of their sheltered places, they sped off, bounding amongst the roaring trees and being twirled and blown and staggered in the awful gale.

The man slid down a crumbling bank into a bouldered creek. There was safety there unless the creek rose. If a tree fell it could not crush him; and trees did fall, but not one nor yet a broken limb caught him. They fell across the creek and rested on the boulders, and beneath it all he was not only safe, but also warm. Just as suddenly as the gale sprang up so it went and, as is usual, it was followed by another great downpour of rain.

He had to climb out of his shelter, and he found a hollowed stump, which served to keep him dry. With the remnant of the wallaby he felt that he could be comfortable until the storm ceased altogether.

After two days the sun came out warm and the vapour steamed off the earth and sailed up through the treetops and into the sky from which it came. He left his shelter and pushed on to the top of a ridge. Shading his eyes with his hand, he peered away over the gum trees, searching the lines of ridges as shown by the colouring of foliage, looking for smoke.

Ah! There was smoke! It was a long way off, but he would make towards it. He knew he would have to walk all day and he set off.

Towards evening he ascended another hilltop and found no vantage point, so he climbed a tree, and from there he saw the smoke again but it was not in the same place, therefore the tribe must be moving, and moving fast.

He decided to camp there for the night, and be fresh to push on in the morning. Now he realised his old age, for each evening, for many evenings, he looked for the smoke and always it seemed as far off as ever. Several times he came across the fires. Once he disturbed the dogs that stayed behind to gather up the remnants of the food. There were often some dry roots or partially eaten meat or bones that had pickings lying about, and upon that scanty fare he did well enough.

He made signal fires but they were unanswered.

The country changed. The basalt rocks—the sharp, brittle, ringing stone—disappeared, and the ridges were ridges of sandstone. The vegetation was different, too, and one day there, just in front of him, was a plant and a flower the like of which he had never seen before. It did not grow in his basalt region.

He plucked it and smelt it and parted its pistils and found it to be full of rich moisture. 'Meewah,' he whispered—'sweet'!

'Waratah,' he said, meaning the most beautiful thing he had ever seen!

Now he grew afraid. What tribe was he following? This was, he knew, far from his country, and he, perhaps, was only travelling into great danger and distress.

So, gathering a bunch of this wonderful flower, he turned about, intending to try to reach his own tribe in another direction.

But he was too late. A couple of men of the travelling people had returned for something, and they spied him and called to him to stop. He did not quite understand their language, but he sensed their intentions. He dropped the waratahs and faced them.

All they did, however, was pick up the flowers and, by pointing, order him off. They did not harm him.

In a few more days he saw other smoke and then he found his own people. He had a great tale to tell. Away in the direction which he showed, a wonderful flower grew. Its bush was beautiful, its form was unique, its colour was gorgeous and it had a sweet juice that he had sipped. It was 'meewah' and 'waratah'—sweet and beautiful.

A few of the daring ones agreed to go in search of it. Selecting the best of their weapons, and, with the old chief to guide them, they sallied out.

It proved to be only about six days' march to the place where the wonderful flowers were growing. The country there was an upheaval and outheaval of sandstone. The rocks were plainly thrown there by static pressure, and they were not caused by fire, but by successive layers of sand washed by running water. And the soil was scanty and poor and full of gravel. It was rich, however, in just what this pretty flower needed, and the roots of the stunted gums kept the soil friable and gave the underground stem of the waratah its proper food.

The party plucked many plants. They destroyed many, too, for they did not understand its habits. They broke the stem from the brittle root and carried it away. Shortly afterwards they went again. By this time the owners of the grounds had found traces of the marauders and they lay in wait.

The men made a great outcry when the intruders came. There was a great hurling of spears and some death cries. The fighting was brief and savage and was soon over.

Not one of the trespassers ever returned to his people.

Now amongst them there was a great sorcerer. He knew more of the mystic signs and the daubing of pipeclay and the sending up of smoke through a hollow trunk than any other of his folk. Often he had saved the tribe. When food was scarce he could find it. When rain was needed he made it with his magic and his smoke magic. And now he was killed.

The people knew what the non-return of the medicine man and the continued absence of the chief meant and the events were rightly interpreted. The chief's son was made leader with all due ceremony. A corroboree was held and every lad who was anywhere near the fighting age was initiated and tried out. At this corroboree the young chief worked himself up into a state of great frenzy and this communicated itself to all those present. He grew passionate with no attempt to check himself. In this way he increased his daring and when he felt himself fit and had engendered sufficient boasting on the part of the young men, he gave the order to go to war. Their medicine man and their chief were to be avenged, or brought back if alive, though none believed them to be alive.

They were only three days following in the wake of their missing people when they found all the evidence of their fate. They went on. The waratahs were in bloom and they marvelled at the glorious sight. But they were bent on retaliation, and they wasted no time.

The scouts of the rearguard of the tribe here were not slow to learn of their coming. They sighted the formidable spears and the huge bark shields. They sighted, too, the determined attitude of this band of fighting men. They reported to their chief, and orders were given for the women and children to go down into a walled-in gully with but one avenue of approach.

The women went down—all but two young ones who trembled for the safety of their lovers, and who ran the risk of defying the old women so that they could watch the battle.

The little band of defenders yelled and rushed upon their enemies and the spears flew. Those from the intruding tribe fell harmlessly but the little band of men who were protecting their country reserved their spears until they were only a few yards from the foremost of the attacking men, and then together, as one man, they hurled theirs. Every one found the intended billet. The great mob of invaders wavered and then turned and fled.

Then came a wonderful and inexplicable thing. It was a great bright light, burning blue, and travelling at an enormous rate. It came down out of heaven and no one knew who had caused it, but all believed that it must have been some sorcerer greater than any ever known.

The earth trembled because of the speed of the visitation. The air was filled with hissing sound. The glare dazzled, and in a fraction of time the thing had struck the earth. The ground heaved and was rent. Stones went up, masses of earth flew, a terrific explosion roared. The noise of the burst was deafening, and it reverberated around and amongst the hills and through the bush until all the world was just a great full noise. The fighting men fell flat, and there they remained until the young women who had stayed to watch the battle came to them, for they were the first to recover their senses.

The girls were full of consternation seeing no men standing up, but all lying as if killed, and each ran to her lover. There was really nothing wrong with the men. They were only stricken with a terror they had never before experienced. They looked up expecting to find, no one knows what, and seeing the girls their spent courage in some measure returned.

But what of the others? There was no trace. The terrible thing had wiped them right out, and of them there remained not a vestige. And just beyond them the waratahs stood serenely, for not one was hurt.

During the ensuing night more heavenly fires darted hither and thither. The frightened people grew somewhat accustomed to them and they watched them. They believed that the fires fell because the waratahs were being taken by those who had no right to them.

In those parts of Australia where the waratah is unknown, shooting stars are said to be souls returning, and often men may be seen searching for them. But, in country where the waratah grows, the coming of a meteor or the shooting of stars is held to be a sign that the bright red blooms were being stolen.

Waratahs were, and still are, quite immune from the effects of such fire. That is why the Aborigines brought the waratah stems to the early blacksmiths, when white people came. They thought that the sparks from the anvil were the same fire as that that came from the sky that day.

MARKS'S CUTTER

E.O. SCHLUNKE

IT WAS A GREAT day when Marks's chaff-cutting outfit came to cut up the hay stooked in our long, 200-acre paddock. It looked like a train, but a magical train that ran without rails along the roads and through our paddocks. It came so slowly that we couldn't believe it would ever arrive.

First the great steam traction engine with its wheels twice as high as a man, puffing out smoke and leaking little jets of steam all over it, reeking of oil and steam and wood-fire and hot metal; then the cutter, not as big or impressive, running on its four small wheels, with a curved iron roof built over it, and a noticeable lean to the left; then the 'travelling kitchen' made of galvanised iron, and mounted on a low platform wagon. Next came the long steam-box with two wheels at the back end and the front attached to the cook's galley.

Last of the train was Marks's old T-model Ford car full of his piratical-looking crew, being towed because there was no point in rushing on ahead. And, following so far behind that we were not quite sure if it belonged to the outfit, was a fat, waddling horse pulling a Furphy water cart, with the wood-and-water-Joey sitting unhappily on the shaft.

Next day we went to see them working, having got ourselves into a fine state of excitement from hearing the steam whistle. Our father said it tooted too often; they must be having trouble if they were starting and stopping so much. He walked so fast across the stubble that we had a job keeping up with him—he always got upset if anything wasn't going properly on his farm.

As we drew near we could smell all the hot engine smells again with a new one added, the sweet, damp smell of steamed hay. Despite the steaming there was a lot of dust about. It came streaming down the wind from the cutter, a million glittering and gleaming particles from the lacquered wheat stalks, looking like the stuff our mother sprinkled over the Christmas tree. We knew, however, from unhappy experience, that it would make our skins itch intolerably, so we began to bear away to the right to avoid it. But father kept straight on ahead.

'You don't want the men to think you're softies?' he said. And we had to follow him, holding our shirt collars tightly round our necks, and rushing through as fast as we could run.

Marks came to speak to our father. He was a tall man with sagging shoulders, his face mottled red all over, looking very strange to us because we had been brought up among sober people. He wore a grin that looked most villainous, showing a few teeth here and there, grown grotesquely long because there were none opposite to keep them worn down. His hands and clothes were black with grease.

Father said gruffly, 'Having a bit of trouble?' And he stared at Marks as if he didn't approve of his light-hearted grin under the circumstances.

'Elevator train broke in the middle of the steamer and we had trouble getting it out.' Then he turned a roving, rolling and roguish eye at us boys and said, 'Pity one of youse wasn't here to crawl up the steamer.'

We looked with popping eyes at the steamer—a long tube made of galvanised iron, with a procession of sheaves of hay running up through it to the cutter, and steam spurting from all its crevices. We moved over close behind our father for protection.

Marks began to talk of less terrifying matters, so we had a good look at how his outfit worked. Where the hay came out of the steamer a fearful, whiskery old fellow, perched on a high, rocking platform, took charge of it and pushed it into the mouth of the cutter. He battled with the hay and the cutter as with mortal enemies, his face contorted with rage. Every now and then he looked up at the skies and cursed the cutter in venomous tones and with a noticeably foreign accent, but all the time his hands flew dexterously.

The band-cutter, noticing our astonishment, said, 'Mad old bastard, but the only man in the country who can get more than half a ton an hour through her.'

At the other end of the cutter where the chaff came out, two men wearing only shorts and sandshoes sewed up the bags deftly, pushing the needle in and pulling it through in one quick movement; then, hoisting the bags on their shoulders, they ran up the pyramid of stacked chaff as nimbly as monkeys.

Suddenly there was a bang and then a grinding noise in the bowels of the cutter, and geysers of chaff were spewed out of various orifices. All the men round the machine yelled, their faces showing various degrees of annoyance because they were on piecework, and the engineer ran to stop the engine.

Marks alone looked good-humoured.

'Only the riddle box,' he said. 'Fix that in a minute.'

But the men looked at each other in sudden anger and condemned their souls if they knew why they stayed with such an old rattletrap outfit.

We looked at our father to see how he was taking all the swearing, because he was very strict with us in that way, but he seemed to be only concerned about getting the machinery going again. Marks and the engine-driver undid some bolts, pulled off parts of the cutter, and let a cascade of chaff flow out. Then the engine-driver crawled in among the chaff, regardless of itch and irritation, to screw and hammer.

A dejected-looking man with a long downward-curving mouth joined father; he was the teamster who carted the chaff to the railway station. He tried to curry favour with father by telling him he had once had a farm of his own but had lost it through sheer bad luck.

Father looked as if he didn't believe any part of the story, so the teamster started sneering at Marks and his outfit. As father hardly bothered to answer, he took a chaff bag and began to bag up the chaff that spilled out of the cutter, for his horses, watching father to see if he was going to make him pay for it.

Presently the engine-driver emerged with chaff leaking out of his sleeves and trousers. The parts were slammed back and the whistle blew. The men rose slowly from where they were sitting and said cynically, 'How long will she go this time?'

The wood-and-water-Joey came trudging along with a load of water slopping out of the Furphy. He stopped about ten yards from the engine, notwithstanding the engine-driver's beckoning and shouting to him to bring it within reach of his hose.

'Come and get it yourself!' he shouted back, and retreated with an anxious eye on the steam-pressure gauge.

He was a very melancholy individual with a long, flattened nose, no teeth, and ragged clothes.

'She'll blow up and kill everybody one of these days,' he told us. 'They've been dodging the boiler inspector for years. Only last week one of the pipes burst just when I was backing up the cart.'

He lifted his rag of a sleeve and said, 'Look.'

The skin had peeled off the entire length of his arm. We didn't feel so contemptuous of his cowardice after that, but gazed admiringly at the engine-driver, who was clambering up and down all the time. He started a pump to get the water out of the cart into the engine, and the extra strain slowed the cutter down to half speed. All the crew gazed apprehensively at the engine.

The next day when we came home from school the outfit was silent. We ran down to see why and found the engine surrounded by heaps of raked-out ashes and pools of rusty water. The engine-driver was somewhere inside the still blisteringly hot engine, trying to find out what had put the fire out. Marks was standing by with his grin, saying reassuringly to his men, 'It's only a bloody pipe. That boiler's all right for another fifty years.'

'Fifty years my fat arse,' one of the bag-sewers said and the others laughed in rueful agreement. Marks laughed, too.

The engine-driver came out feet first, as red, hot and dripping as a well-boiled yabbie coming out of the pot.

'It's only a boiler pipe,' he said, smiling at Marks despite his distress. 'Hand me a Stillson and I'll go in again and undo it.'

The others said, 'You'll kill yourself.'

After he'd gone in again Marks said confidentially to the men, 'He's a good boy.'

The engine-driver had to come out twice for air, but in about half an hour he had the broken pipe out.

'Have to go into town now for a new one,' he said.

There was a chorus of yells—'Room for me?' 'Take me, too?'— and a rush to the car. It was full when Marks arrived, struggling into a torn pullover.

'Ah, you buggers,' he said, 'I don't mind taking a few of you along, but will you be ready to come back again?'

All the men were prepared to pledge their chance of salvation. Marks looked at them unbelievingly and hopelessly, but still grinning.

'Ah, you buggers,' he said again, 'if I find any of you you'll be blind and no use all tomorrow.'

'You'll have to throw us out now,' said the biggest bag-sewer, getting a good grip on a good support.

Marks gave a resigned shrug and squeezed a couple of men over so that he could get behind the wheel.

Next morning the cutter was still idle. We ran down before breakfast and saw that the Ford had not returned. The men who had stayed behind were still asleep—Strelitz, the feeder, in his clean white tent, the cook in his galley, quite a colony on their stretchers under flies attached to the teamster's wagon, and the wood-and-water-Joey, who seemed to have no gear at all and camped in a stook of hay with a couple of chaff bags for blankets.

When we were nearly at school we met the car, the young engine-driver at the wheel with Marks leaning heavily on him, and in the back a heap of tangled limbs, trunks and heads.

When we got home that night our mother was in a scandalised state.

'Don't you go down to the cutter,' she said. 'Mr Marks couldn't find more than half his men last night, and this morning he went to the police, and they gave him enough men from the cells to make up his team.'

We sneaked down as soon as she forgot to keep an eye on us, but it was hard to pick out the jailbirds from the rest of the crew. The engine and cutter were running well, but the output was slow. Half the men were blundering about dizzily, and several were flat out where they had fallen. Many of them were more or less damaged, and even the engine-driver had a black eye.

On the following afternoon the outfit was still running well and the new men looking less awkward at their jobs.

It seemed as if Marks's luck had changed.

Then we saw a man come wheeling a bicycle between the stooks, inappropriately dressed for summer cycling in a town suit, with thick woollen socks pulled over the ends of his trousers.

He leaned his bicycle against Strelitz's tent and carefully dried his face and the inside of his collar. He wiped his hands and then strode deliberately across to Marks. The original members of the crew looked significantly at each other.

The teamster, always eager to tell something to Marks's detriment, came over to us with a malicious grin on his face.

'It's the bailiff,' he said. 'Marks's wife always keeps dunning him for maintenance money.'

Some of the other men, possibly with matrimonial trouble of their own, were all sympathy for Marks.

'The lousy bitch!' they said. 'Always at him as soon as he starts to earn a bit of money.'

'If mine did that,' said another, 'I'd cut her bloody throat.'

We were vastly interested in this glimpse into real-life drama. We stared at the bailiff and edged a bit closer to hear what he was saying. He was a fair, slight man with a mild and pleasant face, and he spoke as if he were merely collecting orders for groceries, or something like that.

'If you just sign this paper,' he was saying helpfully, 'Mrs Marks will be able to get the money straight from the produce merchant who bought the hay.'

It seemed to be a very simple transaction.

But Marks was grinning and swallowing and waving his hands about uncertainly. He pushed his hat back to scratch his head, and when we saw that his hair was white we were suddenly very sorry for him.

'Come on,' said the bailiff briskly, 'I've got a long way to ride home. It'll be all right.'

Marks wiped a greasy hand on his trousers and took the pen.

'By cripes, I hope so!' he said.

He didn't grin so much when the men began to chip him. He stroked his jaw thoughtfully with his black hands and said, 'I don't know how it will turn out. I signed one of them papers before, to get you blokes wages.'

'That will be her funeral,' one of the wife-haters said joyfully.

But the decrepit old wood-and-water-Joey said ominously, 'My word, you've done it now!'

At the tea table that night our mother was inclined to condemn Marks, but father had the severest ideas about wives who took the law against their husbands.

After that there was always something exciting going on at the cutter. They had their breakdowns every couple of days, but we were now more interested in the real-life drama. What we didn't see we heard about from the teamster, who seemed to be having the time of his life.

The bailiff came out again, gave Marks a severe lecture, and got him to sign another and different paper. The wood-and-water-Joey was shocked when he heard about this; he seemed to have a wide knowledge of the various papers people could sign to their detriment.

Several days later two severe and outraged men accompanied the bailiff. They tried hard to make Marks go back to town with them, but after he had refused defiantly several times, and called to the boys to come over and hear what they were trying to do to him, the bailiffs left him, after getting him to sign a paper still another shape and colour.

The wood-and-water-Joey seemed to think that now Marks might just as well go and cut his throat.

In between bailiffs and breakdowns they gradually got the hay cut. Marks did not go to town when new parts had to be procured, but sent the engine-driver. However, there always seemed to be momentous news for him, and we were not really surprised when we saw two large policemen arrive.

Marks had not been at the cutter all that day, and the teamster's guess was that he was 'in the dead centre of your father's big scrub paddock'.

The day came when the last stook was chopped into chaff, and the men began packing up and hooking all the parts of the outfit into a train again.

'He's going to make a run for it now,' the sour teamster said.

That rather amused us, because the traction engine travelled at about two miles an hour and the big wheels left tracks two feet wide wherever they went.

Then suddenly a car came tearing down the road and across our paddock. Some of the men said it was the bailiff and some said the police, and all of them were right.

This time, we could see, there was going to be no nonsense, but we were hardly prepared for what they did. The bailiff read out a paper that left Marks quite speechless and then, while the police stood each side of Marks, the two severe-looking men put seals all over the engine, cutter, steamer, galley and Furphy. The teamster came over and told us gloatingly that they were seizing the plant for debt.

When it was all done they waited there for Marks to leave, but he didn't seem to realise that there was nothing for him to do but go away empty-handed. Finally he got into his old Ford with the engine-driver and as many of the gang as could pile in with him and drove off.

The severe-looking men were suddenly desolated that they had omitted to seize the car.

* * *

The chaff-cutting plant stood there for a long time.

Now and then hopeful-looking bargain-hunters came to inspect it, but none of them bought it. Father was always most discouraging when they asked his opinion of it. Of course he was all for law and order, but he thought it was the ultimate outrage to 'deprive a man of his living'.

The time came round to plough the long 200-acres again, and we had to leave nearly an acre untouched where the plant was standing.

No more chaff-cutting contractors came to look at it, but the scrap-iron merchants began to take an interest. That was in the days when we were selling a lot of scrap iron to Japan. Father told them we didn't know who owned the plant now, trying to make things difficult for them. When they hinted that they'd give him a fiver to say nothing he was so indignant that we saw no more of scrap-iron merchants.

Then, after the next harvest, when we and many of our neighbours were away on holidays at the coast, the plant disappeared. There was heavy rain before we returned and we couldn't see any tracks. Father's explanation to everyone who commented on the disappearance of a landmark was, 'I believe those confounded scrap-iron pedlars dismantled it and frisked it away.'

Sowing time had come again, when one day while we were waiting to go home from town, we saw father talking to a pair of rough-looking men in the street. After he got into the car he kept smiling to himself and our mother looked at him hard several times to see if he'd been drinking. Father began to chuckle.

'You don't know who those two men have been working for, way down in Ganmain,' he challenged us.

Then he gave us a hint to help us guess: 'On a chaff-cutting plant . . . the chaff-cutting plant that used to stand in our paddock.'

'A WALGETT EPISODE'

BANJO PATERSON

The sun strikes down with a blinding glare,
The skies are blue and the plains are wide,
The saltbush plains that are burnt and bare
By Walgett out on the Barwon side—
The Barwon River that wanders down
In a leisurely manner by Walgett Town.

There came a stranger—a 'cockatoo'—
The word means farmer, as all men know
Who dwell in the land where the kangaroo
Barks loud at dawn, and the white-eyed crow
Uplifts his song on the stockyard fence
As he watches the lambkins passing hence.

The sunburnt stranger was gaunt and brown,
But it soon appeared that he meant to flout
The iron law of the country town,
Which is—that the stranger has got to shout:
'If he will not shout we must take him down,'
Remarked the yokels of Walgett Town.

They baited a trap with a crafty bait,
With a crafty bait, for they held discourse
Concerning a new chum who of late
Had bought such a thoroughly lazy horse;

87

They would wager that no one could ride him down
The length of the city of Walgett Town.

The stranger was born on a horse's hide;
So he took the wagers, and made them good
With his hard-earned cash—but his hopes they died,
For the horse was a clothes-horse, made of wood!
'Twas a well-known horse that had taken down
Full many a stranger in Walgett Town.

The stranger smiled with a sickly smile—
'Tis a sickly smile that the loser grins—
And he said he had travelled for quite a while
In trying to sell some marsupial skins.
'And I thought that perhaps, as you've took me down,
You would buy them from me, in Walgett Town!'

He said that his home was at Wingadee,
At Wingadee where he had for sale
Some fifty skins and would guarantee
They were full-sized skins, with the ears and tail
Complete, and he sold them for money down
To a venturesome buyer in Walgett Town.

Then he smiled a smile as he pouched the pelf,
'I'm glad that I'm quit of them, win or lose:
You can fetch them in when it suits yourself,
And you'll find the skins—on the kangaroos!'
Then he left—and the silence settled down
Like a tangible thing upon Walgett Town.

Part 3
DAVE IN LOVE

Here are some 'love stories' from the bush. They range in style from Henry Handel Richardson's insightful examination of adolescent sexual awakening to the stereotypical Victorian melodrama of Marcus Clarke and Ethel Mills.

In between those two extremes are some delightfully well-observed stories which delve into various aspects of the relationships between men and women. Some are poignant, some are amusing, and some are both. What they have in common is a special 'bush' flavour—most of them explore the stoic nature of the outback characters whose tales they are.

Lawson once wrote, 'they say that I never have written of love'. Of course he had, and quite successfully, too. It is, however, a common, ill-informed 'furphy' that our colonial authors did not write well about women and love. I hope this selection of stories proves *that* opinion to be a furphy, indeed.

'TO MANY LADIES'

'DR NIL'
(CHARLES SOUTER)

When you raise your gentle eyes
All the blue fades from the skies.
When your tones so softly ring
All the birds forget to sing.
When you smile, the sea smiles too.
'Tis the same, whate'er you do:
Nature takes her cue from you.

THE WRONG TURNING

HENRY HANDEL RICHARDSON

THE WAY HE HELPED her into the boat was delicious, simply delicious: it made her feel like a grown-up lady to be taken so much care of. Usually, people didn't mind how you got in and out of things, as you were only thirteen. And before he let her step off the landing he took her strap of books from her, those wretched schoolbooks, which stamped her, but which she hadn't known how to get rid of: her one chance of going for a row was secretly, on her way home from school. But he seemed to understand, without being told, how she despised them, and he put them somewhere in the boat where they wouldn't get wet, and yet she didn't need to see them. (She wondered what he had done with his own.)

He was so NICE; everything about him was nice: his velvety brown eyes and white teeth; his pink cheeks and fair hair. And when he took his coat off and sat down, and rolled up his sleeves and spanned his wrists on the oars, she liked him better still: he looked so strong . . . almost as if he could have picked the boat up and carried it. He wasn't at all forward either (she hated cheeky boys): when he had to touch her hand he went brick red, and jumped his own hand away as quick as he could.

With one stroke they were off and gliding downstream . . . oh, so smoothly! It made her think of floating in milk . . . though the water was *really* brown and muddy-looking. Soon they would be quite away from the houses and the little back gardens and allotments that ran down to the water, and out among the woods, where the river twisted like a snake, and the trees hung over the edge and dipped their branches in . . . most romantically. Then perhaps he would say something. He hadn't spoken yet; he was too busy rowing, making great sweeps with the oars, and not looking at her . . . or only taking a peep now and then, to see if she saw. Which she did, and her heart thumped with pleasure. Perhaps, as he was so clever at it, he'd be a sailor when he was a man and go to sea. But that would mean him travelling far away, and she might never see him again. And though she'd only known him for a fortnight, and at first he hadn't liked to speak, but had just stood and made eyes at her when they met going home from school, she felt she simply couldn't bear it if he did.

To hide her feelings, she hung one hand over the side of the boat and let it trail, through the water—keeping it there long after it was stone cold, in the hope that he would notice it and say something. But he didn't.

The Boy was thinking: I wonder if I dare tell her not to . . . her little hand . . . all wet like that, and cold. I should like to take it in both mine, and rub it dry, and warm it. *How* pretty she is, with all that fuzzy-wuzzy hair, and the little curls on her forehead. And how long her eyelashes are when she looks down. I wish I could make her look up . . . look at me. But how? Why, say something, of course. But what? Oh, if *only* I could think of something! What does one? What would Jim say, if he wanted to make his girl look at him? But nothing came.

Here, however, the hand was jerked from the water to kill a gnat that had settled on the other. This was his cue. He parted hastily with his saliva.

'I say! Did it sting?'

She suppressed the no that was on her lips.

'Well . . . yes . . . I think it did, rather.' And doubling her bony little schoolgirl fingers into her palm, she held out the back of the hand for his inspection. Steadying the oars, the Boy leant forward to look, leant so far that, for a wild moment, she believed he was going to kiss the place, and half instinctively, half from an equally strong impulse to 'play him', drew it away. But he did not follow it up: at the thought of a kiss, which *had* occurred to him, shyness lamed him anew. So nothing came of this either. And we've only half an hour, thought the Girl distractedly. If he doesn't say something . . . soon . . . there won't be any time left. And then it will all have been for nothing.

She, too, beat her brains. 'The trees . . . aren't they pretty, the way they hang right down in the water?' (Other couples stopped under these trees, she'd seen them, and lay there in their boats; or even went right in behind the weeping willows.) But his sole response was: 'Good enough.' And another block followed.

Oh, he saw quite well what she was aiming at: she wanted him to pull in to the bank and ship his oars, so that they could do a bit of spooning, she lying lazy in the stern. But at the picture a mild panic seized him. For, if he couldn't find anything to say even when he was rowing, it would be ten times harder when he sat with his hands before him and nothing to do. His tongue would stick to the roof of his mouth, dry as a bone, and then she'd see for sure how dull he was. And never want to go out with him again. No, thank you, not for him!

But talk wasn't everything—by gum, it wasn't! He might be a rotten hand at speechifying, but what he could *do*, that he'd jolly well show her! And under this urge to display his strength, his skill, he now fell to work in earnest. Forward swung the oars, cleanly carving the water, or lightly feathering the surface; on flew the boat, he driving to and fro with his jaws grimly set and a heightened colour, the muscles standing out like pencils on his arms. Oh, it was a fine thing to be able to row so well, and have a girl, THE girl, sitting watching you. For now her eyes hung on him, mutely adoring, spurring him on to ever-bolder strokes.

And then a sheerly dreadful thing happened. So lost was he in showing his mastery, in feeding on her looks, that he failed to keep his wits about him. And, coming to a place where the river forked, he took the wrong turning, and before he knew it they were in a part where you were not supposed to go—a bathing place for men, much frequented by soldiers.

A squeal from the Girl roused him; but then it was too late: they had shot in among a score of bathers, whose heads bobbed about on the surface like so many floating footballs. And instantly her shrill cry was taken up and echoed and re-echoed by shouts, and laughter, and rude 'hullos', as the swimmers scattered before the oars.

Coarse jokes were bandied, too, at the unwarranted intrusion. Hi! Wasn't there nowhere else he could take his girl? Or was she coming in, too? Off with her togs then! Crimson with mortification at his blunder, at the fool he had made of himself (before her), the Boy savagely strove to turn the boat and escape. But the heads—there seemed to be hundreds of them—deliberately blocked his way. And while he manoeuvred, the sweat trickling down his forehead, a pair of arms and shoulders reared themselves from the water, and two hands grasped the side of the boat. It rocked; and the Girl squealed anew, shrinking sideways from the nearness of the dripping, sunburnt flesh.

'Come on, missie, pay toll!'

The Boy swore aloud. But even worse was to come. On one bank, a square of wooden palisades had been built out round a stretch of water and a wooden bath-house, where there were cabins for the men to strip in, platforms to jump from, ropes strung for those who could not swim. But in this fence was a great gap, where some of the palings had fallen down. And in his rage and confusion the Boy had the misfortune to bring the boat right alongside it; and then . . . then . . . .

Inside the enclosure, out of the cabins, down the steps, men were running, jumping, chasing, leap-frogging . . . every one of them as naked as on the day he was born.

For one instant the Girl raised her eyes—one only . . . but it was enough. She saw. And he saw that she saw. And now, to these two young creatures, it seemed as if the whole visible world—themselves, boat, river, trees and sky—caught fire, and blazed up in one gigantic blush. Nothing existed for them anymore but this burning redness. Nor could they escape; there they had to sit, knee to knee, face to face, and scorch, and suffocate; the blood filling their eyes till they could scarcely see, mounting to their hair roots, making even their fingertips throb and tingle.

Gritting his teeth, the Boy rowed like a machine that had been wound up and was not to be stopped. The Girl sat with drooped head—it seemed to have grown strangely heavy—and but a single wish: to get out and away . . . where he could not see her. For all was over between them—both felt that.

Something catastrophic had happened, rudely shattering their frail young dreams; breaking down his boyish privacy, pitching her headlong into a reality for which she was in no wise prepared.

If it had been hard beforehand to find things to say, it was now impossible. And on the way home no sound was to be heard but the dip of the oars, the water's cluck and gurgle round the boat. At the landing place, she got out by herself, took from him, without looking up, her strap of books, and said a brief goodbye; keeping to a walking pace till she had turned the corner, then breaking into a run, and running for dear life . . . as if chased by some grotesque nightmare-shape which she must leave far, far behind her . . . even in thought.

SPICER'S COURTSHIP

EDWARD DYSON

SPICER WAS A SELECTOR. Why he chose to be a selector rather than enjoy comparative ease and affluence as a corporation day labourer or a wharf-hand or navvy is inexplicable. He had taken to the wilderness, built his smart bark hut in the centre of an apparently impenetrable forest, and was now actively engaged eating his way out again. Along the bank of the trickling creek he had cleared an acre or so where a few fruit trees flourished and a methodical little vegetable garden looked green and encouraging. Dick Spicer was a methodical man; what he did he did well, and he was always doing.

Dick was small, and he looked puny lifting his pygmy axe to those mighty gums, and patiently hewing splinters out of the compact bush. Having little or nothing to say to his scattered neighbours, he exchanged small talk with his hens, and favoured Griffin, the low-comedy dog-of-all-work, with his opinion of things.

Mr Spicer was a bachelor, approaching fifty, wiry, leathery, deliberative, and very diffident in company. But, despite his apparent uneasiness when chance threw him into the society of females, Dick was looking about for a wife. The stillness of the long evenings and the solitary Sundays implanted a great yearning for the companionship of a good wife in his lonely heart.

In looking about, the selector's view was very limited. There was not an unmarried woman of suitable years within a radius of twelve miles. Of all the approachable females, he admired Mrs Clinton the most, and his only hope lay in the fact that Clinton was in feeble health and reported to be sustaining life precariously with one lung.

Clinton held a block about a mile up the creek, and Spicer paid him occasional abrupt and unceremonious visits there. Sometimes he would lean against a door jamb, with not more than his head inside, and pass a few remarks relative to nothing in particular, in an irresponsible sort of way; but more frequently he just stood about outside, and criticised the poultry in audible soliloquy, or reflected aloud upon Clinton's ridiculous notions about dairy work and vegetable growing. However, he always displayed a proper neighbourly concern in inquiring after Clinton's health before leaving.

'Y'ain't feelin' no better, I s'pose?' he would ask, with an appearance of anxious interest that quite touched the sick man.

Clinton was always feeling 'pretty bad'. He said as much in his dull, heavy manner, and Dick would go off to indulge in contemplation, and consult his dog.

Spicer did not wish Clinton to die, he did not want to hurry him up; he was a patient, dispassionate man, and the possibility of his neighbour's early demise entered into his calculations merely as a probable circumstance which, however regrettable, could not reasonably be overlooked.

Clinton substantiated predictions, and obligingly died within a reasonable time, and Dick rode solemnly in the funeral cortege, behind the drays, on a lame cart horse borrowed from Canty for the occasion.

After the funeral he looked in upon the widow and, feeling inspired to say something consolatory and encouraging, expressed his belief that she wouldn't mourn much about Peter.

''Tain't worthwhile,' he said.

Dick's command of language was only sufficient to enable him to say the thing he meant once in a dozen tries, and on this occasion he was conscious the moment he had spoken that the sentiment expressed was hardly appropriate to the occasion. Before he could frame an apology the disconsolate widow attacked him with a spear-grass broom and stormed him out of the house. He walked home thoughtfully, afflicted with a nettle-rash and a vague idea that perhaps he had not made an altogether satisfactory beginning.

But Spicer was not cast down. He had resolved upon a plan of courtship, and the object of his first manoeuvre was to break his intentions gently to the widow. This he thought to accomplish by hanging round the house a good deal. He would haunt her selection in the cool of the evening, or, in his more audacious moments, perch himself on the chock-and-log fence running by the side of the house, and whistle an unmelodious and windy jig, which was intended to convey some idea of his airy nonchalance and peace of mind.

It was a long time before Dick progressed from the fence to the wood heap, and meanwhile the widow had not seemed to pay any particular attention to his movements. He sometimes addressed her with a portentous truth bearing upon the dieting of laying hens, or the proper handling of cows, or the medical treatment of ailing chickens; but usually satisfied himself with a significant grin and a queer twist of the head that was his idea of sheer playfulness and waggery.

The neighbours came to notice him overlooking the selection or perched on the fence supervising the weather and things generally, and predicted that there would be 'a marryin' up the creek presently.

Presently!

Spicer did nothing hastily, nothing to lead anybody to believe that he had not all eternity to come and go on. He never considered the flight of time, and had made many calculations that carried him on to the end of the next century without discovering any incongruity.

He did arrive at the wood heap eventually, though. Mrs Clinton's boy John was too young to wield an axe with any effect, and one afternoon Dick lounged over to the logs, took up the axe, and examined it with an air of abstraction. He weighed it carefully in his hand, and satisfied his curiosity by trying it on a log.

When he had chopped about half a ton of wood he appeared satisfied that it was a pretty good axe. That evening he chuckled all the way up the creek, and all the time it took to prepare his tea, and towards bedtime confided to Griffin, with more chuckles, his opinion that it was "bout's good 's done.'

'She can't go back on that,' he said with assurance.

But Spicer lingered at this stage for a long time; he cut all the wood the widow needed, and did other little things about the selection, and often sat on the fence, as usual, and gradually grew to be quite at home there. The widow accepted his services now as a matter of course, and though she was often betrayed into expressions of great impatience, Dick remained oblivious, and worked out his courtship in his own ponderous way.

His next step towards strengthening his position was when he took it upon himself to put several palings on the roof of Mrs Clinton's house. This was a decided advance, and when the buxom little woman thanked him, his odd screw of the face and sidelong nod clearly conveyed the impression that he was beginning to regard himself as a 'perfect devil amongst the women'. There was more chuckling that evening, and further confidences for the dog. After this Spicer ceased working seriously on his own selection, and slowly extended his sphere at the widow's.

He did some gardening, and repaired the fences, and dictated improvements, but it was not till eighteen months after Clinton's death that he made his great stroke. It was on Sunday afternoon that Dick discovered Mrs Clinton in hot pursuit of the boy John, with one shoe in her hand and one on her foot. John was in active rebellion, and yelling his contempt for the maternal authority. Spicer rose to the occasion. He secured boy John, took off his belt, and proceeded to strap the unfilial youth—to give him a grave, judicious, and fatherly larruping—under the eye of his mother. Then the selector drew off to consider and weigh the important step he had taken, with the result that, half an hour after, he hung his head in at the kitchen door, and said abruptly:

'Treaser, when's it to be?'

'Meanin' which?' asked the unconscious widow.

'Meanin' marryin'.'

The widow thought for a moment, and said, just as if she were contemplating the sale of a few eggs:

'This day month'll suit me.'

'Done,' said Spicer.

Then he felt called upon to make some kind of a demonstration, and edged up to Mrs Clinton in a fidgeting sort of way, and when near enough made as if to kiss her, paused halfway in doubt, and then didn't.

'The man's a fool,' said the stout little widow composedly.

They were married though, under conditions of great secrecy, at the parson's house in the township, with the blinds down. It was with great difficulty Dick was convinced of the necessity of witnesses.

DAVE IN LOVE

STEELE RUDD

PLOUGHING AND SOWING ALL over. A hundred acres of the plain-
land under wheat and light showers falling every week. Dad's
good luck was continuing. Yet we were sharing other misfortunes
freely enough. The children were all down with measles, Sarah
with face-ache, Joe with a broken rib, a draught horse broke it
for him (Joe had sandy-blight, and one morning approached the
wrong end of a horse with the winkers), and Dave was the victim
of a fatal malady.

Dave was always the unlucky one. When he wasn't bitten by
a snake or a dog he was gored by a cow or something. This time
it was a woman. Dave was in love. And such love! We could
see it working in him like yeast. He became affable, smiled all
day long and displayed remarkable activity. He didn't care how
hard he worked or whose work he performed. He did anything,
everything, and without help. He developed a passion for small
things, trifles he had hitherto regarded with contempt, purchased
silk handkerchiefs and perfume and conversation-lollies at the
store, and secreted them in the pockets of his Sunday coat, which
he left hanging in his room. Sarah would find them when dusting
the coat and hawk them to Mother, and they'd spend an hour
rejoicing and speculating over the discovery. Sarah never allowed
any dust to settle on Dave's Sunday coat.

Dave went out every night. It amused Joe. He would be on
pins and needles till supper was ready, then he'd bolt his food

and rush off to saddle a horse, and we wouldn't see him again till breakfast-time next morning.

For more than a year Dave rushed off every night. 'Damn! Look at that horse!' Dad used to say, when he'd be at the yard. Then he'd think hard, and begin again when he met Mother. 'This night work'll have t' stop, or there won't be a horse about the place fit t' ride. What the devil the fellow wants chasing round the country for every night I don't know, I'm sure.'

Dad knew well enough.

'Well . . .' Mother would say good-naturedly, 'you were just as bad y'self once, Father.'

'Never, woman!' (with virtuous indignation). 'I never left a horse hanging to a fence night after night to starve.'

But there the matter always ended, and Dave continued his courting without interruption.

It was Fanny Bowman, of Ranger's Rise, Dave was after. She was twenty, dark, fresh-complexioned, robust and rosy—a good rider, good cook, and a most enterprising flirt. Tom Black, Tom Bell, Joe Sibly and Jim Moore all had sought her affections unsuccessfully. And young Cowley climbed into a loft one night and would have hanged himself with the dog-chain because of her inconstancy, only a curlew screeched 'so awfully sudden' just outside the door that he rushed out and fell down sixteen steps and 'injured himself internally'.

Fanny Bowman was a dairymaid, mostly neat and natty and nice. But there were times when she didn't look so nice. She had frequently to go into the yard and milk fifteen and twenty cows before breakfast; and a glimpse at her then, especially in wet weather, with a man's hat on, her skirts gathered round her waist, bare-footed, slush over her ankles, slush on her arms and smeared on her face, wasn't calculated to quicken a fellow's pulse. But then it wasn't at such times that Dave passed judgment on her, any more than the city swell would judge his Hetty while her hair was on the dresser and her teeth in a basin.

Some Sundays Dave used to bring Fanny to spend the afternoon at our place, and Jack Gore very often came with them. Jack Gore was Bowman's man, a superior young fellow, so Bowman boasted, one that could always be depended upon. He took his meals with the family and shared the society of their friends; went to church with them, worked his own horse in their plough, and was looked upon as one of the family.

Dave didn't look upon him as one of the family, though. He was the fly in Dave's ointment. Dave hated him like poison.

When it was time to leave, Dave had almost to break his neck to reach Fanny's side in time to lift her into the saddle. If he were a moment late, Gore would lift her. If he were slow at all in mounting his horse, Gore would coolly ride off with Fanny. If he didn't happen to be slow in mounting, Gore would ride on the near side of her and monopolise the conversation. He monopolised it in any case.

Mother and Sarah used to talk about Jack Gore.

'If I were Dave,' Sarah would say, 'I'm blest if I'd have her carrying on with him the way she does.'

'But Fanny only means it as a sister,' Mother would answer in palliation.

'Does she indeed! . . . Dave's an old fool to bother about her at all, if y' arsk me!' Sarah was developing a keen interest.

Jack Gore left Bowman's service one morning. He left it suddenly. Bowman sacked him, and Mrs Bowman talked to the neighbours about him with the wrath of an insulted mother.

'The cheek of him!' she said to Mother, 'to think he was good enough for Fanny! Why, we wouldn't have kept him a day if we'd thought . . . if we'd even dreamt. Fanny, indeed!'

But she spoke highly of Dave. She moved Mother to tears of admiration for him. And Mother couldn't resist telling Dave all that was said. Dave went to Bowman's a little earlier that night, but returned quite unexpectedly and went to bed in a bad humour.

A change came over Dave. He ceased to smile, and scarcely did any work, and never brought Fanny to see us on Sundays. At last Dave met Fanny on her way to the railway station one day, and when he came home he went straight to the album and took out her photo and jumped on it.

Jack Gore had been away from Saddletop for several months, when . . .

'Girls are more of a trouble than boys,' Mrs Bowman said despondingly to Mother one evening, at the gate. 'Boys is nothing; they can always take care of theirselves. But girls . . .' and she shook her head.

Jack Gore returned to Bowman's one day and neither Bowman nor Mrs Bowman attempted to chase him away. Work was suspended for twenty-four hours, and at midday, a tired, dust-covered parson came to their door astride a poor horse and got down and married Jack Gore to Fanny.

It was a quiet wedding.

When they heard of it Mother and Sarah whispered things to one another, and Dad thought of Dave.

'Thank God!' he said, 'the horses'll have a chance ter get fat now!'

POOR JOE

MARCUS CLARKE

HE WAS THE OSTLER at Coppinger's, and they called him Poor Joe. Nobody knew whence he came; nobody knew what misery of early mutilation had been his.

He had appeared one evening, a wandering swagman, unable to speak, and so explain his journey's aim or end, able only to mutter and gesticulate, making signs that he was cold and hungry, and needed fire and food.

The rough crowd in Coppinger's bar looked on him kindly, having for him that sympathy which marked physical affliction commands in the rudest natures. Poor Joe needed all their sympathies: he was a dwarf, and dumb.

Coppinger—bluff, blasphemous and good-hearted soul— dispatched him, with many oaths, to the kitchen and, when the next morning the deformed creature volunteered in his strange sign-speech to do some work that might 'pay for his lodging', sent him to help the ostler that ministered to King Cobb's coach horses. The ostler, for lack of a better name, perhaps, called him 'Joe' and Coppinger, finding that the limping mute, though he could speak no word of human language, had a marvellous power of communication with horseflesh, installed him as tinder-ostler and stable-helper, and fed him and gave him a bed of clean straw in the stable.

'I have taken him on,' said Coppinger, when the township cronies met the next night in the bar.

'Who?' asked the croniest, bibulously disregarding grammar.

'Poor Joe,' said Coppinger.

The sympathetic world of Bullocktown approved the epithet, and the deformed vagabond, thus baptised, was known as Poor Joe ever after. He was a quiet fellow enough. His utmost wrath never sufficed to ruffle a hair on the sleek backs of King Cobb's horses. His utmost mirth never went beyond an ape-like chuckle that irradiated his pain-stricken face, as a stray gleam of sunshine lights up the hideousness of the gargoyle on some old cathedral tower.

It was only when 'in drink' that Poor Joe became a spectacle for strangers to wonder at. Brandy maddened him, and when thus excited his misshapen soul would peep out of his sunken fiery eyes, force his grotesque legs to dance unseemly sarabands, and compel his pigeonbreast to give forth monstrous and ghastly utterances, that might have been laughs, were they not so much like groans of a brutish despair that had in it a strange chord of human suffering.

Coppinger was angry when the poor dwarf was thus tortured for the sport of the whisky drinkers, and once threw Frolicksome Fitz into the muck midden for inciting the cripple to sputter forth his grotesque croonings and snatches of gruesome merriment.

'He won't be fit for nothin' tomorrer,' was the excuse Coppinger made for his display of feeling. Indeed, on the days that followed these debauches, Poor Joe was sadly downcast. Even his beloved horses failed to cheer him, and he would sit, red-eyed and woebegone, on the post-and-rail fence, like some dissipated bird of evil omen. The only thing he seemed to love, save his horses, was Coppinger, and Coppinger was proud of this simple affection. So proud was he, that when he discovered that whenever Miss Jane, the sister of Young Bartram, from Seven Creeks, put her pony into the stable, the said pony was fondled and slobbered over and caressed by Poor Joe, he felt something like a pang of jealousy.

Miss Jane was a fair maiden, with pale gold hair, and lips like the two streaks of crimson in the leaf of the white poppy. Young Bartram, owner of Seven Creeks Station (you could see the lights in the house windows from Coppinger's) had brought her from town to 'keep house for him', and she was the beauty of the countryside.

Frolicksome Fitz, the pound-keeper, was at first inclined to toast an opposition belle (Miss Kate Ryder of Ryder's Mount), but when returning home one evening by the New Dam, he saw Miss Jane jump Black Jack over the post-and-wire into the home station paddock, he forswore his allegiance.

'She rides like an angel,' said pious Fitz, and the next time he met her he told her so.

Now this young maiden, so fair, so daring, and so silent, came upon the Bullocktown folk like a new revelation. The old Frenchman at the Melon Patch vowed tearfully that she had talked French to him like one of his countrywomen, and the schoolmaster, Mr Frank Smith, duly certificated under the Board of Education, reported that she played the piano divinely, singing like a seraph the whole while. As nobody played (except at euchre) in Bullocktown, this judgment was undisputed.

Coppinger swore, slapping with emphasis his mighty thigh, that Miss Jane was a lady, and when he said that he said everything. So, whenever Miss Jane visited the township, she was received with admiration. Coppinger took off his hat to her, Mr Frank Smith walked to the station every Sunday afternoon to see her, and Poor Joe stood afar off and worshipped her, happy if she bestowed a smile upon him once out of every five times that he held her tiny stirrups.

This taming of Poor Joe was not unnoticed by the whisky drinkers, and they came in the course of a month or so to regard the cripple as part of the property of Miss Jane, as they regarded her dog for instance. The schoolmaster, moreover, did not escape tap-room comment. He was frequently at Seven Creeks. He brought flowers from the garden there. He sent for some new clothes from Melbourne. He even borrowed Coppinger's bay mare Flirt, to ride over to the sheep-wash, and Dick the mail-boy, who knew that Coppinger's mare was pigeon-toed, vowed that he had seen another horse's tracks besides hers in the sand of the Rose Gap Road.

'You're a deep 'un, Mr Smith,' said Coppinger. 'I found yer out sparking Miss Jane along the Mountain Track. Deny it if yer can?'

But Frank Smith's pale cheek only flushed, and he turned off the question with a laugh. It was Poor Joe's eyes that snapped fire in the corner. So matters held themselves until the winter, when the unusually wet season forbade riding parties of pleasure. It rained savagely that year, as we all remember, and Bullocktown in rainy weather is not a cheerful place. Miss Jane kept at home, and Poor Joe's little eyes, wistfully turned to the Station on the hill, saw never her black pony cantering round the corner of Archie Cameron's hayrick. A deeper melancholy seemed to fall on the always-melancholy township. Coppinger's cronies took their tots in silence, steaming the while, and Coppinger himself would come gloomily to the door, speculating upon evil unless the leaden curtain lifted.

But it did not lift, and rumour of evil came. Up the country, by Parsham and Merrydale, and Black Adder's Gully, there were whole tracts of grassland under water. The neighbouring station of Hall's, in the mountains, was a swamp. The roads were bogged for miles. Tim Doolan was compelled to leave his dray and bullocks and ride for his life before the advancing waters.

The dams were brimming; at Quartzborough, St Rey reservoir was running over. It was reported by little McCleod, the sheep-dealer, that the old bridge at the Little Glimmera had been carried away. It was reported that Old Man Horn, whose residence over-looked the river, had fastened a bigger hook to a larger pole (there was a legend to the effect that Old Man Horn had once hooked a body from the greedy river, and after emptying its pockets, had softly started it downstream again), and was waiting behind his rickety door, rubbing his withered hands gleefully.

Young Bartram rode over to Quartzborough to get McCompass, the shire engineer, to look at his new dam. Then the coach stopped running, and then Flash Harry, galloping through the township at night, like the ghost-rider in Bürger's ghastly ballad, brought the terrible news: *the floods were up, and the Glimmera bank and the bank at the old crossing-place were breached.*

'It will be here in less than an hour,' he shouted, under Coppinger's red lamps; 'Make for the high ground if you love your lives!'

And wet, wild-eyed and white, he splashed off into the darkness, that he might warn the poor folk down the river of the rushing death that was coming upon them.

Those who were there have told of the horrors of that night. How the muddy street, scarce reclaimed from the riverbed, was suddenly full of startled half-dressed folk. How Coppinger's was crowded to the garret. How the schoolmaster dashed off, stumbling through the rain, to warn them at Seven Creeks. How bullies grew pale with fear, and men hitherto mild of speech and modest of mien, waxed fiery-hot with wrath at incapacity, and fiercely self-assertive in relegating fools to their place in the bewildered social economy of that general overturn. How the roaring flood came down, bearing huge trees, fragments of houses, grotesquely terrible waifs and strays of household furniture upon its yellow and turbid bosom, timid women grew brave, and brave men hid their faces for a while. How Old Man Horn saved two lives that night. How Widow Rae's cottage, with her light still burning in the windowsill, was swept off, and carried miles downstream. How Archy Cameron's hayrick stranded in the middle of the township. How forty drowned sheep were floated into the upper windows of the 'Royal Mail'. How Patey Barnes's cradle, with its newborn occupant sucking an unconscious thumb, was found jammed in the bight of the windlass in Magby's killing-yard.

How all this took place has been told, I say, by those who were present, and needs no repeating. But one thing which took place shall be chronicled here. When the terror and confusion were somewhat stilled, and Coppinger, by dint of brandy and blankets, had got some strength and courage into the half-naked, shivering creatures clustered in his ark, a sudden terrible tremor went through the crowd, like an electric current. In some mysterious way, no one knew how originating, or by what fed and fostered, men came to hear that Bartram's Dam was breaking. That is to say, that in ten minutes or less, all the land that lay between Coppinger's and the river, would be a roaring waste of water—that in less than ten minutes the Seven Creeks Station, with all its inmates, would be swept off the face of the earth, and that if Coppinger's escaped it would be a thing to thank God for.

After the first sharp agony of self-apprehension, one thought came to each—Miss Jane.

'Good God,' cried Coppinger, 'can nobody go to her?'

Ten men volunteered to go.

'It's no good,' said faint-hearted Riley, the bully of the bar. 'The dam'll burst twice over 'fore you can reach the Station.'

It was likely.

'I'll go myself,' cried brave old Coppinger; but his wife clung to his arm, and held him back with all the weight of her maternity.

'I have it,' says Coppinger. 'Poor Joe'll go. Where is he?'

No one had seen him. Coppinger dashed down the stairs, splashed through the yard into the stable. The door was open, and Blackboy, the strongest of King Cobb's horses, was missing.

Coppinger flashed round the lantern he held. The mail-boy's saddle had disappeared, and faintly mingling with the raging wind and roaring water, died the rapid strokes of a horse galloping.

Poor Joe had gone.

*   *   *

The house was already flooded out, and they were sitting (so I was told) with their arms round each other, not far from where poor Bartram's body was found, when the strange misshapen figure, bestriding the huge horse, splashed desperately through the water, that was once the garden.

'Rescue,' cried Frank, but she only clung to him the closer.

Poor Joe bit his lips at the sight of the pair, and then, so Frank Smith averred, flung him one bitter glance of agony, and dropping his deformed body from the back of the reeking horse, held out the bridle with a groan.

In moments of supreme danger one divines quickly. Frank placed his betrothed upon the saddle, and sprang up behind her.

If ever Blackboy was to prove his mettle, he must prove it then, for already the lightning revealed a thin stream of water trickling over the surface of the dam.

'But what is to become of you?' cried Miss Jane.

Poor Joe, rejecting Frank's offered hand, took that of Miss Jane, patted it softly, and let it fall. He pointed to Coppinger's red light, and then to the black wall of the dam. No man could mistake the meaning of that trembling finger, and those widely opened eyes. They said 'Ride for your lives ride!' plainer than the most eloquent tongue owned by schoolmaster could speak.

It was no time for sentiment, and for the schoolmaster there was but one life to be saved or lost that night. He drove his heels into the good horse's sides, and galloped down the hill.

'God bless you Joe,' cried Miss Jane. Poor Joe smiled, and then, falling down on his knees, waited, straining his ears to listen. It was not ten minutes, but it seemed ten hours, when, through the roar, he heard a distant shout go up. They were saved. Thank God! And then the dam burst with a roar like thunder, and he was whirled away amid a chaos of tree trunks.

*   *   *

They found his little weak body four days afterwards, battered and bruised almost out of recognition, but his great brave soul had gone on to judgment.

STRAWBERRY: A LOVE STORY

J.J. POYNTON

JOCK CONDON WAS OVER forty as years count. He was grey in patches, and wrinkled and fat. His hands were swollen from hanging listlessly, and bad weather had distorted his face. By proper reckoning he was getting old, but, measured by the standard of experience, he was only a youth. And all because he was slow; other men had lived through their lives, had tasted of the world, the flesh and the devil, had married and given in marriage, and had even made their final bow while Jock was travelling to that point in existence whereat monumental marble ceases to be uninteresting.

But, having reached that point, Jock began as a matter of course to court the young girls of the district, instead of the mothers who had borne or the maiden aunts who had nursed them; and he met with ridicule. Even his experience with Maggie Johnston only acted as a temporary check. He went on grinning upon one after another in his amorous fashion, putting the inevitable question when chance offered, till there was not in the whole neighbourhood a single young woman unasked.

Then Jock became miserable. He sat before the fire in his lonely hut and thought, and thought; and it seemed to him that life was blacker than the darkness that covered the earth. No mate was his, and years were going by. Fielding was dead, whom he remembered since they were boys together. Morton was dead; and Joyce. He, too, would be called upon some day, the dream within his heart unrealised.

Suddenly his face brightened. He stirred the fire nervously and rubbed his hands. 'Take the sheep round that way tomorrow,' he muttered. And so the die was cast.

She was not an angel, this newest of Jock's chosen. Even he guessed that. Her history no man knew; and as for her name—they called her 'Strawberry'. She came a stranger to that place, but whence or how no tongue ever told. This only the Dogwood people knew: she had possessed herself of a hut and strip of land in their midst; she wrought, and tilled, and delved as men do, and she lived somehow.

Now, Jock was vaguely conscious that Strawberry would not make an ideal wife, but he was desperate. So he bore up along the bank of the creek next day, stooping to keep under cover, and made his attack.

Strawberry was hoeing a row of potatoes near the fence. Jock could see the back of her head rising and falling with every stroke, and his heart thumped. He had often seen her thus, and he wished now that he had introduced himself before—it would have made the task so much easier. However, he crept up to the fence, and on hands and knees spent some time looking through a hole.

Presently he stood up and whistled, but bobbed down again immediately, with his heart thumping louder than ever. Strawberry worked on. A pebble was lying at his hand. He picked it up and threw it over gently, so that it would not hurt. But the pebble fell short in the soft ground, and the hoe came down with its rhythmic beat.

Jock got another stone, and, standing up, put his best effort into the aim. This time it hit Strawberry on the ankle just where there was a big hole in her stocking, and she wheeled round in time to see a grinning face disappear behind the logs.

That was enough for Strawberry. Hoe in hand, she rushed to answer the challenge. But Jock made off backwards, grinning and showing all possible signs of peace. He wanted the lady to understand that this was merely his playful way of introducing himself, but he stammered badly, and she was forcing matters.

'You dashed gorilla!' she called out, climbing the fence; 'I'll teach you!'

But just then Jock fell flat into the creek with a splash that startled the birds a hundred yards off. He struggled out on the other side dripping, with hat in hand, only to find his lady-love still brandishing the hoe.

'Will yer marry me?' he called out across the water.

The hoe was gradually lowered.

'Eh! What's that?'

Jock put the question again, adding, 'That's what I came for.'

'Well, why didn't you say so, you grinning idiot?'

Jock looked pleased at the compliment.

'Who the devil are you, anyway?' she went on.

He told her.

'Well, come over here!'

He waded through and stood meekly on the bank. Then they sat on the fence for a while, and later on Jock helped to carry her things to his hut.

There was not much romance about it as the world judges, but poor old Jock was satisfied at the time. And even afterwards, when Strawberry took command and upset all his household arrangements, when she was spending his money freely on visits to the township, and bullying him of nights, he was very patient.

Throughout long days, while following the sheep, he discussed the matter with his dogs; but Rover showed plainly that he had no opinion whatever concerning marriage, and Laddie only wagged his tail.

At length, Jock came to regard his experience as natural, and this bred in him a kind of helpless pity for all married men. He began secretly to long for his lost solitude, and his face grew sullen.

Then, one night, after yarding the sheep, he found a visitor at home. A big, heavy-browed man it was, dark-looking as a Spaniard. He nodded carelessly as Jock entered, and took no further notice, while Jock sidled into a corner to sulk. All the evening, the stranger talked familiarly with Strawberry. They laughed and joked coarsely, and about ten o'clock the stranger turned abruptly to Jock: 'About time you sloped, isn't it?' he said

Jock stared like an owl.

'About time you got!' repeated the stranger.

'Where to?' Jock asked, stupidly.

'To blazes—I don't care. Ain't room for three here, anyway.'

Jock had come to that conclusion also, yet he was inclined to protest.

'But . . .' he commenced.

'No buts,' the visitor interrupted, standing before the fire. 'There's a hut down by the creek. Come on, now—get! This here's my missus.'

Jock turned pale, and his eyes rolled.

'Her?' he asked, jerking his thumb.

Strawberry went towards him and said, more softly than he had ever heard her speak before, 'You'd better go. Take a blanket and some tucker with you.'

She made a bundle silently and opened the door, and when it closed again the shepherd realised that this had been his home for over thirty years.

The man within laughed harshly. 'Strange old bloke, that!' he remarked.

The woman did not answer for a while, then she said, 'He's not a bad sort, Bob.'

Next day Jock met the ration-cart near the main road.

'You needn't go down to . . . to the hut today. I'll carry the stuff,' he said to the driver.

The bag was handed out. 'How's the missus, Jock?' the young fellow asked with a grin.

'She . . . oh, she . . . the bag isn't heavy,' Jock answered, as he hurried away.

So Jock lived in the hut that used to be Strawberry's, and cooked his own meals again, and muttered, and stirred the fire just as in years gone by. And when about a month had gone a swagman passed towards the setting sun, and Jock knew that Strawberry, too, was alone.

Then began a struggle. Should he go back to her? Should he claim his own hut? The dogs did not know; and while he was still pondering, and wearing himself to a skeleton, came a day when the sheep were not liberated. Another followed, and by noon Strawberry took his place. She let the hungry animals out and sought the shepherd by the creek. He was sick—was very sick. And she set to work to nurse him back to health.

All day she watched his sheep, at night she yarded them, and came to sit beside the bed; and, while he lay thus unconscious in summer heat, a fire broke out. At sundown it seemed far away, but the north wind rose and urged it on, and by midnight the sky was red for miles, and the woman could hear the crackling grass and leaves. She thought of the penned-up sheep, and, single-handed, burned a strip around the yard. Then, with set face, she hurried back to the hut and stood on guard. And later, when the Dogwood people came, they saw against the broad front of the fire the solitary figure of a woman fighting as never woman fought before.

So she worked and watched till Jock got well again, and together they went back to his hut. There she made a garden and planted fruit trees; she helped him with the flock; she saved money. They even enlarged the hut in the course of years; and when sickness came again it was Jock who bore the burden of the toil and the watching; and he it was who was left to mourn.

He came home one day and found their visitor of years before waiting, his brows even more shaggy, his skin even darker.

'Gone?' the fellow asked laconically, pointing to the closed door.

'Dead!' Jock answered simply.

The stranger started.

'No! . . . She was my wife,' he said quickly.

'The gravestone says Missus J. Condon,' was the response; and there was a touch of pride in the old man's voice.

A BOX OF DEAD ROSES

ETHEL MILLS

THE OLD LADY WAS a most amusing creature, and she had a past, which was a record amongst pasts. Only that she was rich enough to buy the whole district, its 'society' would have 'cut' her long ago; as it was, people only talked about her with meaningful looks and whispered condemnation.

At least, the generation to which she belonged did that; the younger one only looked and wondered. Bent with rheumatism, bushy-browed, fierce-eyed and hard-featured, there remained no trace of the beauty and charm which (so reports said) had sent more than one good man to the devil.

On sunny days she would have her chair moved onto the wide, vine-sheltered verandah. She liked to see what was going on; and she said that in Australia most things happened on verandahs. This particular verandah had been planned and built in early pioneering days, and had, no doubt, seen many ups and downs of varied incident.

One could listen to her by the hour when she was in the vein for remembering pages from her own life or from other lawless lives of early days, when all country west of the station was unknown Australia.

Like most old people, she was given to repetition, but she told me a story once which neither I nor anyone else could ever induce her to tell again.

It was about a young wife, the most innocent of brides, who thought the world of her husband, and had no wish or look for other men. Yet the house was full of other men in those days, and they all gave thoughts or looks, more or less, to the prettiest woman in the district.

Every evening she used to stand at her bedroom door, looking along the verandah, until she saw her husband returning from his work; and every evening he brought her a rose from the big bush by the steps. That was during the first months of her marriage.

Next year, the rose bush bore as abundantly as ever, but the man often forgot to pick a flower for her and, after a time, he forgot altogether.

The young wife was painfully ideal and long-suffering, and never gave him a word of reproach; she was still so much in love with him that she was shy, and blushed like a girl when he came near her unexpectedly. 'Fancy: after two years of married life!' And the old lady smiled wickedly, and continued.

'She was tired one night, and went to bed early, leaving her husband smoking and reading in the dining room; but it was so hot that she presently got up, threw on a gown, and strolled along the verandah in the shadow for a breath of cool air. The sultriness of the air brought out the strongest scent of the moonflowers. Just there, at the corner near the rose bush, she saw her husband with his arms round a woman, kissing her lips over and over again; they were full, very red lips, such as men like to kiss.

'The woman was one of the housemaids, the soft-voiced, self-contained, velvet-footed one who usually brought in the tray for supper, and whose eyes never left the floor as she did so, a girl who seemed to have no thought beyond her duties.

'The wife heard enough to show her that the woman had thoughts for many things besides. She heard enough to tell her that those kisses were not the first by any means; that the man's life had been a long lie, except, perhaps, during the very early days of marriage. She liked to think that he was all hers then. A delusion also, possibly; but a harmless one.

'As it was, she stole off to bed without saying a word. I call that a "verandah tragedy", my dear; because her whole nature changed in a few moments. Not that there was much to notice one way or the other at first, except that she said she could not bear the scent of the moonflowers, and had the creeper taken up at the roots.

'She did not even send away the housemaid. Why should she? But things were a great deal more pleasant for the "other men" afterwards—a great deal, my dear! She used to sing and play to them, and dance with them, and flirt with them, and fill the house with visitors, and so on. In fact, she was a beauty, and had only just awakened to a knowledge of her power. You see, the station and money belonged to her; so she was freer than most wives.

'There was the baby, of course, a lovely, soft-faced little thing that used to take its midday sleep in a string hammock, swung up there by the trellis. She was fond of the child; yet, when it died and was buried by the lagoon in the garden, she used to sit dry-eyed, looking at the hammock that swung loosely in every breeze without its accustomed burden.

'She even said she was not sorry; because the boy might have grown up to break some woman's heart, and the world was well rid of the breed. Perhaps it was best so; though, looking at the other side of the question, he might have lived to blush for his mother.

'One day her husband was brought in dead, kicked by the horse he was trying to catch in the yard. They carried him straight up the verandah to the big spare-room, and the blood was dripping—dripping all the way.

'She was a tidy, methodical woman always, and she sent for the housemaid, the velvet-footed one, and bade her wash the boards. The girl had a wonderful power of self-command usually and yet, at sight of that blood, she shivered and trembled like one with the palsy. Sentimental people said the wife was perfectly inhuman to think of the state of her verandah at such a time and, of course, a kind friend told her what was said.

'She laughed as she replied, "No! I am not heart-broken. I went through that experience two years ago."

'Well, my dear,' (and here the old lady's voice sounded a little tired), 'she lived a long, long life, and rather a varied and interesting one, from an outsider's point of view, at any rate.

'I often sit and think of her and of many things that happened on this old verandah, but of late years I forget a great deal. I like best to remember the days when the young wife used to stand listening, listening for the husband's step. It was the sweetest music in the world to her.

'No doubt she was an arrant little fool and bored him to death. I think, now, that he was no worse than the majority of men: a clever, interesting woman could have managed him. She became all that afterwards . . . for other men. But, as I said before, she was a totally different woman then.

'Live every inch of your life, my dear!' the old lady concluded, impressively. 'One life, one love! Why, the idea is perfectly absurd.'

*   *   *

Two years later I saw the old lady again, feebler, worn in body and mind. She still sat in sunny weather on the verandah, but now she always had a little cardboard box on her lap, caressing it with her withered fingers.

'Look, my dear!' she said, 'this box is full of dead roses; they all came off that bush by the corner, years ago.

'I may die at any moment and young people are so careless and forgetful. Unless I had these with me they would never remember to bury them in my grave. They are the dearest things I possess; but the reason why they are so dear I shall carry as a secret to my grave also.'

The old lady had forgotten that she had ever told me a story with roses in it.

DRIFTED BACK

HENRY LAWSON

THE STRANGER WALKED INTO the corner grocery with the air of one who had come back after many years to see someone who would be glad to see him.

He shed his swag and stood it by the wall with great deliberation; then he rested his elbow on the counter, stroked his beard, and grinned quizzically at the shopman, who smiled back presently in a puzzled way.

'Good afternoon,' said the grocer.

'Good afternoon.'

Pause.

'Nice day,' said the grocer.

Pause.

'Anything I can do for you?'

'Yes; tell the old man there's a chap wants to speak to him for a minute.'

'Old man? What old man?'

'Hake, of course—old Ben Hake! Ain't he in?'

The grocer smiled. 'Hake ain't here now. I'm here.'

'How's that?'

'Why, he sold out to me ten years ago.'

'Well, I suppose I'll find him somewhere about town?'

'I don't think you will. He left Australia when he sold out. He's . . . he's dead now.'

'Dead! Old Ben Hake?'

'Yes. You knew him, then?'

The stranger seemed to have lost a great deal of his assurance. He turned his side to the counter, hooked his elbow on it, and gazed out through the door along Sunset Track.

'You can give me half a pound of nailrod,' he said, in a quiet tone. 'I s'pose young Hake is in town?'

'No; the whole family went away. I think there's one of the sons in business in Sydney now.'

'I s'pose the M'Lachlans are here yet?'

'No; they are not. The old people died about five years ago; the sons are in Queensland, I think; and both the girls are married and in Sydney.'

'Ah, well! . . . I see you've got the railway here now.'

'Oh, yes! Six years.'

'Times is changed a lot.'

'They are.'

'I s'pose . . . I s'pose you can tell me where I'll find old Jimmy Nowlett?'

'Jimmy Nowlett? Jimmy Nowlett? I never heard of the name. What was he?'

'Oh, he was a bullock-driver. Used to carry from the mountains before the railway was made.'

'Before my time, perhaps. There's no one of that name round here now.'

'Ah, well . . . I don't suppose you knew the Duggans?'

'Yes, I did. The old man's dead, too, and the family's gone away, Lord knows where. They weren't much loss, to all accounts. The sons got into trouble, I b'lieve—went to the bad. They had a bad name here.'

'Did they? Well, they had good hearts, at least old Malachi Duggan and the eldest son had . . . You can give me a couple of pounds of sugar.'

'Right. I suppose it's a long time since you were here last?'

'Fifteen years.'

'Indeed!'

'Yes. I don't s'pose I remind you of anyone you know around here?'

'Nnn . . . no!' said the grocer with a smile. 'I can't say you do.'

'Ah, well! I s'pose I'll find the Wilds still living in the same place?'

'The Wilds? Well, no. The old man is dead, too, and . . .'

'And . . . and where's Jim? He ain't dead?'

'No; he's married and settled down in Sydney.'

Long pause.

'Can you . . .' said the stranger, hesitatingly. 'Did you . . . I suppose you knew Mary . . . Mary Wild?'

'Mary?' said the grocer, smilingly. 'That was my wife's maiden name. Would you like to see her?'

'No, no! She mightn't remember me!' He reached hastily for his swag, and shouldered it. 'Well, I must be gettin' on.'

'I s'pose you'll camp here over Christmas?'

'No; there's nothing to stop here for . . . I'll push on. I did intend to have a Christmas here . . . in fact, I came a long way out of my road a-purpose . . .

'I meant to have just one more Christmas with old Ben Hake an' the rest of the boys . . . but I didn't know as they'd moved on so far west. The old bush school is dyin' out.'

There was a smile in his eyes, but his bearded lips twitched a little. 'Things is changed. The old houses is pretty much the same, an' the old signs want touchin' up and paintin' jest as bad as ever; an' there's that old palin' fence that me an' Ben Hake an' Jimmy Nowlett put up twenty year ago. I've tramped and travelled long ways since then. But things is changed—at least, people is . . .

'Well, I must be goin'. There's nothing to keep me here. I'll push on and get into my track again. It's cooler travellin' in the night.'

'Yes, it's been pretty hot today.'

'Yes, it has. Well, s'long.'

'Good day. Merry Christmas!'

'Eh? What? Oh, yes! Same to you! S'long!'

'Good-day!'

He drifted out and away along Sunset Track.

'THE FREE-SELECTOR'S DAUGHTER'

HENRY LAWSON

I met her on the Lachlan Side—
A darling girl I thought her,
And ere I left I swore I'd win
The free-selector's daughter.

I milked her father's cows a month,
I brought the wood and water,
I mended all the broken fence,
Before I won the daughter.

I listened to her father's yarns,
I did just what I 'oughter',
And what you'll have to do to win
A free-selector's daughter.

I broke my pipe and burnt my twist,
And washed my mouth with water;
I had a shave before I kissed
The free-selector's daughter.

Then, rising in the frosty morn,
I brought the cows for Mary,

And when I'd milked a bucketful
I took it to the dairy.

I poured the milk into the dish
While Mary held the strainer,
I summoned heart to speak my wish,
And, oh! Her blush grew plainer.

I told her I must leave the place,
I said that I would miss her;
At first she turned away her face,
And then she let me kiss her.

I put the bucket on the ground,
And in my arms I caught her;
I'd give the world to hold again
That free-selector's daughter!

Part 4

THERE'S A PATRON SAINT OF DRUNKS

The pub was the social centre of most small country towns when I was living in the bush. They used to say that the perfect town was one that had two pubs, 'the one you drank at . . . and the other one'. The 'other pub' was often the 'bloodhouse' or 'the one you drink at when you're barred from the good one'.

Every town also had a resident 'town drunk'—in fact, most had more than one. Dipso Dan is an amalgam of several town drunks I got to know while living in bush towns.

The stories here include a couple of Kenneth Cook's downright scary accounts of the behaviour of men affected by alcohol in the bush. These stories are even more scary, and oddly amusing, because they are so close to the truth. Anyone who has lived in the bush for any length of time and seen the effects of alcohol on certain blokes can attest to that.

Frank Daniel's well-observed story, based on his childhood memories, has a gentle, nostalgic humour to it and reminds me just how much attitudes and lifestyles have changed in less than a lifetime. It contrasts sharply with Lennie Lower's zany and satiric, but also oddly accurate, account of visiting 'the bush'.

There are lots of laughs in these stories of inebriation, but not far beneath the storylines lie some rather sobering thoughts and reflections on what is, or was, considered 'acceptable behaviour' in the bush.

'DRUNKS'

'SYD SWAGMAN'

Wild drunks, mild drunks, weary drunks and sad,
Drunks that 'knowed your dad, me son, when he was a lad',
Tall drunks, small drunks, tubby drunks and thin.
Drunks that seem to cheek the cops until they get run in;

Square drunks, lair drunks, moody drunks and loud,
Drunks that will not drink with drunks because they are too proud.
Tough drunks, rough drunks, dirty drunks and fat,
Drunks that shicker with the flies and shicker on their pat;

Poor drunks, sore drunks—heads as big as tanks,
Drunks that keep the town alive with their funny pranks;
Glad drunks, mad drunks, yellow drunks and white—
Somehow I meet a lot of drunks whenever I get tight.

SNAKES AND ALCOHOL

KENNETH COOK

'THERE'S TWO THINGS THAT don't mix,' said Blackie slowly and pompously, 'snakes and alcohol.'

It would never have occurred to me to mix them but I nodded solemnly. Nod solemnly is pretty well all you can do when you're talking to a snake man because they never actually converse—they just tell you things about snakes.

Blackie was a travelling snake man. He travelled in a huge pantechnicon which had wooden covers on the sides. Whenever he found a paying audience—a school or a tourist centre—he would drop the wooden covers and reveal a glass-walled box the size of a large room. This was his snake house, inhabited by a hundred or so snakes ranging from the deadly taipans and browns to the harmless tree snakes.

Blackie was like all the snake men I've ever met, cadaverously thin, very dirty, extremely shabby and without a second name. I think he was called Blackie because of his fondness for black snakes, or perhaps because his eyes were jet black—he had the only eyes I've seen that were black. He looked as though his enormous pupils had supplanted his irises, but if you looked closely you could see the faint outline of the black pupils inside them. I tended to feel uncomfortable looking into those two round patches of black and the suffused and bloodshot eyes (all snake men have suffused and bloodshot eyes—I think it's because snakes bite them so often).

I met Blackie just north of Mackay in Queensland where we were both camping on a little-known beach named Macka's

Mistake; I don't know why it's named that. I was trying to finish a novel and Blackie was doing something complicated with the air-conditioning of his pantechnicon, so we were thrown together for about a fortnight and became firm friends.

Blackie was so good and confident with snakes that he imbued me with much of his own attitude. I would often go into his snake house, sit on a log and talk to him while lethal reptiles regarded us torpidly within striking distance or slid gracefully and slowly away from the smell of our tobacco smoke.

Now and then a black, brown or green snake would slide softly past my foot and Blackie would say, 'Just sit there and don't move. It won't bite you if you don't move.' I wouldn't move and the snake wouldn't bite me. So, after a time, I became more or less relaxed with the snakes, provided Blackie was there.

Nothing would have induced me to go into the snake cage without Blackie, but I was convinced he could actually talk to the things, or at any rate communicate with them in some way which both he and they understood. It seemed to me at times fancifully possible that Blackie might have some drops of snake blood in his veins. Or perhaps the venom he had absorbed made him somehow *simpatico* with the creatures. Mind you, I did notice that the snakes had black eyes too, and that made me wonder.

There was only one other camper at Macka's beach, Alan Roberts, a fat and friendly little photographer who had set up a tent and was making a study of seabirds. He, Blackie and I would usually meet in my campervan for drinks in the evening.

Only the previous night, Blackie had been expounding to me and Alan the dangers of mixing alcohol and snakes. Of course, this took place over a bottle of whisky and I was considerably disconcerted when I called on him in the morning to find him unconscious in his own snake house, two empty whisky bottles by his side and his body festooned with deadly snakes.

The snakes were lying quite still, apparently enjoying the warmth of Blackie's motionless body. I assumed he was alive because of the snores that shook the glass windows of the snake house. But I had no idea whether he had been bitten and was in a coma, or had simply drunk himself insensible, or both.

The snakes resting on Blackie were, as far as I could make out: one taipan (absolutely deadly) two king browns (almost as deadly) a death adder (very deadly) three black snakes (deadly) and one diamond snake (harmless).

My first impulse was to run screaming for help, but there was nobody in sight, and if Blackie jerked or turned in his drunken or moribund torpor, at least seven deadly snakes would probably sink their fangs into him simultaneously. Then, no doubt, the other eighty or ninety variably venomous snakes would stop lying peacefully round the snake house and join the fray. Blackie's chances of survival would be slight.

I knew the snake house door did not lock. Normally when not in use it was covered by a wooden shutter, so I knew I could get in. But did I want to?

I didn't consider that in his present state Blackie would be able to provide his normal protection against snakes. Going in with Blackie like this would be worse than going in alone. A treacherous voice within me whispered that it would be better to run away and let Blackie wake up naturally. The snakes were used to him and he would probably instinctively act in the proper way with them.

Sadly, the treacherous voice wasn't convincing. Besides, I didn't know whether Blackie had already been bitten and needed medical help urgently.

I looked around for a weapon. Under the pantechnicon I saw a rake that Blackie used for clearing his snake house. I picked it up and cautiously and very slowly opened the door. There were several snakes between me and Blackie and I wasn't sure of their species. They all looked lethal. I poked at them gently with the rake and all of them, except one, resentfully slithered off to the other side of the snake house with no apparent intention except of going back to sleep. The one, a big king brown, raised itself on its coils and began hissing, throwing its head back to strike. I knew enough about snakes now to know that as long as I stayed the length of the snake's body away from its fangs, they couldn't reach me. Equally I knew that if I tried to pass this snake to get at Blackie, it could get to me.

I poked at it with the rake again and it struck, its fangs making a tiny ringing sound against the iron prongs. Blackie had told me that this sort of thing was bad for a snake's fangs. I didn't care. I poked at it again and it sank to the ground, wriggled over to Blackie, worked its way onto his back, then coiled again and began looking at me threateningly. It seemed much more agitated than before; no doubt its teeth hurt. The snakes already using Blackie as a mattress stirred fitfully, but didn't go anywhere.

A black snake detached itself from a group near the wall and came towards me. I banged it with the rake and it retired, probably mortally hurt. Again, I didn't care.

The king brown was hissing like a leaking steam pipe and the death adder appeared to dislike this. It made its way off, taking a path over Blackie's motionless head. There were still eight snakes on Blackie, seven of which were deadly.

I pushed tentatively at the king brown and it reared back, but didn't strike again. The movement disturbed the diamond snake and it went off to a quieter place. But that wasn't any real advantage, as it was harmless anyway.

A couple more black snakes started circling the walls and I remembered that the door behind me was open. There was a reasonable chance that within minutes the population of the snake house would be ravening around Macka's Mistake beach. I preferred they should escape rather than remain in the snake house with me, but I didn't want them waiting just outside when, if ever, I managed to drag Blackie through the door. I banged the rake on the floor in front of them. They stopped, considered this phenomenon, then retreated. I went back and pushed the door almost to.

What was Blackie's great maxim about snakes? Handle them very gently and slowly and they'll never bite you. I eyed the waving, hissing, tongue-flicking king brown on Blackie's back and decided I didn't believe this. Possibly if this king brown would just vacate

Blackie's back I might be able to prod the rest away, gently and slowly.

However, the king brown showed no inclination to move and it was so angry now I felt that if Blackie so much as twitched an ear it would have him. I was sweating with terror and the rake handle was slippery in my grasp. The tension in my body was so great I knew that if I didn't solve this quickly I would collapse or run weeping from the snake house.

The devil with treating snakes slowly and gently, I thought; you can also treat them quickly and violently. I swung the rake at the weaving king brown with every intention of decapitating it if possible. It ducked. The rake missed. The snake struck. It became entangled with the prongs and I was holding the rake in the air with the king brown on the end of it. It sorted itself out quickly, coiled itself around the handle of the rake and began moving towards my hands. Convulsively I flung the rake away. It fell flat on Blackie's body, stirring the current inhabitants into a frenzy.

Fortunately, they all seemed to think they were being attacked by other snakes. They whipped up onto their coils and began threatening each other. Then, presumably trying for more advantageous positions, they all slipped off Blackie and began retreating towards the walls. Only one, the taipan, came near me.

All I could do was try the standard procedure of not moving and hope it would not notice that I was trembling uncontrollably. It went past and took up a position near the door.

Blackie was clear of snakes for the moment. He still hadn't moved. But now seemed safe to try to wake him.

'Blackie!' I screamed and prodded him with my foot. He didn't stir. 'Blackie!' I screamed again and kicked him hard in the ribs. He still didn't stir.

All the snakes were awake and active now, but inclined to stay near the walls. The only immediate problem was the taipan against the almost-closed door. Obviously there was no chance of rousing Blackie, so I leaned down and grabbed him by the shoulders. He half turned and belched. The alcohol-loaded gust of breath was the only thing I have ever encountered to approach a camel's breath for sheer noxiousness. The rake was still across Blackie's back. I grabbed it with one hand and grabbed him by the collar with the other.

The collar came away in my hand. I grabbed him by his sparse hair, but there wasn't enough of it to get a good hold. I grabbed him by the back of his shirt. A great patch of it came away, revealing a bony, dirty yellow back. There was not much left to grab him by, so I took him by the hand and began hauling. Fortunately the hand held together.

Blackie was no great weight and I began inching him across the floor, brandishing the rake at the taipan guarding the door and desperately aware of the sea of serpents to my right and left and behind me.

A carpet snake, quite harmless, wriggled within a handspan of my right foot and I hit it with the rake out of sheer spite. I was close to the door, just out of range of the taipan, which showed no sign of moving. I pushed at it with the rake but it ducked disdainfully and stayed where it was, weaving slowly and keeping its evil eyes fixed, I was sure, on my bare, exposed and palpitating throat.

I was desperately tempted to throw Blackie at the taipan and probably would have done, except that it's hard to throw a man anywhere when you've only got him by the hand.

I had, of course, been bellowing my head off for help for some minutes now and it came in the form of Alan Roberts, the photographer who, seeing through the plate glass what was happening, gallantly flung open the door to come to my help.

The violently pushed door caught the taipan fair in the back of the neck and squashed it against the wall. I went through the door, hauling Blackie after me.

'What the bloody hell . . . ?' Alan was saying.

Blackie had somehow stuck on the steps of the snake house. The taipan, apparently undamaged by the door, was very close to his exposed ankle, which it was inspecting curiously. The other snakes were mercifully milling some distance away, hissing among themselves.

'Help me get him out!' I gasped. Alan went through my routine of trying to grab Blackie by the collar, hair and back of shirt and ended up with handfuls of collar, hair and shirt before he grabbed Blackie's other hand. Together we hauled him through the door and slammed it in the face of the taipan, which seemed anxious to follow.

Blackie folded into a grubby heap on the ground and I leaned against the glass and tried to start breathing, which I had apparently stopped doing some time before.

'Has he been bitten?' said Alan.

'I don't know,' I croaked. 'Get an ambulance.'

Alan, a competent man who was not about to ask foolish questions, turned to go. Blackie jack-knifed to his feet, opened the door of the snake house and tried to go back in.

Alan and I grabbed him by the shoulders and slammed the door.

'Blackie!' shouted Alan. 'What's wrong with you?'

Blackie, immobilised, stared at the closed door bemusedly.

'He's very drunk,' I said. 'I don't know whether he's been bitten or not.' I was beginning to doubt it. I didn't think people came out of snake poison comas quite so abruptly. If he was out of a coma.

'Blackie,' I said, 'are you awake? Has a snake bitten you?'

Blackie focused on me and said disdainfully, 'Snakes don't bite me.'

'I think he's just drunk,' I said quietly to Alan, and then to Blackie, 'Better come up to my campervan and lie down for a while, Blackie.'

'Sure,' said Blackie, 'just lie down in here.' And he turned and tried to get in with the snakes again. Alan and I grabbed him.

'Come on, Blackie, come up to the van and have a sleep.'

But Blackie had looked through the plate glass and seen his beloved snakes rushing backwards and forwards or coiled and waving and hissing.

'Something's wrong with my snakes!' he roared, and began to struggle with us to get free.

'Blackie, Blackie,' said Alan, 'take it easy. You've had a few drinks . . .'

''Course I've had a few drinks,' said Blackie. 'Can't a man have a few drinks?'

'Of course you can, Blackie,' I said soothingly, 'but you were passed out with snakes all over you. We just hauled you out.'

Blackie looked at me closely. 'So that's why my snakes are all upset,' he said.

'That's right, Blackie.'

Blackie thought about that. 'Ah well,' he said after a while, 'I suppose you meant no harm. Don't do it again, though.'

And the wretched man pulled away and tried to get in the door again. Alan and I could hold him easily, but we weren't prepared to do it indefinitely.

'Now listen, Blackie,' I said firmly, 'just come over to my van and have a few hours' sleep and you can come back to your snakes.'

'I'm going back to my snakes now,' said Blackie. 'Get your hands off me.'

We let him go, but Alan slipped between him and the door. Blackie considered this new problem.

'I'm going in there,' he said quietly and threateningly.

'Calm down, Blackie,' said Alan reasonably.

Blackie took a wild and ineffectual swipe at him. Alan and I looked at each other helplessly. I mouthed the word 'Police?' behind Blackie's back and Alan nodded regretfully.

'Can you keep him out of there?' I asked.

'Yes,' said Alan confidently. I thought he could, too; Blackie was far too drunk to put up much of a fight.

The trouble was I didn't know where the nearest telephone was. As far as I knew I might have to go into Mackay, eighty kilometres away.

I drove at incredible speed down to the highway and was delighted to see a police patrol car go past at the junction of the roads. I sped after it with my hand on the horn and it stopped. I leaped out of my van and ran to the police car. Two solemn Queensland policemen, both fat, red-faced, without humour, eternally middle-aged, looked at me expressionlessly.

'I wonder, would you follow me?' I said breathlessly. 'I've got a friend who's very drunk and who wants to sleep with his snakes.'

There was a long pause.

'What?' said the two policemen eventually, simultaneously.

'I've got a friend who's very drunk who wants to sleep with his snakes,' I said again, but this time I could hear my own words.

There was another long pause.

'Could you explain a bit more, sir?' said the driver policeman. Even then I could wonder at the talent of policemen for using the word 'sir' as an insult.

'Oh the hell with it, it's too difficult to explain. Just follow me, will you? It's urgent.'

I thought they probably would follow me, if not necessarily for the reason I wanted them to. I was right. They did and we arrived back at Macka's Mistake to find Blackie pinned to the ground with Alan Roberts kneeling on his shoulders. The snake house was still a whirl of activity. Blackie was shouting obscenities with considerable eloquence. I don't say the policemen put their hands on their guns, but they looked as though they might any minute. It was all too difficult to explain, so I just gestured at the strange tableau of Blackie and Alan in front of the snake house. 'What seems to be the problem?' said one of the policemen. Blackie stopped shouting when he saw the uniforms. Alan let him go and he stood up, stared for a moment, then looked reproachfully and unbelievingly at me. 'You called the cops,' he accused.

'What is all this?' said the policeman.

Blackie saved the necessity for an explanation by feebly trying to punch the policeman's nose. They took him off to Mackay and charged him with being drunk and disorderly.

Alan and I waited through the day until we felt he must be reasonably sober and then went down and bailed him out. Blackie was silent until halfway through the journey back when he suddenly and tearfully asked, 'How could you do this to me?'

Alan and I explained the sequence of events to him. 'Is that true?' he said.

'Perfectly true, Blackie. We had to do it.'

'I can see that. Funny, I don't remember any of it.'

I tactfully made no reference to the two empty bottles of whisky.

'I'm really sorry,' Blackie said. 'Just goes to show, though, snakes and alcohol don't mix.'

THERE'S A PATRON SAINT OF DRUNKS

JIM HAYNES

THERE'S A PATRON SAINT of drunks. Someone looks after them. It's almost impossible for a drunk to hurt himself and it's very difficult to get the better of a drunk.

I'm not really talking here about part-time drunks or weekend drunks. I'm talking about genuine drunks, those who make a vocation of being drunks, whose character is defined by the fact that they're drunks. We had a few like that in Weelabarabak, but the most memorable of them all was the 'town drunk' for many years, Dipso Dan.

His real name was, I believe, Daniel Harvey. The whole town, however, referred to him as 'Dipso Dan', and to his face he was called either just 'Dan' or 'Dipso'.

Dipso Dan wasn't born in Weelabarabak. Like most town drunks I've known he drifted into town from somewhere else, found a place to camp, did a bit of casual work now and again and got on with the job of being the town drunk.

It was rumoured that he had grown up in Melbourne and come to the bush as a sideshow worker. He'd even fought in boxing tent shows many years ago and was 'pretty handy' according to some of the older blokes around town. Old Nugget reckoned he remembered him going a few rounds with some of locals many years ago at the Weelabarabak Show, when he was a regular member of King Riley's Travelling Boxing Show.

As the grog slowly got to Dipso he had slipped down the carnival pecking order, becoming a rigger and a 'rousie' and eventually, when he couldn't perform any regular productive work, he had been left behind in Weelabarabak to become our town drunk.

Dipso wore old woollen army pants tied with rope in place of a belt, a flannel shirt of an indeterminate shade and shoes that varied in type and colour depending on charity. I remember that he never wore socks and his old army pants ended about six inches above his shoes, revealing a fair bit of bony shank. He was always accompanied by his dog, Digger.

Dipso was a fairly happy drunk, though he could be an absolute pain in the neck if you were trying to have a couple of quiet ones and a bet at the Tatts on Saturday. He always tried to tell you yarns about his illustrious punting career and wanted to know if you had 'a good thing in the next'. But there was no malice in Dipso; he wasn't a 'fighting drunk' in spite of his reputed past career in the ring.

He was painfully thin and seemed incredibly uncoordinated for an ex-boxer. He moved with a strange, jerky dancing motion that I found fascinating when I was a kid. Perhaps it was a combination of his boxing days, dancing around the ring, and the effect of years of booze.

One year the famous Tintookies Marionette Theatre came to Weelabarabak and put on a show. The whole school was marched down to the CWA hall and sat on mats at the front, near the stage, while the adults who weren't working sat in chairs behind us. The show was a ripper too, although I don't remember the plot or the characters very well. What everyone in town does remember is what happened when the curtain opened. The first marionette, a swaggie character, appeared on stage. The strings that operated the puppet gave it that jerky walking action that marionettes have. Half the kids on the infants and junior school mats called out in unison, 'It's Dipso Dan!' It almost brought the show to a standstill.

The poor puppeteers must have wondered what these kids were yelling about.

They no doubt also wondered why the adult audience was in stitches before the action had even begun. I bet they thought we were a very odd lot and were pleased to move on to the relative civilisation of Coopers' Junction for their evening performance.

Us kids used to imitate Dipso quite a bit, especially after we saw the marionette theatre performance. Kids can be pretty insensitive and cruel and, although Mum warned us that it was wicked to make fun of drunks like old Dan, my cousin Gerald and I used to pretend to be Dipso whenever we had creaming soda, a soft drink that developed a creamy head like beer if you shook it up before pouring it.

Dipso was always getting barred from the Tatts. He had even been barred from the Royal a couple of times, which was pretty rare. He didn't mind that too much; publicans changed fairly regularly at the Royal and they were always desperate for customers, so Dan wasn't usually barred for long.

What did terrify Dipso was the thought of being barred from the Royal by Dot the barmaid while he was still barred from the Tatts by Dougie.

Dipso lived in mortal fear of Dot, who worked most of the evening shifts at the Royal. If he was barred by Dot he had to rely on getting a sneaky drink from Happy Harold at the Royal before Dot came to work. This meant his evenings would be very dry and lonely affairs. It was rumoured that, under these circumstances, Dipso drank metho down in his camp near the river.

I know for a fact that this was more than a rumour because of a conversation I had with Dipso one Friday afternoon at the Tatts. I must have caught him at the very start of a bender because he was quite articulate.

'How's a boy?' he asked.

Dipso always slurred his words slightly and his head, arms and shoulders were never completely still when he spoke. You got used to it after a while but it could be very disconcerting at first. He also spoke with a constant slight hesitation that never quite became a stammer.

'Got a winner for t . . . termorrer?'

'No, Dan, haven't even had a look at the form yet,' I answered.

The trick was to be polite, not make eye contact, and hope he'd move on. It worked maybe one time in every three, but not that afternoon.

'Well, you t . . . tell me when you've p . . . picked one,' he said, patting me on the shoulder. 'And how about making an old digger happy and buying me a drink?'

'You're not an old digger, Dan,' I replied, trying to keep my head in the paper.

'I know that,' Dipso chuckled, 'but I got a d . . . dog called D . . . Digger and he'd be happy if you bought me one.'

He could be quite funny sometimes.

So I bought him a seven-ounce glass of beer and he told me about his recent troubles with Dot and Dougie.

'Trouble was I think I p . . . peed me pants on the carpet and Dougie hates that,' he confided to me. 'I'm glad he's let me back in anyhow, a man could end up drinkin' metho!'

'Well Dan, things aren't that crook yet,' I said. 'Anyway, I don't know how anyone could actually *drink* metho.'

'Well it's not easy,' he replied, 'you need a t . . . terbacca tin and you pour it in real shallow and mix it with condensed milk or s . . . soft drink cordial mix, or boot polish if that's all you've got, then you can usually get it down.'

I was stunned by the matter-of-fact nature of his reply. 'Strewth, that sounds bloody awful Dan!' I said.

'Well it t . . . tastes worse than it sounds too,' he assured me, 'but it's even worse if you've got nothing to go with it, then you have to light the fumes and drink it out from under them—straight from the t . . . terbacca tin.'

Dipso went on to tell me all the names metho had when mixed in different ways. It was 'white lady' when mixed with condensed milk, 'red' was the boot polish mix—and there was a lot more that I've forgotten and thankfully never needed to remember!

That conversation changed my attitude to Dipso Dan. I didn't mind buying him the occasional beer once I knew something about the alternatives. I even offered him a lift home once or twice, but he told me he was 'orright' and said the sergeant usually got him 'back to camp' if he couldn't manage it himself.

Dipso's camp was an old shack down on the river just out of town. Between 'benders' in town he lived there with Digger. Dipso told me dogs were great to talk to when you were drunk and 'no other bastard would talk to you'.

He had his dog Digger from when I was a teenager until long after I left town. Digger was a little brown kelpie that Old Nugget had given him as a pup. He was out of Nugget's good working bitch but was born a runt with a deformed back leg, so Nugget gave him to Dipso for two reasons.

Firstly, Dipso had just lost his previous dog to a brown snake down at their camp. Secondly, it meant Nugget didn't have to 'hit the poor little bugger on the head'—Nugget was very soft-hearted for an old bushman.

Digger followed Dipso everywhere and always waited for him outside the pub. Digger was much more popular around town than his master. All the kids would pat him as they passed the pub and my Uncle Lennie used to feed him regularly at the back of the fish and chip shop.

At least Digger ate regularly. Dipso wouldn't eat at all when he was on a bender. Sometimes he didn't get home for days at a time. He'd sleep in Anzac Park or at the back of whichever pub he got thrown out of at closing time, with Digger to keep him warm.

If someone caught him up and about before the pub opened Dipso might be offered something to eat; I think Uncle Lennie fed him occasionally at the back of the fish and chip shop, as well as Digger. Mostly, though, he'd drink for days at a time and then he had two 'plans of action'.

Sometimes he'd get some provisions at the general store (a few loaves of bread and tins of camp pie which he'd share with Digger) and go home to dry out for a while. On other occasions he'd put himself in the lock-up, if the sergeant hadn't already put him in there for being drunk and disorderly.

Often Mrs Sayer, the sergeant's wife, would discover Dipso in the unlocked cell when she went to clean up in the morning. 'Did Bill put you in there or did you put yourself in, Dan?' she would ask.

'I put meself in, missus,' Dipso would reply. 'I'm real crook too.'

'Well you can have some lunch now and a proper meal tonight, but you're out in the morning,' she'd reply, matter-of-factly.

'Orright, Missus Sayer, thanks,' Dan would say politely. 'Can you give Digger a feed too, please?'

It was mostly observing Dipso Dan that led me to believe there's a patron saint of drunks. He was indestructible. I've seen him fall down on the concrete outside the cafe and not even drop his shopping. I've seen him fall over the pub verandah at the Royal without breaking the two bottles of beer he had wrapped in brown paper. He would stagger erect in one jerky movement and continue on his wobbly pilgrimage as if nothing had happened.

The other amazing thing was that you could never get the better of him. I remember Dougie calling the sergeant to remove him from the Tatts one night when he'd been particularly obnoxious. Big Bill Sayer appeared within minutes and, filling the door of the pub in his police uniform, said, 'C'mon Dan, you're coming with me. You drink too much!'

Dipso didn't miss a beat. 'Don't be s . . . silly, sergeant,' he slurred, swaying on the spot, 'you can't!'

My favourite Dipso Dan story concerns the time he supposedly backed a winner with the SP bookie and made a real nuisance of himself until Dougie threw him out of the Tatts. Eddy Pierce's cab was parked outside and Dipso jumped straight in. With his mind totally befuddled by booze he told Eddy he wanted to go to the Tatts for a drink.

'We're at the Tatts now,' replied Eddy.

'Strewth, so we are!' yelled Dipso, fumbling in his pocket and staggering out of the cab. 'Here's your money and you shouldn't drive so bloody fast!'

As I wasn't there when that happened, I can only assume it's true. I've seen Dipso do some pretty funny things. I can see him now, in my mind's eye—weaving and bouncing jerkily along the main street of Weelabarabak, talking non-stop to Digger as he goes.

And the more I think about him and that crazy dancing motion of his, the more convinced I am that there's a patron saint of drunks. Perhaps it's St Vitus.

THE EVENIN' BEFORE LEAVIN' HOME

STEELE RUDD

IT WAS DRAWING CLOSE to New Year when Sam Condle sent me word to get ready to go shearin' down the rivers with him an' some other chaps.

I was ready to go anywhere with anyone, not because there weren't plenty work about Vinegar Hill, but because Connie told me straight out one evenin' that she didn't want me comin' to see her any longer. An' after all th' conversation-lollies I bought her, an' all th' wood I chopped for her too! By cripes, it made me furious.

'I'm off in th' mornin',' I sez to th' old lady. 'An' might never come back to these parts again.'

'Frankie, if I was you I wouldn't,' she sez, with a terrible sad look on her.

Ah, an' when I think of how she coaxed an' coaxed me to stay, brings the tears to me eyes!

'Me boy, you are not strong enough to shear beside men as old as your father,' she would say, 'so wait till you get set an' have more practice.'

Of course I didn't tell her about Connie, but I quoted Jack Howe shearin' his three hundred a day to her, an' reckoned if I couldn't hack me way through a couple o' hundred I'd eat me hat.

'An' th' terrible floods they have in them rivers,' she went on, 'carries horses an' men away; an' th' wild blacks. Oh, they'll massacre you all in th' night!'

I never heard anythin' before about blacks bein' down th' rivers, an' it made me hair stand up when she mentioned them.

'We'll give them all th' massacrin' they want, mother,' I sez, treatin' it lightly, but at th' same time makin' up me mind to ask Sam how many there was down there.

'An' y' can't go without seein' your father,' th' old lady continued, 'there he is not over his birthday yet. Oh, th' terrible fool of a man that he is, an' gettin' worse instead of better every year. Where he'll find th' money to pay Dollar his wine bill when it's all over, I'm sure I don't know. This is no life for me an' your sisters to be livin', Frankie, an' if you're goin' to go away it will be far worse.'

'He's been down there too jolly long, no doubt about that,' I said, waggin' me head in agreement with her, and appearin' wise at th' old man's expense. 'An' if he ain't home be eight o'clock tonight I'm goin' down to bring him.'

'He might come for you,' the old lady answered with a sigh, 'but if I go near him there'll only be words, an' then he won't come at all.'

When eight o'clock arrived, o' course th' old man wasn't home, an' down I goes to Dollar's.

Near Codlin's corner I sees a light comin' along th' road, an' hears a wheel squeakin', then a cove starts singin' loud an' another chap tells him to 'hold his tongue'. For a while I couldn't make out what sort of a trap they was drivin', but I could tell it was th' old man who was singin' by th' sort of 'cooee' he used to begin th' lines with. He always sung like a dingo howlin'. But when we got close together an' I sings out, 'Hello!' they stopped. An' there was th' old man squattin' as comfortable as you like in a wheelbarrow with his back to th' wheel an' his legs danglin' over the back an' a lighted candle stuck on each side of him, an' a big square bottle o' wine in his arms, an' old 'Scottie' nearly as screwed as himself in th' handles of th' barrow.

'By cripes!' I sez to them, 'this is a nice sort o' thing.'

'Thash you, Frankie?' sez th' old man.

'Of course it's me,' I growled at him. 'This is a nice sort of business; an' them sittin' up waitin' for y' at home.'

'Yer needn't go down to (hic) Dollar's for me. I'm comin' home (hic) meself. Ain't we, Scot-(hic)-tie?'

'Aye, comin' home in (hic) Dollar's motor car, d' y' see, Frankie.' An' raisin' th' handles of th' barrow, Scottie proceeded to propel th' old man over stones an' ruts at a vigorous and reckless speed again.

I trotted along beside them actin' as a guide, an' thinkin' of the reception they would get from th' old lady when they reached home, an' silently wonderin' if all the horrors of drink wasn't more than compensated for by th' humours of it.

Every hundred yards or so Scottie would stop an' puff hard, an' tell th' old man he was as 'heavy as yon German lassie i' th' wine (hic) shop'.

'Take another drink,' an' th' old man would hold out th' bottle to him. 'An' make me a bit (hic) lighter for yourself.'

Then Scottie would drink, an' off again.

Arrivin' at th' house th' old man broke into fresh song, an' th' dorgs begun barkin' an' th' old lady followed by th' girls come runnin' out. I knew they'd get a surprise when they saw him in th' barrow between th' candles like a blitherin' Chinese god. An' they got one too.

'I've brought him home to y' in a (hic) motor car, d' y' see,' Scottie said to them, stickin' to th' handles to keep himself from fallin'.

But they just stood starin' as if they had no tongues to talk with.

Last th' old man who kept blinkin' an' hiccupin' at them, an' thinkin' of th' blokes he saw givin' up their seats to ladies in th' tram th' time he took Fogarty's bull to th' exhibition, opens his mouth an' sez:

'You'll (hic) 'scuse me, ladies, for keepin' me (hic) seat.'

Th' girls an' me bust out laughin', but th' old lady lost her block.

'You beast!' she shouted, an' grabbin' one of th' candles nearly burnt off his whiskers with it. Then she kicked the barrow over, an' th' other candle went out an' old Scottie fell on top of th' old man an' they both started roarin' an' bitin' each other, an' I got ready to run. But seein' th' others wasn't frightent I waited too.

'A lovely pair! Two beautiful specimens of men! Come away, girls, come inside an' leave th' brutes.'

An' carryin' what was left of th' bottle o' wine which she rescued when th' barrow went over, th' old lady bounced inside an' I after her.

Next mornin' first thing I rolled me swag up an' strapped it on th' pack horse along with a jackshay an' a pair o' greenhide hobbles that I made on purpose about three months before.

Soon as breakfast was over I grabs me hat an' sez, 'Well, I got to meet th' rest of th' chaps at Hodgson's Creek in about an hour.'

Then th' hand shakin' an' th' cryin' commenced, which was always the worst part o' goin' away. Anyone who's never left a home in th' bush don't know what that means.

'Look after y'self Frankie while you're away,' th' old man who was the last to shake sez, 'an' if ever ye see any drinkin' or gamblin' goin' on, keep away from it.'

THE SIX O'CLOCK SWELLS

FRANK DANIEL

SIX O'CLOCK CLOSING AT the pubs was supposed to be the law when we were growing up. In our town this law might have existed—but it wasn't really enforced.

When I was a kid women didn't go into pubs—and I didn't know any women who drank beer. As I grew older I discovered a lot of ladies drank beer, but they didn't always let on. Some even smoked cigarettes.

Ladies who drank beer weren't very nice. Neither were ladies who smoked cigarettes. Mother didn't drink beer or smoke cigarettes— and she didn't like other people doing either. However, I don't recall her ever treating them any differently from those who didn't.

As a youngster I had a lot of Aunties and Uncles, most of whom were not even related to our family. The titles were used instead of calling them 'Mister' and 'Missus', just as a mark of more familiar respect.

As I grew older I sorted all this out and gave the family tree a real pruning. I already had enough relations without cultivating any more.

One day around 1951, we met a new 'uncle' and 'aunty', who arrived unexpectedly from Albury on a Friday afternoon.

He was a large bloke with a big belly. He'd known my father during the war and thus, on arrival, was automatically promoted to the rank of 'uncle'. His wife, our new 'aunty', was a thin quiet lady.

They were towing a thirteen-footer Sunliner caravan behind their 1950 model Ford Custom Sedan. Uncle said his car was a 'Single Spinner'. The bullet-shaped chrome piece in the centre of the grille was apparently known as a 'spinner', and there was only one.

Useful information of course! It would be handy to know stuff like that when we used our expert knowledge of Uncle's Ford to impress our mates.

The car was also a V8, and had a 'ton a guts' to tow the plywood caravan 'smack bang round Australia'.

Dad kicked the tyres and tapped his fist on the mudguards and said how solid the car was. He said that we would get one like it one day, 'Soon's we get a few more quid.'

Our car was a Willys Overland. It was a big square old tub. It had lots of room inside, and a rack on the back for carrying luggage. The Willys also had a draw-down blind on the rear window. The Ford didn't have a blind but it had large chrome hubcaps. The Willys had wooden spokes.

My parents showed the visitors around the house and the yard and gave them a look at our modest garden. Mum explained that water was the greatest problem on our farm, and that we had to be very careful as we were down to about two thousand gallons in the tanks.

'It will need to rain soon,' said Dad.

The surprise arrival of our guests caught us low on supplies and Mum asked Dad to run into town and get some things from the shop. It was a rare occurrence, rushing to town like that. Any other time we always managed to 'make do' with whatever could be scraped up.

These visitors must have been very important. They looked as if they were pretty 'well off'. They didn't look like us. They didn't dress like us. They didn't sound like us.

My older brother Jim was much chattier and less shy than me. He soon found out that they didn't know anything about sheep and they didn't even know how to ride a horse.

What sort of people could they be?

Maybe they were what Mum called 'swells', or even 'snobs'.

Dad drove us to town in the Willys—our new Uncle and me and Jim.

We felt that we should have been taken for a drive in the big Ford, but the offer wasn't made, though our visitor made a lot of comments about our old 'faithful', comparing it with his new 'Henry'.

As he talked his big fat arm, outstretched across the back of the front seat, was blocking my view of the speedometer, which was in the centre of the dashboard. I liked to keep a good eye on the speedo to see if Dad ever got the old thing over thirty miles per hour, which was about its limit.

Uncle talked a lot about real estate and extolled the virtues of 'keeping up with the times' and not letting his cars get too old. Dad looked a bit uncomfortable, but generally seemed to agree with his mate.

The gathering up of the groceries wasn't any great problem. Mr Hogan, the 'General Merchant', was 'pleased to meet' Uncle, who didn't seem terribly pleased to meet Mr Hogan. Uncle kept looking at his watch and at the pub, which was just two doors from the store.

With all the goods loaded, Uncle suggested that he and dad 'should imbibe a little before they ventured home'.

'Uh-oh!' I thought to myself, 'Mum will go crook,' especially if imbibing meant drinking beer, which I figured it did.

Then he gave me and Jim a two-bob piece and told us to go and get an ice-cream and some lollies at the milk bar up the street, while he bought our father a few beers.

Why had we ever had suspicions about this man from Albury? He'd turned out to be a real good bloke. In fact he was a bloody beauty, shouting lollies for us and buying Dad's beer too! Gawd, that would save Dad a heap of dough. He'd soon be able to buy that new Ford that he was interested in.

We didn't realise that buying Dad a few beers meant that Dad had to buy a few more for Uncle. Nor did we realise that if a couple of the locals met Uncle, and then bought him a beer, that meant that Dad and Uncle had to join that 'shout' and drink a few more to square up.

For us kids, the pub was one of the 'Wonders of the World'. Peering through the doorway into that dark mysterious place felt to us like we were encroaching into the secrets of some exotic religious sect. It was a bit like us wondering what it was like inside the Church of England, where the nuns said we were forbidden to ever go.

Drinking beer was a complicated arrangement, accompanied by a continual hubbub of noise and lots of laughter—and it always seemed to last until well after six o'clock.

Hanging around waiting didn't concern us too much on this occasion as Uncle slipped us a few more bob and told us to 'disappear for a little bit longer'; he also advised us 'not to tell the women' that he and Dad had been drinking.

'Blimey!' said Jim, when Uncle went back into the pub; 'we ain't never had more than a shilling at the one time before in our lives.'

He was right too.

When the publican decided that he had overstepped closing time by a sufficiently profitable margin of about two and a half hours, but it was still early enough not to annoy the local constabulary, he evicted all his patrons from the bar.

We watched the exodus and it was hard to imagine that so many people had been able to fit inside the bar at the same time. They were all laughing and some were wobbling—and one bloke fell over.

Two others tried in vain to help him to his feet and finally Dad came to their assistance and helped get the bloke up.

Evidently they were shearers from one of the sheds down near the Lake having a 'cut-out'. As they staggered away Dad commented that some blokes didn't know when they'd had enough.

The trip home in the faithful Willys was memorable—and at times a little scary. We were pleased to see that Dad was not really 'that drunk' after all. He must have been OK because he managed to bring the car back onto the roadway without any trouble on more than three occasions. Jim kept turning to see if the guideposts were still in place as we went along.

Big fat Uncle was sitting quietly in the front with his left elbow out the window, but every now and then he'd suddenly make a comment.

'Hang on to her there, mate!' he said, as Dad battled with the Willys on a bend at about twenty miles an hour.

'She'll be right mate,' said Dad, 'the old girl knows the way home on her own.'

'Bore it up 'er!' burped Uncle.

He wasn't sounding too much like a swell now. He was as red as beetroot and he kept doing little hiccups, which puffed his cheeks out and made his lips pout and give a little hiss each time he exhaled. His face looked fat and round as if he had a mouth full of something and he had three chins now, instead of the two he had when he arrived. At times, in the intervals between hiccups, he looked like he was about to explode and, sure enough, about halfway home he let go a huge fart that made the car stink.

That gave Jim and me the giggles, which gradually got out of control. Finally our hysterical giggling roused Dad, who tried to give us a clout by swinging his arm at us over the back of the front seat.

We were pretty safe in the Willys as the rear seat was too far back for him to reach us, but his attempt to discipline us caused the car to leave the main part of the gravel road for a while, before finding its way back to where the grader had been and the road was smooth.

After that we'd snort and start giggling again whenever one of us looked at Uncle. What a funny fat old geezer he seemed to be now.

When we reached our place there was a fight over who would open the front gate. Jim was first out and away and then Uncle decided that he had to get out too, to 'shake hands with his best mate'.

I thought that meant that he'd developed a sudden affection for Jim and wanted to show his respect for him volunteering to open the gate by giving him a manly handshake.

Once he got out, though, he seemed more intent on something else.

He had a pee on the gatepost and while he was busy doing that it must have slipped his mind to shake hands with Jim.

Back at the house Mum and Aunty had managed to gather some bits and pieces together for a meal and only needed a few essentials from the grocery box after all. Some mention of our late arrival was made, but we didn't dob about the men going to the pub.

Dad and Uncle stood outside in the dark, talking and laughing for some time until they were called for tea. Of course they tried to look sober and make out that they hadn't been drinking.

The light from the kerosene lamp in the centre of the table seemed to give Uncle and Dad a kind of rosy glow. Aunty's face had a serious look and her steely eyes were fixed on Uncle. His eyes, on the other hand, were a bit watery and glistened in the flickering glow of the lamp, and he still hiccuped quietly now and then as he ate.

Mum was busy making sure that everybody had enough to eat but Jim and I were not hungry for some strange reason. We'd eaten about four bob's worth of ice cream and chocolate and still had pockets full of lollies.

Then Uncle hiccuped loudly and we started giggling again. Mum went crook on us but Dad said nothing, for fear that his speech might betray his drinking, I suppose.

We had almost controlled our giggles when Uncle reached for a slice of bread and let out another loud fart.

All hell broke loose.

We just couldn't contain ourselves. In an uncontrollable fit of hysterical giggling, Jim slipped off his chair and disappeared under the table. The last we saw of him were his two hands holding a knife and fork, which clawed the tablecloth in an endeavour to slow him down.

Dad did his block. 'Shut up and eat ya tea!' he roared through a mouthful of meat, peas and potato.

Dad gave Jim a kick under the table, which brought him to the surface smartly. In the process he cracked his head on the edge of the table.

Now, Jim had finally put a slice of mutton in his mouth where there was already a well-sucked boiled lolly just before Uncle farted.

When he hit his head he let out a yelp and then started to choke. Before anyone could do anything to help he coughed out the mutton and the lolly and made a bolt for the back door.

The screen door from our kitchen to the back verandah was abused so many times in emergencies like that. Once again it was flung wide open beyond the manufacturer's wildest expectations and then slammed shut.

The mood changed very quickly. Suddenly things didn't seem that funny anymore.

Jim went to sit on the paling fence behind the shearer's hut, which was a good defensive vantage point. Should an attack come from the house yard he could drop down into the orchard and make for the tank-stand behind the laundry. An attack from the rear could be countered by a quick drop into the house yard, where a number of escape routes were available. The safest hiding place of all was under our beds, should access be available through a vacant house.

By the time the meal was over it was way past our bedtime. We had a wash outside by the laundry in an enamel basin, which sat on a large chopping block.

Cold water and Sunlight soap soon put a shine on my face again and about then Jim decided that it was all clear to return to the ranks.

Some vestige of the earlier hilarity returned when we got to bed. We giggled in whispers until Mum came in and said, 'Quieten down and go to sleep now and you can have another talk to Uncle in the morning.'

But our visitors had a very early breakfast and left straight after.

We never saw them again, ever.

Dad, it seemed, had been convinced about the virtues of keeping up with the times and bought a new car from Heats Motors in Goulburn a few weeks later.

He didn't buy a Ford.

Our new car was a Standard Vanguard.

WHERE THE COOLER BARS GROW

LENNIE LOWER

I'M ONLY A CITY boy. Until a short time ago I'd never seen a sheep all in one piece or with its fur on. That's why when people said to me, 'Go west, young man, or east, if you like, but go,' I went.

Truth to tell, I thought it would be safer. I had a shotgun and a rifle, and a bag of flour, and two sealed kerosene tins of fresh water in the luggage van. I thought of taking some coloured beads for the natives, but decided it was too expensive.

I forget now where it was I went. Anyhow, it was full of wheat silos and flies, and there was a horse standing on three legs under a tree. There were no other signs of life except a faint curl of smoke coming from the hotel chimney.

When I walked into the bar there was nobody there, so I walked out the back into the kitchen and there was nobody there. I went out on the verandah and saw a little old man picking burrs off his socks.

'Good-day!' I said.

'Day!' he replied.

'Where's everybody?' I asked.

'Never heard of him. Unless you mean old Smith. He's down by the crick. You're a stranger, aren't you?'

'Just got off the train. Where's the publican?'

'Do you want a drink?'

'Yes.'

'Orright!'

So we went into the bar and had a drink.

'I want to book a room here,' I told him.

'Don't be silly!' he replied. 'Sleep on the verandah with the rest of us if you've got blankets. They're decoratin' the School of Arts with the sheets. You going to the dance?'

'I can't dance!'

'Strike me pink, who wants to? We leave that to the women. There ought to be some good fights at this one. When I was younger there wasn't a man could stand up to me on the dance floor. Here comes somebody now.'

'Day.'

'Day. Don't bring that horse into the bar! Hang it all, you've been told about that before.'

'He's quiet. I broke him in yesterday. Hear about Snowy? Got his arm caught in the circular saw up at the timber mill.'

'That's bad.'

'Too right it is! They've got to get a new saw. Whoa there!'

'Take him out into the kitchen. The flies are worryin' him.'

'Goodo. Pour me out a beer.'

'Pour it out yourself.'

'Go to bed, you old mummified ox!'

'I'll give you a belt in the ear, you red-headed son of a convict!'

'Give it to your uncle. Giddup!'

'One of me best friends,' said the old man, as the horse was led into the kitchen.

'I suppose,' said the red-headed one, returning, 'it'll be all right if he eats that cake on the kitchen table? Won't do him any harm, will it?'

'That's for supper at the dance!'

'Well, I'll go and take it off him. There's a good bit of it left.'

Outside on the verandah voices were heard.

'I wouldn't sell that dog for a thousand pounds.'

'I wouldn't give you two bob for 'im.'

'You never had two bob in your life. You ever seen a sheep dog trial? That dog has won me more prizes at the Show than ten other dogs.

'Why,' he continued, 'you could hang up a fly-veil, point out one particular hole in it and that dog could cut a fly out of the bunch and work him through that hole.'

'Good-day!'

'Day!'

'No sign of rain yet.'

'No. I heard tell of a swaggie who had to walk eighty miles to get water to boil his billy, and when he got there he found he'd forgotten his cup and saucer, and by the time he walked back for his cup and saucer there was a bush fire in the waterhole, it was that dry.'

'Don't bring your horses into the bar!'

'Don't take any notice of the old crank. Why don't you put this beer out in the sun to get cool? If it was any flatter you'd have to serve it in a plate. Going to the Show this year?'

'Of course I am. Why don't you teach that horse manners?'

'Good-day, Mrs Smith.'

'Who put that horse in my kitchen?'

'Is he in the kitchen? Well, what do you think of that!'

'Fancy him being in the kitchen!'

'In the kitchen, of all places!'

'Who could have let him in?'

'Never mind about that. Get him out at once, Jack! Wipe up that counter. I told you to cut some wood this morning. And put the dog outside and get the broom and sweep up the bar. Wash those glasses first.'

By this time we were all out on the verandah.

'She hasn't found out about the horse eating the cake yet,' said somebody.

'Better go for a walk somewhere, eh?'

*   *   *

But that was all years ago. They've got radios and refrigerators in the bush now, and that's why you see me mournfully wandering about the cattle stalls at Show time. I'm thinking of the good old days before the squatters all took up polo and started knitting their own berets. When men were men and women were useful about the farm when the plough horse took sick.

Wrap me up in my stockwhip and blanket
And bury me deep down below
Where the farm implement salesman won't molest me,
In the shade where the cooler bars grow.

Ah, me!

ONE HUNDRED STUBBIES

KENNETH COOK

To UNDERSTAND HOW THIS could happen, you have to know something about where it happened—Coober Pedy, an almost impossible town in the arid centre. Coober Pedy is an opal-mining town. The name is Aboriginal for 'white man in a hole'. The 'hole' refers to the mines and to the houses, which are caves dug into the sides of low hills. In the summer the temperature averages around fifty degrees Celsius. You spend most of your time underground or in a pub, or you die.

I had driven up from Adelaide in an air-conditioned car and I thought I was going to die.

I saw Coober Pedy in the distance as thousands of tiny round bubbles in the shimmering desert heat haze. Soon these bubbles resolved themselves into the waste piles from the opal mines that stretch endlessly out from the town in all directions.

The whole area looks as though it is infested by the termites that build those huge nests of mud. Many of the mines are deserted and local legend has it that they contain the bones of reckless men who have welshed on gambling debts or tried robbing mines. I never actually heard of a skeleton being found.

The sight of the pub in Coober Pedy automatically brought my car to a halt. I needed cold beer, and lots of it. The heat out there is almost solid and you can feel it dropping on your head when you step out of the car. I trotted across to the pub, my whole being yearning for beer, totally unaware that I was about to witness an event that would put me off beer drinking for months.

The pub was moderately full of pink men. Almost all the men in Coober Pedy are pink because they are opal miners and the pink dust of the mines becomes ingrained in their skins. Or perhaps they never wash, because the water there is pretty foul stuff.

I ordered beer, found it deliciously cold as beer always is in outback Australia, often the only evidence of any form of civilised living, and began tuning in to the talk around me, as is my habit.

Two pink men quite near me were having a conversation which was absurd, like most conversations in outback pubs by the time everyone has had five beers. The two of them were leaning on the bar peering earnestly into each other's deep-etched faces. Like two grotesque dolls, they carried on a nonsensical argument.

'He can.'

'It'd kill him.'

'It'd take four hours.'

'It wouldn't kill him. Nothing would.'

I leaned closer. Their voices were beginning to hit an hysterical note. Like buzzsaws, their shouts rose above the hubbub of the other drinkers. They were obviously used to yelling at one another fifteen metres underground with jackhammers going full blast.

'A hundred stubbies in four hours. Do you reckon that would kill him?'

'It'd kill anybody.'

'He's not anybody.'

They stared into each other's faces, the importance of the topic growing in their minds as the beer ran down their throats.

'Why are you so bloody sure?'

'Because I'm bloody sure.'

One of them was almost middle-aged, with grey hair all over his exposed shoulders. At least, it would have been grey if he had washed off the pink dust. His face was dulled and brutalised by years of grubbing away in the ground all morning and drinking beer all afternoon. Or perhaps he had been born with a dull and brutal face.

His companion was younger, probably not thirty, a little fat but with the heavy shoulders and arm muscles of the opal digger. If men keep on digging in the ground for opal for a few generations, they will probably develop forequarters and arms like wombats. This younger man looked like a hairy-nosed wombat because of the three-day growth on his face. Not exactly like a wombat, though, because a wombat has some expression on its face if you look hard enough, while this character's face was just a blob of pendulous blankness. With its pink-dusted stubble, it looked like a discarded serving of blancmange growing a strange mould.

'Well, if you're sure, will you bet on it?'

'Sure I'll bet on it.'

You couldn't tell who was speaking because their voices sounded identical, like knives scraping on plates at an unbearably high volume. But you could tell the sound was coming from them and gradually a pool of silence was forming around them as the rest of the bar tuned into their conversation.

'What do you reckon, Ivan?'

Now you could see who was speaking because the older man turned and addressed himself to the drinker alongside him.

Ivan turned slowly and I realised I was looking at a monster. He stood barely a metre and a half high and was almost as wide across the shoulders. His chest, black-singleted and covered with dust, stood out like a giant cockerel's, a vast billow of muscles with dark streaks running over the pink dust as the sweat made its own little rivers. One great arm hung disproportionately low by his side, the other rested on the bar with an enormous pink hand almost totally concealing a glass of beer. His hair was short and closely cropped and he carried a comb of bristles over a face that for one mad moment made me wonder whether it is possible to cross a crocodile with a hippopotamus.

This was a face that displayed a complete lack of interest and malice, with a blank complacency that made it obvious no thought had ever disturbed the brain that nestled just under that absurd cockscomb of hair.

He was wearing shorts, and two massive legs, not unlike those of a hippopotamus except that they were pink and hairy instead of grey and wrinkly, propped up his body. It was as though the body was resting on the legs rather than being joined to them, because he seemed to have no waist; he was tree-trunk thick all the way down until suddenly he had legs. The junction was concealed by the baggy shorts, but I got the impression that the legs might walk away at any moment, leaving the body standing there.

'What do you reckon, Ivan? I reckon you could drink a hundred stubbies in four hours.'

''Course I could,' said Ivan. His voice was flat and deep, almost pleasant by comparison with those of the other two, but only by comparison.

'There,' said the older man, turning to his companion as though everything had been proven.

'Bet you he couldn't.'

'Bet then. Go on, bet!'

'What do you mean, bet?'

'I mean what I say. What'll you bet he can't drink a hundred stubbies in four hours?'

'Bet you five hundred bucks.'

The older man thrust his hand into his hip pocket and brought out a wad of notes. He counted ten fifties onto the counter. The younger man looked on impassively while Ivan, losing interest, turned back to his pint.

'Match that.'

The younger man, having waited until the last fifty was laid down, dived into his own pocket and counted out his bundle of fifties. He paused before laying down the tenth.

'Who's paying for the beer?' he asked cunningly.

There was a long pause while this was pondered.

'Take it out of the centre,' said the older man at last.

'All right, Ivan. Here's the biggest beer-up of your life, and on me,' said the older man, grabbing Ivan by the shoulder. 'Come on, Bill,' he said to the barman, 'set up ten stubbies. Ivan's gonna sink a hundred.'

Bill didn't react, just reached into the refrigerator and lined ten stubbies up on the counter. 'Off you go, Ivan. Remember, I'm betting on you.'

'He's gotta be standing at the end,' said the younger man, sullenly, now sounding worried.

'He'll be standing. Come on, Ivan. Sink 'em.' Ivan was looking at the ten stubbies.

You could see he was thinking by the contortions on his face. You could almost hear him. The three men were now the centre of a large circle that had formed as the concept of the bizarre bet was grasped by the other drinkers. Money was appearing from dusty pockets as side bets were laid. Ivan was still thinking.

'Come on, Ivan.'

'I want a hundred bucks,' said Ivan.

The older man was shocked. 'What do you mean, you want a hundred bucks?'

'I mean I want a hundred bucks.'

'Whaffor?'

'Drinking the beer.'

'But you're getting the beer free.'

'I want a hundred bucks.'

Conversations tend to be limited on the opal fields.

'You can go to hell.'

'Right.'

Ivan turned back to the bar and ordered another beer. The older man looked at this disbelievingly. Ivan downed his beer. Obviously he intended to stand by his position.

'All right then,' said the older man desperately, 'if you drink all of the hundred stubbies, I'll give you a hundred bucks.'

'A hundred for trying,' returned Ivan, without even turning around.

'God Almighty. What happens if you drink fifty beers and pack it in? Do I still give you a hundred dollars?'

'A hundred for trying,' said Ivan.

The older man stared at the impossibly broad and unyielding back. You could tell that he was thinking, struggling for a solution. 'Tell you what,' he said finally, 'a hundred and fifty if you make it, nothing if you don't. How's that?'

Ivan was thinking. A long pause. 'All right,' he said, and reached for the first stubby.

'Take if off the top,' said the older man to his companion, which presumably meant that the winner would have to pay Ivan's fee.

This seemed reasonable to the younger man, but he was slow to make up his mind. By the time he had nodded assent, Ivan had already drunk six stubbies.

His technique was impressive. He picked up one of the little squat bottles in each hand and flicked the tops off with his thumbs. Most men need a metal implement for this, but not Ivan, he had thumbnails he could use as chisels. Then he raised his right hand, threw back his head and poured the beer into his gaping mouth all at once, the whole bottleful, one continuous little jet of beer until the bottle was empty. Then he did the same with the bottle in his left hand. Both bottles empty, he put them down neatly on the counter and reached for two more.

There are 375 millilitres of beer in each of these bottles. Legally, if you drink three in an hour, you are too drunk to drive a motor car. One hundred bottles would be 37,500 millilitres. The mathematics are beyond me, but it must be a monumental weight of beer. I timed him. It took just on eight seconds to empty a bottle, one second to put the two bottles on the counter, one second to pick up two more, one second to flip off the tops. He was swallowing a stubby every eleven seconds.

Swallowing's not the word. There was no movement in his throat. He was just pouring it straight down into his stomach. A stubby every eleven seconds. At that rate, he would be able to drink 100 in 1100 seconds—that's less than an hour. But he couldn't keep that up. For obvious reasons; he'd burst, for one.

I wasn't the only man in the bar making these calculations. In the great circle that now surrounded Ivan, men were looking at their watches and counting. To save time the barman had put twenty cold stubbies on the counter just as Ivan downed the tenth. Ivan didn't pause. He was drinking, or working, as rhythmically as though he were on an assembly line: pour down one bottle, pour down the next, both bottles on the counter, pick up the next two, flip off the tops, pour down one bottle, pour down the next.

The only sound in the bar was the slap of the bottles on the counter and the metallic rattle of the bottle tops hitting the floor. All the drinkers were silent, watching in an almost religious awe, their own glasses held unnoticed.

I realised for the first time that the clock hanging above the bottles at the back of the bar had a chime. It chimed six o'clock just as Ivan finished his fortieth bottle of beer. As if it were a signal, he slammed the two bottles on the bar and paused. The silence became intense as everybody started leaning forward slightly, wondering. I was convinced Ivan would drop dead.

Ivan stood motionless, his hands on the bar, his body inclined slightly forward. The pause lengthened, the silence deepened, if silence can deepen. I could even hear the clock ticking. Suddenly, Ivan's back muscles convulsed and a monumental belch erupted through the bar, breaking the silence like a violent crack of thunder. I swear the front rank of spectators reeled back. There was a burst of cheering and laughing and clapping.

Ivan reached for the next two bottles and was back to his rhythm again. Forty-five bottles, fifty, fifty-five, sixty. The impossible was being translated into reality in front of our eyes. Then came a piece of virtuosity: Ivan flipped the tops of two bottles but instead of raising his right hand, he raised both hands and poured the contents of two bottles down his throat simultaneously. It took just eight seconds. Seven hundred and fifty millilitres of beer in eight seconds to join the flood that was already coursing through his stomach, intestines, bloodstream.

Technically he had to be dead. No human tissue could withstand an assault of alcohol like that. Perhaps Ivan wasn't human; perhaps he had never been alive. He had stopped again. He glanced around the circle of spectators.

'Had it, Ivan?' said one hopefully.

Ivan ignored him.

He looked to his principal, the older drinker. There was something he'd forgotten, a condition in the contract that hadn't been spelled out.

'Time out to leak?' he said, a little plaintively.

'Sure, get going,' said his backer.

Ivan was away from the bar for five minutes, which wasn't surprising. I wondered whether he had regurgitated some of the beer, but this didn't seem to occur to anybody else.

At eighty bottles, Ivan stopped again. We waited expectantly for the mighty belch, but it didn't come. He paused for about fifteen seconds and then reached for two new bottles. But there was a change of pace. The mighty fingernails fumbled slightly before the bottle tops flew off. His movements were deliberate and ponderous. Once he missed his aim and a jet of beer splashed onto his chin. I wondered whether this counted as a whole bottle but nobody raised the point. He was pausing each time he set down the bottles.

I was aware that gently, almost whispering, the whole bar was counting: 'Eighty-five, eighty-six, eighty-seven, eighty-eight.'

The count was slowing as Ivan's drinking rate slowed. By now he was taking fifteen seconds a bottle, then eighteen, nineteen. At ninety-five bottles, Ivan stopped again, one half-full bottle in his left hand. He leaned forward. We waited again for the belch, but there was no sound.

Ivan shook his head from side to side. I saw his eyes. They had gone completely white, like a blind man's.

Ivan started to sway.

'Come on, Ivan, into 'em, boy!'

Ivan's massive body swung around in a slow circle, his feet still firmly on the floor. But then he steadied himself and the giant hand was raised. But this time he put the bottle to his lips. It did not go down in one unbroken stream. He swallowed many times with great effort. He put the bottle on the counter and reached for two more. He couldn't get the tops off; the barman whipped them off for him. Slowly, painfully, his eyeballs rolled deep into his head, his body swaying in ever-increasing circles, Ivan drank each bottle.

'Ninety-nine!' It was a roar.

Then Ivan drank the ninety-ninth bottle. By then he was spinning quickly, inclining his body at an impossible angle. Only the weight and size of his legs can have kept him upright.

Somebody had to put the hundredth bottle into his hand. Obviously he couldn't see it, or anything else for that matter, but somehow his hand found his gyrating head and he got the bottle to his lips.

Down went the beer, slowly, terribly slowly. But down it went, all of it.

'One hundred!' It was a mighty animal scream. The empty bottle crashed to the floor. Ivan had drunk one hundred stubbies in just under an hour.

Three or four men tried to stop Ivan spinning and there was a general hubbub as bets were settled and fresh drinks ordered.

Then Ivan brought instant silence with a vast bellow.

'Vodka!' he shouted.

The word, as much as the level of Ivan's thunderous voice, brought the silence.

He turned to the bar and thumped it.

'Vodka!'

Dazed, the barman poured him a nip of vodka.

Ivan brushed the glass off the bar with a sweep of his hand that demolished half a dozen other drinkers' glasses as well.

'The bottle!' he roared.

There was silence.

Then timidly, terrified in the presence of mystical greatness, the barman put a bottle of vodka on the counter. It was open, but Ivan broke its neck on the bar in a ritual gesture. Apparently he could see again, although his eyes were still just blank white.

He raised the vodka bottle until the jagged neck was a handspan from his mouth, then poured a gush of the clear spirit down his throat. Half the bottle gone, he slapped it down on the counter; it rolled on its side and the vodka slopped onto the floor. Nobody noticed.

Arms by his side, eyes pure white, body rigid, Ivan made for the door of the bar. A quick passage cleared for him and he went through in a stumbling rush, like a train through a forest. He crashed into the swinging door, the bright flash of late sunlight illuminating his huge frame, and plunged headfirst out into the street, hitting the dust with a thud that seemed to shake the building. Just once his head moved, and then he was a motionless heap of sweat-sodden humanity in the dust.

'We'd better get a truck to take the poor bastard home,' said somebody.

'Yeah.' And two of the drinkers, kindly men, wandered off to organise the truck.

'He's forgotten his money,' said someone else.

'I'll keep it for him,' said the barman. 'He'll be back in the morning. Probably have a head.'

'THE ALCOHOLICS' CREED'

ANON

Our lager
Which art in barrels
Hallowed be thy foam
Thy will be drunk
Thy pints be sunk
At home as it is in tavern.
Give us this day thy foamy head
And forgive us our spillages
As we forgive those who spill thee against us
And lead us not to incarceration
But deliver us from hangovers
For thine is the sin done, the headache, the guilt trip,
For ever and ever . . .
. . . Barmen.

Part 5
TO THE CITY

A trip to 'the big smoke' has become a 'standard' in Australian storytelling. The contrasting lifestyles and attitudes of city slickers and bush folk, and the ever-present danger of losing your true values and sense of self in the city, or finding redemption and peace in the bush, are themes that occur again and again.

The 'city slicker' versus the 'country hick' has been a constant source of inspiration for stories, verse, yarns and jokes from the earliest colonial days, through the era of gold rushes and 'new chums', and through to the stories of Steele Rudd and Henry Fletcher.

Many of Banjo Paterson's most famous poems, like 'The Man From Ironbark', 'Geebung Polo Club', 'Been There Before' and 'Clancy of The Overflow', are based on contrasting city life to rural life.

The iconic figures of the gullible bushie and the confidence man, or 'spieler', turn up in many guises. The many ruses used by the 'spieler' to outwit the 'bushie' include some, like the 'Uncle from Fiji', which became stereotypes in themselves.

The opening poem by Edward Dyson (written for *The Bulletin* under his pen-name 'Billy T'), in which a woman's ingenuity proves to be more than a match for both bush caution and spieler, is one of my all-time favourites.

The story by Gavin Casey adds a different and darker dimension to the old theme of bush camaraderie and alienation in the city.

'SIMPLE SISTER GOES TO SYDNEY'

'BILLY T'
(EDWARD DYSON)

When Flo resolved to go to town
From brothers three a yell went up,
Predicting ruin and distress.
Bill, in his horror, dropped a cup.
'Gorstruth!' he said, 'in Sydney there,
What is a simple girl to do?
They took *me* down. I lost me watch
And seven quid. What 'ope for you?'

Ben turned on her in pale dismay.
'Look here, me girl, ain't you bin told
How one of them there spieler blokes
Done me for twenty pound in gold?
He was as nice a gentleman
As any in the blessed shops:
He got away with all I had,
And took a luner at the cops."

'Me, too,' said Dave, 'that time I went
To Sydney town to see the Show
One trimmed me for me bran' new suit.
You stay where we can watch you, Flo.'

Flo packed. 'If spieler comes at me
His finish will be sharp,' she said;
And when the boys next heard of her
She'd got a bloke, and then was wed.

She wrote: 'He's rather nice, I think,
And I am putting him to work.
Next Chrissmiss we are comin' up
To see yous people back o' Bourke.'
And when he came he brought for Bill
A silver watch and seven quid,
For Dave a bran' new suit of check,
A ruby tie-pin and a lid.

To Ben he handed twenty pounds,
In nice new minted sovereigns, too.
And still the brothers gaped at him,
And still their great amazement grew.
He was a natty kind of chap,
With gentle manners, small and slim.
And when they spoke 'twas as one man.
'So 'elp me Flo', they said, 'it's 'im!'

THE WAYBACKS GO TO SYDNEY

HENRY FLETCHER

CHAPTER ONE: DADS WAITS A FEW MINUTES

Everyone at Dingo Flat, and far beyond, to the Wallaby Ranges, knows the Wayback family—old settlers, corned beef and pumpkin eaters; tall, lanked, ring-barked folk; hair sun-bleached, and features contracted to a pucker in the brow in the contest with flies and vivid sunlight; true children of sun, sorrow, and scrub.

Old Ted had been going down to Sydney any time this last score years, but had never gone. When he had the money, he lacked the time, and when time hung on his hands his pockets were empty.

Ever since they could remember the children had heard of that wonderful journey ahead: 'When we all go to Sydney!' They had come to regard it as a visionary mirage, an instalment of Paradise only to be realised in dreams.

So that, when Old Ted, having sold his mob of fats at a fat price, suddenly said that the time had come for them all to go to town and see the Commonwealth celebrations, and join in the festivities, no one could credit it.

'Oh, Dads!' said Mums, 'How can we go now? That's just like you. Why didn't you say so last week before I sat the three broody hens? Who will look after the chicks?'

'Oh, hang the broody hens! Haven't you been bothering to go this last twenty year? Said you was buried alive, and ther children ought to see life, and I don't know what else? And now yous talk about broody hens! How was I ter know last week that Price would come along and give ten pounds a head?'

'But we've got nothing to wear Dads,' said Mums, looking fearfully at the nine children, who had paused in their eating as though petrified at the news. Jabez held a potato on a fork halfway to his mouth, Tilly had her teeth fast in a chunk of damper, Sarah Jane held a cup of tea aloft as though she were an iron drinking fountain, Euphemia had her mouth wide open, Rube held his spoonful of sugar half over the table, Delia's lips were stuffed with pumpkin, Little Sid's eyes had opened so wide that his forehead had vanished, Cris held his bread in mid-air like a newspaper; while Bubs, alone unaffected by the general paralysis, grasped the moment with both paws, and collected all the titbits from the plates of his brothers and sisters that were within reach or grab.

'Nothin' ter wear!' said Dads. 'Why yous not naked!'

'That's just like you,' replied Mums, 'you never takes a hit of notice as long as there is some sort o' rags over our backs. What would people in Sydney say about us even in our Sunday things? Why Tilly wants new everything; Sarah Jane has outgrown all the tucks I've let out of her skirt; Euphemia's boots have no toes in 'em; and, as for Delia, I'm fair ashamed ter see the child. Then there's the boys' pants; I'm just sick o' mendin' 'em. I believe Rube thinks his mother's a sewing machine. I've patched his knickers five times this month if I . . .'

'Oh, all right,' said Dads, 'if we can't go we can't, and there's an end o' it; but I thought yous wanted ter go.'

'Now, there you are, flying off and jumping down a body's throat before they have opened their mouth; I never saw such an unreasonable man. Who said we's couldn't go? The celebrations are weeks ahead yet and . . .'

'I see by ther papers, Jane, that all ther hotels are chock a block and folks that wait will have ter camp in ther streets and eat their meals on ther kerbstone. None o' that fer me, Jane! If we goes now, before ther rush. The last beast in ther paddick gets ther worst grass. Not me, Jane, not me!'

'Oh! Are we really, truly going Mums?' eight voices asked with a single shout.

'By cripes!' yelled Jabez, and he ran onto the verandah and threw a stone at the cat.

'I must have a new dress now, Mums!' cried Tilly.

'An' me, an' me!' echoed the others as they caught hands and waltzed around the room.

As for Rube, the house could not hold his delight; he had to rush into the yard and throw rocks at the dog.

Bubs had crawled over the table; his movements covered by the general riot, and now sat in the gravy while he pulled over the cruet.

Crash!

Howl!

Spank!!!

'Oh, you wicked child, why didn't you mind him, one of you? Now, look at that; I hope you'll wash it up, I shan't! I declare it's enough to vex a saint!'

*   *   *

Bright and early the following morning the male Waybacks and Mums drove into Barjo in the cart, the father and the boys to fit on new suits and get their hair cut, the mother to buy much dress material.

Dads took seven in ready-mades across the shoulders and four around the waist, so that the new coat hung at the back in two gracefully draped box pleats from the shoulderblades. The storekeeper said it fitted like a glove; and, as Dads had never worn a glove, he could not well contradict him; besides, he was mighty anxious to get the job over.

'That's all right, Boss, fits me tip-top,' and the suit was boxed up.

Mums had all the boys' suits on the rack pulled down, while her lads stood in a row like railway signals, flopping their arms up and down as they tried on the coats. After all the fuss, Mums took the ones she had seen first, then she sat down in the drapery department as if she owned it and meant to camp there a week.

Seeing this, Dads went over to the Dodrop Inn to have a nip and pass the time with Sullivan. He came back in an hour.

'Are you ready, Mums?'

'In a few minutes, Dads.'

Dads went over and had another nip. He met Regan, from Duckhole and, of course, they both shouted.

Regan warned Dads about the confidence men down in Sydney and how a bloke he knew got took down for fifty quid. Dads, looking at the clock, saw another hour had gone by, and went over to the store.

'Are you ready, Mums?'

'Only just another minute, Dads.'

Dads went over for another nip and met Allsop, from Longswamp, Allcorn, from Seven Acres, and Fegan, from Cowshorn, and they all had to relate to Dads what they had 'heard tell' of the pitfalls of city life. Dads felt he was being posted up to worldly wisdom of the latest date and armoured against all the wiles of the wicked, and took more nips to sink the advice into his memory.

Dads did not go over to the store again. Later on, when Mums had really finished and the boys had all been harnessed up, they helped Dads into the cart, where he sat on the bale of drapery and sang songs all the way home.

'It's extraordinary,' said Mums, 'how a man can't wait a few minutes without making a fool of himself!'

*   *   *

It was the night before the journey. For a week the house had been in the possession of the dressmaker, the sewing machine, and the fashion plates from *The Young Ladies' Journal*. Snips of lining fluttered in the wind and covered the floor; the girls were always taking on and taking off the raiment, and Dads had to get his meals anyhow he could in the slab kitchen.

*   *   *

The train starts from Barjo at 6 a.m. Dingo Flat is two hours' drive, so naturally the Waybacks started at 2 a.m., to leave a safe margin of time. Mums had a new hat with three ostrich feathers that the milliner at Barjo had said was 'the very latest from Paris'. Mums said she did not care a pin what she wore, only for the sake of the family she did not want the Sydney folks to laugh at her; thus, from a strict sense of duty, she bought the hat.

Now, a two hours drive in the Bush when the dew falls is ruination to the curl of feathers; so when the Wayback family got into the two spring carts Mums had her fine new hat in a paper bag, to be carefully preserved till they got to the station. In the meantime she wore her old milking bonnet. Bubs howled all the way to Barjo, where Mums nursed him to sleep in the waiting room.

All Barjo and Dingo Flat seemed to have congregated to see the Waybacks off. Till now they had no idea how many dear friends they had; for it is when they are going to get rid of you, if only for a time, that true fellowship declares itself.

When at last the train did come in, Dads and Mums rushed to hold it as though they feared it might change its mind. In they jumped, father, mother, boys and girls, bags and parcels, packets and wraps, and then everybody that could find a place leaned out the windows and grinned at the neighbours on the platform.

Cousin Jonas was there to take the carts home, and he kept saying, 'Now mind you take care of yourselves.'

Then there was a whistle, a banging of doors, and the train moved out of the station.

'Hi! Hi! Stop!'

It was Jonas, rushing along the platform waving a parcel in his hand.

'Good gracious!' cried Mums, 'I've forgotten my hat. Tell them to stop, Dads! Oh, tell them to stop!'

Dads shouted out the window of the train, the children shouted in the carriage, Bubs howled in sympathy. But the train, regardless of the most frantic appeal, carried off Mums in her old milking bonnet to see the Commonwealth celebrations.

CHAPTER TWO: THE EMU COFFEE PALACE

'By cripes, Dads, this must be Sydney! We're going inter a lashing big station, my word! Beats Barjo an' no mistake!'

It was Jabez who spoke, his body half out of the carriage window.

'Now, get all yer things ready, children!'

Everybody stood up and grabbed a parcel or bag with a desperate resolve to be first out of the carriage. Other passengers acted on the same impulse, so that when the train pulled up, the platform was, of a sudden, a dense mass of hurrying humanity.

'Come on, kids! Let's get out of this!' cried Dads, as with Bubs under one arm he dragged Mums with the other. As for Mums, she held three parcels and towed little Sid, who held Cris, who held Delia, who hung onto Rube, who had grabbed Euphemia, who clung to Sarah Jane, who was fastened to Tilly, who helped Jabez carry a portmanteau.

'Now, don't yous let go, anyone!' shouted back Mums, as the long line of Waybacks swayed to and fro in the crowd, 'or you'll be bushed!'

They rounded up under the clock near the front of the station.

'Now, just bide a bit here,' Dads said, 'till the crowd's gone.'

They waited and waited, standing like an island in a moving sea of rushing people. Dads' eyes opened wider and wider as the rush continued unabated.

'What's up, Mums? Do yer thinks it's a bush fire? Hi, mister,' and he clutched hold of a porter pushing a luggage trolley, 'what's up here?'

The porter gave Dads a pitying look, 'Price of damper's rose a penny a pound,' he said sarcastically, and hurried on.

'You're mighty smart,' Dads called after him, 'I suppose yer thinks I come from the country.'

'Let's get on ther bus, Dads,' said Mums, pointing at the electric tram.

'I'm waitin' fer 'em to hitch the team on,' said Dads. 'Don't tell me them there carriages is pulled far with that piece o' fencin' wire! Take my tip; there'll be a bloomin' accident pretty soon!'

But, as time passed and no damage was reported, the Wayback family gained confidence and finally boarded the car and were whirled away up George Street.

* * *

'Is this here the Emu Coffee Palace and boarding place?' It was Dads who spoke.

'That's it,' said the clerk as he struck two dinner tickets on the file and handed key 24 to one of the boarders.

'I'd like ter know,' said Dads, 'if yer serve tea as well as coffee. Yer see, we's not too strong on coffee up Barjo way.'

'Buckets o' tea, anytime you like,' said the clerk, now busily collecting dinner tickets with both hands.

'That's all right, then,' said Dads, a great anxiety lifted from his mind. 'Can yer let us have a bit of a shake-down, then, fer the lot of us?'

'Here you are, 72, 73, 74,' said the clerk, handing over three keys to the liftboy after he had entered the Waybacks' name in a big book and tucked away a five pound note as if it was a pipe-lighter.

The boy pulled a door open to show what appeared to be a room five by five.

'No yer don't, Sonny,' said Dads, 'eleven of us can't sleep in that, not even if we all stood up!'

After a while the liftboy persuaded them to all enter the lift.

'Oh crikey, Dads!' cried Jabez, as all the children howled in a chorus, 'ther blanky house is fallin' inter the cellar!'

'Well, I'll be hanged!' said Dads, as the whole party, white and trembling, stepped out of the lift onto the landing, 'if that don't beat everything! Take my tip, that catapult will go up through the roof to glory one o' these here days when the wire breaks off. It's a bit too sudden, that's what it is!'

Before the liftboy left them, Dads asked, 'Say, sonny, is there a waterhole handy? We wants a bit of a wash.'

'There's a bathroom, mister, at the end of the passage.'

When Dads and Jabez opened the bathroom door they had grave doubts about entering. It reminded them too much of the lift, and they sounded the floor carefully with each foot to make sure it would not fall down or jump up with them.

*   *   *

Crash! Crash! Crash!

It was the boarders' dinner gong going that resounded up the stairs.

'Hi! Hi! Where are they?'

It was Dads with nothing but his pants on, who rushed out into the corridor, caught up a tray some waitress had left and started banging like a demon as he ran. Jabez followed, hammering a tin lid, and all the little Waybacks swarmed into the passage armed with hairbrushes, water bottles, boots, or anything handy that would make a noise.

It was a fearful row. All the doors flew open and anxious boarders rushed out, certain at the very least that the house was on fire.

'Throw dust on 'em, mister! Throw dust!' shouted Dads to a bald-headed man who was rushing for the stairs.

'Throw dust on what?' enquired an alarmed chambermaid.

'On ther bees, of course! Isn't there a swarm? An' didn't you start to ring 'em down?'

Then everybody laughed.

'You've got to be quick an' lively after bees. No time to ask questions,' explained Dads. 'Dust is real good; but water's better if it's handy. Rub some honey in ther box if yer want to make 'em stop. Now, at Barjo . . .'

But the fat man had reached his room and banged the door, so Dads was obliged to finish his discourse on bees to the liftboy.

*   *   *

The Waybacks descended to the dining room.

'Where's ther dog?' enquired Jabez of a waiter.

'What dog, sir? I've not seen one.'

'Ter throw the bone to! What'll I do with ther bone if there ain't no dog?'

'Now, Cris,' cried Mums, 'don't put yer knife so far inter your mouth. Knives is meant to scoop up the gravy, not to cut yer throat with. Keep yer legs still Sid, an' don't put all yer fingers in yer plate at once. Remember you're in Sydney an' be a little gentleman. Gentlemen only take taters with one hand at a time. Euphemia, if you want to drink up your soup, ask Sarah Jane to hold the dish fer yer, or you'll spill it all down yer new frock. Now, Delia, don't catch flies at mealtimes, it's not manners; shoo 'em off and eat all those bits on yer plate. There's many a poor child has come to want through leaving bits. Wipe the gravy off yer mouth Jabez and I wish, Tilly, you would look after Bubs and stop him making post-holes in all the loaves of bread. Perhaps ther folks here won't like it. Have a little sense, do!'

After dinner was over, the Waybacks drifted down to George Street to see the sights.

'What I'd like to know,' said Dads, 'is why all these here people is allowed ter walk up and down, up and down, doin' nothin'? Look at 'em, hundreds of 'em, thousands of 'em; not like us, just come ter see ther sights fer once in our lives, but just loafin' along, lookin' at nothin', doin' nothin'.

'Surely ter goodness they could find a bit o' clearing or stumping ter do. I'd give all those gals hoes and set 'em to chippin'. Take my tip; they wouldn't want ter put on all that paint on 'em.'

The progress of the party was slow. Every shop window had to be surrounded in turn, and calls and counter-calls drew them to and fro.

'I say, Cris!'

'Look here, Sarah Jane . . .'

'Oh, ain't that spiffin'!'

'Euphemia, how'd you like ter wear that?'

'Delia, come an' see, come an' see!'

'By cripes, look at that, now!'

'Talk about clocks an' watches, look at that Mums!'

The family pushed on and forward. If they had only been on the Wallaby Ranges, in dense scrub or heavy timber, there is no doubt that their method of exploration would have kept them together and within touch and call; but, in the wilds of George Street south, the precipices of Brickfield Hill, the gorges of Pitt Street and the undergrowth of Sussex Street, bushcraft altogether failed.

Undaunted, Dads kept on, but though moving quickly, he progressed slowly, for he had to zigzag through the crowd and it often happened that when he dodged, the man in front dodged also.

Dads began to falter; he was getting tired. He had already cannoned against one hundred and fifty-seven persons and, while a few bumps more or less don't count, when you get over seven score in less than thirty minutes, a certain soreness is left on even the toughest.

Dads had been called a blanky fool more times in the last half-hour than in all his life before, and, although he had taken the remarks in a friendly spirit, they began at the last to pall and Dads began to have a vague doubt that a verdict so unanimous must have some justification in fact.

CHAPTER THREE: THE BENEVOLENT STRANGER

'Say, mate, can you tell me the way to the railway station?'

The man who spoke was evidently a country man; stiff-jointed, round-shouldered, face bronzed and blotched with tan.

'I'm a stranger myself, hereabouts,' said Dads, 'but I just passed the station and now I'm going back.'

'Now, that's lucky!' said the stranger, 'for I'm no hand at all at this street work. If it was the Myall Ranges, now, it would be a hard job to bush me, and I guarantee I can cross-country with any man. But, the fact is, I have only just come up by train. I started out to find the Emu Coffee Palace, but I've got bogged somehow, so I reckon I'll go back to the railway and make a fresh start.'

'Goin' to ther Emu, are yer?' said Dads, 'Now there is the most extraordinary thing as I ever heard tell of; I'm staying there myself.'

'By cripes! You don't say so?' replied the stranger. 'Do you think it's a safe place for a cove to camp? One who has a few beans, you know. I don't want to get took down.'

'You've just about sized things up, mate,' said Dads, 'but seeing as I only arrove this mornin', I can't give yer many points about ther Emu. Keep yer door locked; carry yer beans in yer hip pocket and strap yer belt tight. Don't talk ter strangers and, if a bloke mentions an uncle in Fiji, call a policeman.

'But, if yer stops at ther Emu, take my tip about one thing. Don't get in that there little room that fires yer up the house like a gun with two charges of powder in her. I'll allow it's quick, but give me the stairs for safety.'

'They tell me a bloke can't be too careful; Sydney's full of spielers,' said the countryman, 'and you've got to sleep with both eyes open, or get your eye teeth drawn. Anyhow, come and have a drink; that looks a decent sort of pub.'

Dads had a drink, then he shouted, and the stranger would shout again; and, to be more at their ease, they sat down in a room off the bar and here Dads, taking pity on the stranger, began to post him up in all the villainies by which the Sydney sharpers took down country mugs, the wiles of confidence men and the fatal lures of spielers.

'I tell you I'm just watchin' fer 'em, an' I'll give 'em Fiji, I promise you, if they start to tackle me. Now, mind you be keerful an' don't yer be took down by none o' those blokes as want yer to show 'em money.'

'By cripes, mate,' said the other, 'if what you say is true, and I could not doubt your words fer a moment, I can always tell an honest man when I see him, I think I had best take the next train home again!'

'Don't be afraid, now,' said Dads. 'I'll stand by yer, we'll be mates up there at ther Emu; you'll be alright if yer keeps in my tracks. Hold yer money tight, and beware of "Fiji", and yer as safe as ther Wallaby Ranges.'

While they were talking two strangers entered the room. The taller, who was most elegantly dressed, offered to shout to the crowd, and he was such a nice, genial man, Dads could not refuse.

The man who shouted said he had just come into a lot of money; up till now he had been a poor selector, working on the land. He knew what hard graft and harder fare was, to his sorrow, and till the longest day he lived should always feel sorry for the poor 'cockie'. So much so that he had decided to help one poor man every day, till he had got through £4000. He had helped one yesterday, and one the day before, and if he did not help one today he would not sleep that night.

Here the stranger pulled out a big bundle of notes, and turned to explain his idea to Dads.

'I want to help those who help themselves; it's not a bit of good, I've tried it, giving a cheque to a man without bean. He may be a good sort of fellow, but the chances are 1000 to one the cash will do him harm, and all go in the cursed drink. No, let me see that a man is a careful, saving chap, and has got a little stuff, and I'll double it for him; then he will take care of it, and it will do him good!'

Dads thought the stranger talked most rationally; it was a kind of charity he understood, and his eyes were fascinated by the huge bundle of notes, but his friend, the countryman, seemed more sceptical, and when the two strangers had turned away, he whispered to Dads:

'We had best be careful now. I've got my doubts of those two: but I tell you how we can be on the safe side. I don't mind showing them twenty-five quid, if you show another twenty-five, and you hold the lot. No letting it out of your hands, mind. If they give us another fifty you can hold that while I make an excuse, and slip out and fetch a policeman. If they are spielers they will clear when they see him; if they are on the square, it won't matter. Anyhow, we stand to make sure fifty, which won't be too bad for two bushies their first day in town.'

With this the countryman produced a pocketbook, with twenty-five notes, and handed it to Dads, who felt pleased all over himself, and quickly produced his own share of notes.

'Hi, mate,' said the countryman, 'we are two poor men, the sort you want, and can show you fifty quid.'

'You can?' said the amiable stranger. 'I'm dashed glad to hear it. Two of you, too! That will save me looking for a man tomorrow. Show me, and I'm as good as my word.'

The countryman took the pocketbook, and carefully counted over the fifty notes, and Dads was pleased to see how careful he was not to let go of them. The stranger, quite satisfied, handed over another fifty in five tens, and was so pleased, he called for more drinks for all hands.

The countryman put all the notes in the pocketbook, handed it to Dads, thanked the stranger for his kindness, and saying he had a friend outside he must call in to tell his good luck to, turned to go, and giving a knowing wink to Dads, he was gone.

Dads, sitting firmly in his seat, grabbed the pocketbook securely in both events, and sat chuckling to himself with glee.

'Now, if that's not the smartest thing I ever heard tell of. We've got ther stuff, all right, whichever way it works out. We're not all fools at Barjo, take my tip.'

'Your friend's a long time away,' said the genial stranger, after a long pause; 'I want him to join in another drink. I'll go and call him in,' and off he went.

Later the third man said he must look for the second. He said he could not think what was up.

Still Dads smiled. Happen what would, he held the pocketbook, and was safe from all wiles, real or pretended.

Minutes passed, half an hour, an hour. Dads still sat, solid and satisfied.

The barman came in and asked what he was waiting for.

'That friend o' mine I came in with,' said Dads. 'I 'spect he's lost his way again; yer see he don't know Sydney.'

'Well he ought to,' said the barman. 'I've seen him knocking about here for the past five years.'

Dads began to feel uneasy. Was it possible that after all he had been done?

With shaking hands he opened the pocketbook, only to find there a fat bundle of blank pieces of paper.

'Well, I'm damned!' said Dads. 'But how was I to know? Never a word did they say about Fiji or the rich uncle there!'

'Lord love me!' said the barman, reading the whole story in Dads' amazed face. 'The likes of you ought to be led about with a string!'

A ZACK TO CENTRAL

FRANK DANIEL

THERE WAS NOTHING GRAND or exciting about my last day at school.

It wasn't a big deal; it just meant that I didn't have to come back the next day, or any other day for the rest of my life.

There was no fanfare, just the traditional dunking ritual.

My head was held under a running tap at the water tank, which stood at the western end of the school building. There was a bit of jostling and some friendly wrestling in feigned objection, and then the four-mile ride home on my pushbike with my haversack filled with books and other paraphernalia that I considered to be of no further use, but took home anyway.

In those days kids could leave school at fourteen but, in an endeavour to please my mother and to further my education, I'd stuck it out until I was fifteen.

Working at home on the family farm was the only occupation available to me at the time and, after a few months of that, I'd saved five pounds.

Five pounds! A 'fiver'! It seemed a lot of money and, considering I wasn't being paid wages but just 'pocket money' for my services, it was a lot of money!

I was still being fed and clothed by my parents and no one seemed to consider a weekly wage necessary. My parents were too cunning to ever mention wages.

Anyway, being a man of means, I thought it was time I visited the 'big smoke'.

I'd been to Sydney with my family in the past, to visit relatives, but now I felt that a trip to the city on my 'Pat Malone' would be in order, without having to visit aunts and uncles.

I broke the news to Mum and, rather surprisingly, there were no objections. In fact she was more than helpful and gave some good advice.

'First of all,' she told me, "when you ride your bike into town, leave it at your mate's place where it won't get pinched, and walk up to the railway station.'

I hadn't even thought of anyone lifting my bike while I was away.

'Then, when you get to the station, tell the stationmaster that you want a return ticket. That way, you'll be sure of getting home. Make sure you get a *return* ticket!'

Mum didn't bother with any more details. She always assumed that everyone knew what she was talking about.

I thought I knew what she meant but wasn't a hundred per cent certain; I didn't let on, though. I couldn't have her worrying that her son, the great world traveller, didn't understand the fundamentals of purchasing a ticket for a ride on a train.

I reckoned things would sort themselves out as I went along.

I picked a date for my journey and, when the day arrived, Mum packed a few spare items of clothing in my old school haversack with a couple of fresh mutton and tomato sauce sandwiches wrapped in newspaper, some Anzac biscuits and a couple of apples.

I was ready.

The ride into town was quite exciting; it was my first such trip since leaving school. Now, however, I was heading into town in the late afternoon instead of heading for home at that time, as I had done for so many years.

I left my bike at my mate's house and walked to the railway station. There I was met by the stationmaster, who was waiting on the 'five-o-clock' to come in.

'And what can I do for you, Sir?' he asked formally. 'The train will be in shortly. If you want to buy a ticket you should really have come earlier than this.'

His manner put me a little off my stride.

'Arrhh,' I said, 'I want a *return* ticket, please!'

'Where to?' he asked.

'Back here,' I said.

'You've got to go somewhere before you can come back,' he said, looking at me over his spectacles. 'Where are you going?'

I felt a little silly by this time and, to add to my dilemma, I didn't really know the name of my destination.

'Arrhh . . . Sydney . . .' I said hesitantly. I just hoped there'd be a station called Sydney.

He sighed and went into the ticket office, directing me to the ticket window on the other side, in the waiting room.

Before I could blink he punched out a ticket, took my fiver and handed me some change and the ticket through the little window. Then he dropped down the window's heavy wooden security shutter with a bang.

I left the waiting room clutching my ticket and the stationmaster met me again on the platform, where quite a few others were waiting for the train.

There, much to my embarrassment, he explained the workings of the ticket in a voice loud enough to be heard up and down the platform.

'See this?' he said pointing to my ticket, which read 'Bungendore to Central' on one half and 'Central to Bungendore' on the other.

'Yair.'

'Well, when you get to Central Station, that's the big station in Sydney where the line ends, you give your ticket to the ticket collector at the gate and he'll give you back the half with 'Central to Bungendore' on it. Do you understand?'

'Yair.'

'Now don't lose that half, or you'll be stuck in Sydney. OK?'

'Yair, I know,' I lied.

It made sense, but it was all news to me. At least now I knew that 'Central' was the name of Sydney's railway station.

The trip was long and uneventful. Darkness fell shortly before we arrived at Goulburn.

Some passengers got off to buy a hurried meal and a cup of tea, but I refused to budge in case the train moved on without me. Besides, I had the sandwiches that Mum had prepared.

As it turned out I had plenty of time and, when some passengers returned with packaged salads and pies to eat on the train, I had another revelation. It was the first time in my life that I had ever seen a take-away meal.

Goulburn to Sydney in the dark was a bit scary, as the train passed through a number of tunnels along the way. Pulling over on loop lines to allow more important rail traffic through was also a bit of a worry. There was always a chance that someone might sneak onto the train while it was stopped in the dark, people who were 'up to no good'. I was happier when the train was moving. There was no chance of anybody boarding the train if it was moving.

The station identification signs along the way gave me something to read as well as telling me where I was: Marulan, Moss Vale, Mittagong, Picton, Camden, Liverpool—followed by a bewildering number of suburban station names until, finally, 'Central' appeared in all its glory.

Central from the train was a multitude of platforms adorned with lots of lights, huge signs, wooden seats and vending machines, and crowds of people all hurrying in one direction.

I stumbled from the carriage and followed the mob.

Once off the train Central became a noisy maze of tiled walls, stairways and passageways, directional signs and large arrows that meant nothing to me.

I found myself in a huge space filled with people where there was a huge clock and enormous timetables with smaller clocks showing departure and arrival times. There were newspaper stands and shops, and loudspeakers barked directions while motorised trolleys towed multiple trailers piled with ports, suitcases and all sorts of luggage.

People were ripping and tearing in all directions. Everyone appeared to be in one hell of a hurry, all bar me. I didn't know where I was or what to do next. I thought I was worried on the train, but I was really worried now!

I finally found a sign indicating the way to George Street and, because I'd heard of it before, I reckoned it must be the main street of Sydney, so I headed in that direction.

Things didn't improve when I left the station; there were huge buildings and busy roads and cars and people and trams and buses going in all directions, and traffic lights!

I negotiated my way across an enormous intersection by following the crowd going the same way as me and went along George Street for a number of blocks till I came to a big old three-storey hotel.

I forget the name of it, 'Prince' something or other, I think. I ventured in and hesitantly asked if I could stay for a couple of days.

The bloke in the little office asked my name and wrote it down and took some money and gave me change. Then he told me to go up the stairs to the second floor, turn left and find room number fourteen.

I did.

Inside room fourteen was a single bed with a grey blanket and a pillow, a small wardrobe with a mirror, a chair, a sink and a window from which I could view the city traffic. Rain had just started to fall and it all looked a bit strange and unfriendly.

It was an uneventful night. I slept with my clothes on and my schoolbag in the bed just in case there might have been need for a hasty escape, seeing that there was no key or lock to the door.

The next two days were nice and sunny and I spent them taking in some of the sights. I saw the Harbour Bridge, Hyde Park Fountain and the 'Fairy Terminal'.

I rode on the 'Manly Fairy' across the harbour and back without getting off and then shouted myself a ticket to Taronga Park Zoo where I gazed at animals I'd only ever seen in picture books.

Close to sundown I caught a ferry back to 'Circular Kway', where I noticed a large crowd of people boarding another ferry to Luna Park.

I knew Mum wouldn't be too happy with me staying up after dark, but how the Hell would she know?

Off I went to see the famous great laughing mouth and explore its attractions. I was on my own but that didn't bother me, it was all new and fascinating. I went on a few rides and even scared myself half to death alone on the ghost train, but I spent most of the evening watching the city slickers having fun and taking in the sights and sounds.

With the 'fairy rides' and a drink and sandwich now and again I'd been spending a 'zack' here and a 'bob' there and realised that soon the only thing in my pockets would be my two hands.

Besides, it was now over three full days since I'd left home; I was getting homesick. All the excitement of Sydney and my holiday was fading and I thought about making tracks. I decided to have one more walk around next morning with my haversack and then make my way back to Central—and home. As a reluctant Catholic with a pious mother I had one thing to do before I left. I had to look at St Mary's Cathedral, at least from the outside.

Next morning after looking at St Mary's Cathedral for a few minutes and then staring at the Archibald Fountain splashing water in all directions for a bit longer, I wandered across the grass and found myself standing on a corner at one end of Hyde Park.

I was trying to figure out exactly where I was when I saw a large double-decker 'Gov-a-mint' bus approaching.

'Struth!' I thought suddenly, 'I haven't had a ride on one of them yet!'

I put my hand in my pocket to see how much money I had left.

I only had a threepence and two pennies—five pence left out of five quid!

I quickly checked all my other pockets but all I could come up with was half a railway ticket with the words 'Central to Bungendore' printed on it. I put that safely back into my pocket. I was more than pleased that I still had it.

I ran to where the bus was heading and when it stopped I called to the conductor who was perched on the little platform at the back, casually holding onto the metal pole that helped you get on board.

'Hey mate!' I called out, 'How much is it from here to Central Station?'

'Sixpence,' he replied expressionlessly.

Blow! I only had five pence and I needed a zack.

I really wanted a ride on that bus, and then I had an idea.

So, I ran behind the bus, keeping pace with it for five or six blocks. It was hard going with all the crowds and my haversack and I lost touch for a bit, but I managed to keep it in sight and put on a bit of a spurt and finally caught up again when it stopped at a big intersection, many blocks further along the road.

'Hey mate!' I panted at the conductor, 'how much is it from here to Central Station?'

'Eight pence,' he replied laconically, without even appearing to look at me. 'You're running the wrong way.'

The bus moved off and left me standing there.

It was a long walk back to Central.

THE DOWNFALL OF MULLIGAN'S

BANJO PATERSON

THE SPORTING MEN OF Mulligan's were an exceedingly knowing lot; in fact, they had obtained the name amongst their neighbours of being a little bit too knowing. They had 'taken down' the adjoining town in a variety of ways. They were always winning maiden plates with horses which were shrewdly suspected to be old and well-tried performers in disguise.

When the sports of Paddy's Flat unearthed a phenomenal runner in the shape of a blackfellow called Frying-pan Joe, the Mulligan contingent immediately took the trouble to discover a blackfellow of their own, and they made a match and won all the Paddy's Flat money with ridiculous ease; then their blackfellow turned out to be a well-known Sydney performer. They had a man who could fight, a man who could be backed to jump five-feet-ten, a man who could kill eight pigeons out of nine at thirty yards, a man who could make a break of fifty or so at billiards if he tried; they could all drink, and they all had that indefinite look of infinite wisdom and conscious superiority which belongs only to those who know something about horseflesh.

They knew a great many things never learnt at Sunday school. They were experts at cards and dice. They would go to immense trouble to work off any small swindle in the sporting line. In short the general consensus of opinion was that they were a very 'fly' crowd at Mulligan's, and if you went there you wanted to 'keep your eyes skinned' or they'd 'have' you over a threepenny-bit.

There were races at Sydney one Christmas, and a select band of the Mulligan sportsmen were going down to them. They were in high feather, having just won a lot of money from a young Englishman at pigeon-shooting, by the simple method of slipping blank cartridges into his gun when he wasn't looking, and then backing the bird.

They intended to make a fortune out of the Sydney people, and admirers who came to see them off only asked them as a favour to leave money enough in Sydney to make it worthwhile for another detachment to go down later on. Just as the train was departing a priest came running onto the platform, and was bundled into the carriage where our Mulligan friends were; the door was slammed to, and away they went. His Reverence was hot and perspiring, and for a few minutes mopped himself with a handkerchief, while the silence was unbroken except by the rattle of the train.

After a while one of the Mulligan fraternity got out a pack of cards and proposed a game to while away the time. There was a young squatter in the carriage who looked as if he might be induced to lose a few pounds, and the sportsmen thought they would be neglecting their opportunities if they did not try to 'get a bit to go on with' from him. He agreed to play, and, just as a matter of courtesy, they asked the priest whether he would take a hand.

'What game d'ye play?' he asked, in a melodious brogue.

They explained that any game was equally acceptable to them, but they thought it right to add that they generally played for money.

'Sure an' it don't matter for wanst in a way,' said he, 'Oi'll take a hand bedad. Oi'm only going about fifty miles, so Oi can't lose a fortune.'

They lifted a light portmanteau onto their knees to make a table, and five of them—three of the Mulligan crowd and the two strangers—started to have a little game of poker. Things looked rosy for the Mulligan boys, who chuckled as they thought how soon they were making a beginning, and what a magnificent yarn they would have to tell about how they rooked a priest on the way down.

Nothing sensational resulted from the first few deals, and the priest began to ask questions.

'Be ye going to the races?'

They said they were.

'Ah! And Oi suppose ye'll be betting wid thim bookmakers, betting on the horses, will yez? They do be terrible knowing men, thim bookmakers, they tell me. I wouldn't bet much if Oi was ye,' he said, with an affable smile. 'If ye go bettin' ye will be took in wid thim bookmakers.'

The boys listened with a bored air and reckoned that by the time they parted the priest would have learnt that they were well able to look after themselves. They went steadily on with the game, and the priest and the young squatter won slightly; this was part of the plan to lead them on to plunge. They neared the station where the priest was to get out. He had won rather more than they liked, so the signal was passed round to 'put the cross on'. Poker is a game at which a man need not risk much unless he feels inclined, and on this deal the priest stood out. Consequently, when they drew up at his station he was still a few pounds in.

'Bedad,' he said, 'Oi don't loike goin' away wid yer money. Oi'll go on to the next station so as ye can have revinge.' Then he sat down again, and play went on in earnest.

The man of religion seemed to have the Devil's own luck. When he was dealt a good hand he invariably backed it well, and if he had a bad one he would not risk anything. The sports grew painfully anxious as they saw him getting further and further ahead of them, prattling away all the time like a big schoolboy. The squatter was the biggest loser so far, but the priest was the only winner. All the others were out of pocket. His Reverence played with great dash, and seemed to know a lot about the game, so that on arrival at the second station he was a good round sum in pocket.

He rose to leave them with many expressions of regret, and laughingly promised full revenge next time. Just as he was opening the carriage door, one of the Mulligan fraternity said in a stage-whisper: 'He's a blanky sink-pocket. If he can come this far, let him come on to Sydney and play for double the stakes.' Like a shot the priest turned on him.

'Bedad, an' if that's yer talk, Oi'll play ye fer double stakes from here to the other side of glory. Do yez think men are mice because they eat cheese? It isn't one of the Ryans would be fearing to give any man his revinge!'

He snorted defiance at them, grabbed his cards and waded in. The others felt that a crisis was at hand and settled down to play in a dead silence. But the priest kept on winning steadily, and the 'old man' of the Mulligan push saw that something decisive must be done, and decided on a big plunge to get all the money back on one hand. By a dexterous manipulation of the cards he dealt himself four kings, almost the best hand at poker. Then he began with assumed hesitation to bet on his hand, raising the stake little by little.

'Sure ye're trying to bluff, so ye are!' said the priest, and immediately raised it.

The others had dropped out of the game and watched with painful interest the stake grow and grow. The Mulligan fraternity felt a cheerful certainty that the 'old man' had made things safe, and regarded themselves as mercifully delivered from an unpleasant situation.

The priest went on doggedly raising the stake in response to his antagonist's challenges until it had attained huge dimensions.

'Sure that's high enough,' said he, putting into the pool sufficient to entitle him to see his opponent's hand.

The 'old man' with great gravity laid down his four kings, whereat the Mulligan boys let a big sigh of relief escape them.

Then the priest laid down four aces and scooped the pool.

The sportsmen of Mulligan's never quite knew how they got out to Randwick. They borrowed a bit of money in Sydney, and found themselves in the saddling-paddock in a half-dazed condition, trying to realise what had happened to them. During the afternoon they were up at the end of the lawn near the Leger stand and could hear the babel of tongues, small bookmakers, thimble riggers, confidence men, and so on, plying their trades outside. In the tumult of voices they heard one that sounded familiar. Soon suspicion grew into certainty, and they knew that it was the voice of 'Father' Ryan. They walked to the fence and looked over. This is what he was saying:

'Pop it down, gents! Pop it down! If you don't put down a brick you can't pick up a castle! I'll bet no one here can pick the knave of hearts out of these three cards. I'll bet half-a-sovereign no one here can find the knave!'

Then the crowd parted a little, and through the opening they could see him distinctly, doing a great business and showing wonderful dexterity with the pasteboard.

There is still enough money in Sydney to make it worthwhile for another detachment to come down from Mulligan's; but the next lot will hesitate about playing poker with priests in the train.

TO THE CITY

STEELE RUDD
(EXCERPT FROM *ON AN AUSTRALIAN FARM*)

A WARM AND GLORIOUS sunshine lit up the land. The fields of waving wheat breaking into shot-blade were pictures good for man to see. The great pine trees towering round the snuggling home were a-song with birds and all the family were up to their eyes with the final preparations for the trip to the city.

For a week and more Mrs Dashwood and the girls had been overhauling and organising their wardrobes, and packing boxes and bags and portmanteaux, so that no hitch would happen and no time be lost when the hour for starting arrived. Tilly, who had had more experience in travelling than the others, was careful to send Maria, her married sister, instructions to do likewise, and warned her to leave nothing to the last. And Maria sent a message to say that she and the baby were ready to start at any moment.

Preparations for a church picnic, or for attending a race meeting, are exciting enough events in the country, but this trip to the city excelled all things in the history of 'Fairfield'. Nothing had ever so disorganised and dislocated the family nerve and general placidity.

There is no class on earth so easily and speedily demoralised as the country person when under the spell and influence of a 'trip to the city'. But the demoralisation lasts only until their feet touch the floor of the railway carriage, and they feel the grip of the ticket and the carriage window. Then, with a gulp and a gasp, the temporary disorder passes away like the evil effects of green lucerne leaving a bloated cow when proper remedies are applied.

Old John, arrayed in a shining black suit with a heavy gold chain stretched across his great stomach, strutted into the dining room and surveyed himself in a self-satisfied sort of way. A big man was old John, and done up and posing as he was now, looked all over a prosperous alderman.

Granny in a motherly way looked him up and down, then took him in charge and tugged at the sleeves and tails of his coat to coax them into position. Then, taking out her pocket-handkerchief, she proceeded to brush him all over.

Peter, dressed like a shop window, in a loud check suit, a cunning-looking tweed hat—the only one of its kind in the land—a high-coloured collar, a variegated necktie, and carrying a spanking new leather bag in each hand, skipped breezily into the room.

For a moment John's breath threatened to leave him. He stared long and hard at his artistic-looking son. Peter paraded the room as if for inspection. Old John started to smile.

'Well,' said old John, 'if I wouldn't a'thought you was just come back from heaven.'

'By Jove, then, Father,' Peter rejoined enthusiastically, 'you don't look too bad yourself. You'd pass for a king in those clothes.'

James, carelessly dressed in a common tweed suit, and wearing a soft felt hat, sauntered in search of luggage to convey to the buggies standing in the yard. His eyes rested on Peter and he stopped abruptly, and stared.

Old John, looking at James, said, 'Don't you know him, lad? Did you think he were the Dook o' York?'

James burst into merriment and, turning on his heel, retreated down the corridor. The next moment he was heard calling to the girls.

'What is it, James?' Tilly answered. 'We'll be ready now in a moment.'

'For heaven's sake,' James said, 'just go and look in at the dining room!'

Neither Tilly nor Polly could resist curiosity. Clad in their sombre travelling dresses they hurried to the dining room and looked in curiously and expectantly. For a second or two they experienced only disappointment, for their eyes rested only on the forms of Granny and old John. When, however, the gorgeous and smiling figure of Peter standing rigid and erect took shape to them, they simultaneously shrieked and fled.

'They be a'laughin' at you, lad,' old John remarked with a grin at Peter.

'Those who laugh last, Father, laugh longest,' Peter said. 'Wait till we get to the city, and see who'll be laughed at then, not me. Ha, ha, ha!'

Mrs Dashwood and Maria and the baby assembled in the dining room and dumped a consignment of small luggage on the table.

'Did anyone see Maria's basket?' Mrs Dashwood asked.

But Maria, herself, stifled a reply. 'Oh *Peter*!' she exclaimed on beholding her brother. Then she started to laugh.

'Well, I'm blowed if I know what you all see wrong about me to laugh at,' Peter protested. And once more he stepped out round the room in a gallant parade.

'Really,' Maria said advisedly, 'you don't show a bit of taste, Peter, not a bit.'

'Don't show a bit of *taste*?' Peter echoed. 'There's a good joke in there somewhere, Father, but I'm blessed if I can get it off my tongue.'

James, who had returned quietly to the room, started to grin. 'If there's a better joke there than himself,' he remarked slyly to Maria, 'I'll be very much surprised.'

William appeared, and announced that everything was ready and advised them to get a move on.

Polly and Tilly, with their hats in their hands, paid final visits to the mirror. Granny put up a hue and cry about the loss of one of her woollen 'mitts' that all the while was in her pocket, and started the others off on a wild goose chase.

'Now then, for the city,' Peter cried, lifting his hand and adjusting his quaint little hat.

'Oh, wait just a minute!' Polly exclaimed excitedly. 'What on earth did I do with my umbrella?'

They turned the place upside down in search of the umbrella and eventually discovered that Granny was nursing it all the while.

Out in the sun Polly and Tilly tittered and said, 'Just look at Peter!'

Then they clamoured and climbed into the four-wheeler. James opened and closed the big white gate. The whip cracked and away they rolled to the railway station.

A sharp twenty minutes' drive past McFlaherty's farm, around Catherton's corner, and they reached the station.

The bulk of the luggage, which had preceded them on Smith's wagon, occupied a whole end of the platform. The stationmaster and his porter were busy engaged disfiguring it all with labels.

The stationmaster raised his cap to the ladies, all of whom smiled graciously upon him, and passed pleasant remarks to old John on his appearance and expressed envy at his freedom and prospects of a good time in the city.

'Ahh, I be goin' to enjoy meself, Johnson,' old John assured him. 'It be the first trip we've taken and we're a'goin' to do it in style.'

'I don't blame you,' the stationmaster said. 'Peter looks like he is going to have a good time, Mr Dashwood.'

With a 'Ha, ha, ha!' Peter spun around three times on one heel.

'Ahh,' said old John with a smile, 'Peter thinks he is a'going to take the city by storm.'

'I don't know about taking the city by storm,' the cheerful stationmaster answered, 'but he might take some of the city girls by storm.'

'Ha, ha, ha!' and Peter made several revolutions on his other heel.

The stationmaster, glancing towards the ladies to see they were not within hearing, placed his mouth close to old John's ear and said something confidential.

'Hoh, hoh, hoh! I don't think he would go *thet* far!' old John roared.

'Then he's a lot different to what his father was at his age, I bet,' the stationmaster replied.

Old John broke into another loud, 'Hoh, hoh, hoh! Look here Johnson,' he laughed, 'I'll have you dismissed at headquarters, when I gets to the city.'

Meanwhile Mrs Dashwood and Maria and the girls were busy swapping and changing and arranging the smaller items of luggage. Polly required a certain bag taken into the carriage and Tilly a particular box, while Mrs Dashwood and Maria expressed grave doubts as to the safety of a trunk in the van.

'All travelling "first", Mr Dashwood?' the stationmaster enquired, as he procured the tickets.

'Aye, all first,' old John answered, taking out his purse.

'What about Peter?' the official smiled significantly.

'Peter?' answered old John, turning and eyeing the magnificently dressed one. 'Ahh, but now you haven't anythin' better 'n "first" have you Johnson?'

'Not here,' the other answered, prodding the tickets into the date stamp. 'But I dare say we could get the Governor's carriage if we wired right away.'

'Ha, ha, ha!' Peter went off. 'I'd look as well in it as old thing-a-me-bob the Lieutenant Governor.'

'You'd look a jolly sight better, if you ask me,' the stationmaster broke into a chuckle.

'He'd look better in the dog-box,' James drawled, gazing out at the railway yard.

Just then the mail whistled and a scramble set in.

'That's her!' the stationmaster cried.

Old John and James and Peter snapped up articles of luggage. William kissed Maria and the baby and said 'goodbye' to the others.

The train drew up to the platform and one after the other the family crowded noisily into it, much to the annoyance of two 'commercials', who lay full stretch on the seats. The stationmaster banged the door noisily after them, then stood on the carriage step and wished them all a good time and a safe return. Old John and James waved to those on the platform. The train whistled and puffed, strained, and off it went.

*   *   *

After passing through mile upon mile of smouldering, smoking wastelands over which a fierce bush fire had obviously been raging for many days, after flying past Mullungangerina and Niccoloconjoorooroo, and Bibleback, and Howe, and many other strange places, large suburban residences with luxuriant gardens and white paling fences about them began to show up.

A succession of small shops took shape; pedestrians and motors and bikes began to come along in numbers, and the ascending spires of lofty churches elevated on hills, and volumes of black smoke curling into the sky could be seen from the windows.

Through the last cutting the train rushed, then the great city in all its age, in all its youth, in all its glory, in all its grime, in all its grandeur and in all its dirt and dust burst full before our country friends.

Excitement! There *was* excitement! None of them could remain still a minute longer. Not even Granny, who woke up and wished to know where she was, and how long she had been asleep. They were all in a flurry.

The door flew open and a railway porter bounced in.

'Tickets, please!' he cried sharply.

'Tickets,' Polly and Tilly repeated, looking at old John.

'Ahhh,' and old John started fumbling in his pockets.

'I saw you get them from Mr Johnson, Father,' Peter remarked.

The others regarded old John with anxious eyes.

The porter regarded him as an outrage. 'Can't you find them?' he said, impatiently.

'I put 'em somewhere,' answered old John, screwing and twisting his body about to fit his big hands into his pockets.

'You surely can't have lost them, Father?' Mrs Dashwood murmured with increased anxiety.

'You haven't got them, Mother?' Tilly suggested, looking at Mrs Dashwood.

Mrs Dashwood shook her head and said she hadn't even seen them.

The official lost patience. 'I can't wait on you all night,' he snapped. 'Oh, you'll have to come to see the SM,' and opening the door commanded them to follow him to the magnate's office.

They seized their luggage and, like Brown's cows, followed him. Some of them looked solemn; some looked convicted of bigamy; some looked amused.

Tilly and Polly hid their faces with things they were carrying and tittered.

'Goodness gracious me!' Tilly said. 'What on earth will people think of us!'

The great platform along which they trailed was thronged with people. Some of them were scrambling and jostling for possession of luggage; some running up and down peering into railway carriages; some hugging long-lost brothers and sisters; and a great number staring curiously at the cortege that trooped at the heels of the swaggering railway man.

Hotel porters and boarding-house touts thrust their advertising cards into old John's hand, and into the hands of every member of the family, and shouted the virtues of their respective establishments into their ears.

The crowded shelves of the open book-stalls with their glaring flaring placards inviting people to purchase the 'newest wonder' in the literary line arrested the wondering gaze of our mutual friends. But the porter was in a hurry, and they were not permitted to linger and look.

They were approaching the door of the SM's office. Old John suddenly stopped.

'Ahh, hold on,' he said with a smile.

Old John seemed to have remembered something.

'Have you found them, Father?' the family cried, with joyful expectation in their eyes.

Old John took a tobacco pouch from his pocket, out of which he slowly extracted the missing tickets.

'That be 'em,' he said, handing them to the porter.

'A very stupid place to put tickets!' the porter remarked disappointedly, as he handed back the return halves.

'Ha, ha, ha!' laughed Peter. 'You got 'em, eh, Father?'

'Oh, I knew I had 'em soomwheres,' said old John.

And they turned and departed.

MINER'S HOLIDAY

GAVIN CASEY

THEY POURED TOM AND me onto the Sunday train just as it started to move, and we collected our bottles and found our compartment. There were four other chaps in it, one we knew and three we didn't know. One of the strangers didn't seem to like us much, but the rest brightened up when they saw how many bottles we had. We settled down and loosened our ties and collar studs, and Tom took his shoes off and kicked them under the seat. We arranged the luggage so it wasn't in the way, and smoked and watched the dumps and smoke stacks disappearing over the horizon.

'Goodbye and good riddance!' said Tom. 'All you chaps goin' right to the coast?'

They said they were, and we began to talk about the city and the fields and the great times we were going to have for the next couple of weeks. It was a hot summer, and there was nothing to look at through the windows except mangy inland bush. I thought about the long rows of foamy breakers at North Beach, and we drank a couple of bottles. It was already smoky and stuffy in the carriage, and I liked the beer, but I was looking forward to the coast and thinking of yachting on the river and among the islands a few miles out.

'We'll have to look after the bottles,' said Tom. 'She gets a bit dry down the line in the middle of the night.'

'There's a pub next stop,' said one of the chaps. 'If we make it quick we can nick across and get a few more there.'

We got some more beer and started knocking them over quicker. A bottle with plenty of head on it sprayed over the stranger who wasn't drinking, and we thought that was the best joke ever. A bloke from the next compartment came and stood in the doorway and glared at us as if he'd like to say something. We laughed and offered him some beer, and he glared harder than ever and went away. Somebody found a pack of cards, and they started on poker, but I didn't play. I was full of beer and excitement and didn't feel like cards.

I sat there in the smoky carriage drinking more beer and listening to the wheels bump over the rail joints. I wondered how long each section of rail was and how much closer to the coast each *clankety-clank* took us. It would be great down there in the green, rain-washed country between the rolling coastal ranges and the sea. It would be good to see the rows of streets in which every house had lawns and flowers and the trees were different shapes and colours. Not like the fields, where the broad red roads are flanked by everlasting pepper trees and picket fences.

Then they put up the sleepers, and, though the mob kept playing cards and making a row, I dozed. The rumble of the train became the roar of surf, and I was back at North Beach, riding the breakers like I used to six years ago, before we went to the fields.

When the train pulled in next morning we were all dry and a bit sick. Our holiday suits were crumpled and ugly and the luggage was heavy and covered with corners. The buildings weren't as big and fine-looking as I had remembered them, and they were a dirty smoke colour. It was as hot as hell, hotter than it had been on the fields. We walked out of the station and across the road and had a long, cool pot at the nearest pub. It was what we needed, and we had a couple more.

'Where're you blokes going to stay?' asked one of our new cobbers.

'We want to find a place at one of the beaches,' I said.

'Aw, right in town's the place to stop,' said someone. 'Y' can always go out to the beaches, but if you live there you might as well die after dark.'

'We want a spell,' I said. 'We won't care if it's quiet.'

'Funny idea of a spell,' said someone. 'Wantin' to lug all his baggage another twenty miles as soon as he gets here.'

'I'm stoppin' right where I am,' said another chap. 'I'm goin' to book a room. This pub looks good to me.'

'Why don't we book in, too, Bill?' said Tom. 'We can shift to the beach in a couple of days. We can have a spell here first.'

'We can stick together an' have a bit of fun for a start,' said someone.

It was sensible, I thought. I was tired, and I wanted a bath. There was a whole fortnight ahead. We'd collected a good bunch on the way down, and though it was hot in the streets it was cool in the pub. The beer was good, and I was hungry too. The chaps were all laughing and arguing about it, but I was too tired to argue. I just agreed. We had a couple of rounds to celebrate the fact that we were going to stay together for a while.

That pub was hard to leave. The concrete pavements get your feet when you're not used to them, and the pub was always cool. Every evening I'd think about getting out to the beach next day, but something would always interfere. On the Tuesday Pat Stanford and Johnny Josephs turned up from the fields, and the mob of us made a day of it. On the Wednesday there were thunderstorms. We trotted around the shops and we bought some stuff, but we always finished up in a pub. Tom was enjoying himself, but I got restless.

'Look here,' I'd say when we got up in the mornings, 'we came down here for a change, an' what are we doing? Roaming from pub to pub just like we would on the fields! We're shifting today, Tom. We'll get our things out after breakfast.'

Tom would grumble a bit, but he'd agree. Then one of the other chaps would roam in, fuzzy-headed and yellow-looking.

'What a night!' he'd say. 'Hell! There's so much fur on me tongue I think I must have a cat in me mouth.'

'We're skipping after breakfast,' I'd say. 'We're off out to the beach, where they don't have any cats.'

The chaps were laughing at me, I knew. Always one of them would dig out the rest and they'd decide that we had to have a drink before Tom and I left. An hour would pass in the bar, where it was quiet and cool, and then there'd be no bus for half an hour and we'd have a few somewhere else to pass the time. Someone from the fields would show up, or some bloke one of us knew at the coast. I'd check the clock and worry while they all talked and drank and made a row, but after a while I'd forget about it. We'd eat wherever we happened to be, and the money would flow out of our pockets fast and easy. And Tom and I would always land back at the pub with the mob about midnight. We made a lot of noise, but nobody minded because we spent plenty.

Then the weekend came and half our holiday was gone, and I stuck out for going to the beach.

'Christ! Why bust the party up?' said someone. 'We're gettin' on all right an' havin' a good time, aren't we?'

'This's the best place in the city on Sunday,' said another of them. 'We're boarders, an' it's no trouble to get served.'

'Why don't you all come out?' asked Tom. 'Come out for the day, anyway. It'll do you good.'

I didn't want them all at the beach. I only wanted Tom and me there. But they liked Tom's suggestion.

'Cripes, yes!' said someone. 'We got t' see the water before we go home. Why not now?'

We got a taxi and a lot of bottles and we all piled in and went zooming off to the beach. We went through the suburbs, and I got a good look at the gardens for the first time since we'd arrived. When we were a mile from the coast I smelled the sea. Then we dropped over the last sand hills with the sound of the breakers booming away in our ears, and the car pulled up where we could see the whole beach, speckled with people and bright in the sunshine. The sand glared and hurt our eyes, but it did me good to see the beach with brown bodies all over it. There were a lot of improvements, flash pavilions and lookout towers and so on, but it was the same old beach. I remembered the first day I'd spent trying to ride a surfboard, and a lot of other occasions.

None of the chaps except Tom and I wanted to go in, but they felt they had to, and they pulled each other's legs about it until we were all in the dressing rooms. We peeled off our clothes, and I wished I'd bought a new swimming suit. Not that I'm fussy about how I look, but most of them were wearing trunks, and my old bathers were baggy as well as out of date. The men in the rooms were as brown as I used to be, and our mob seemed white, even their forearms and faces. You don't get sunburnt underground, or in pubs either.

When we went out the glare on the sand seemed worse, and we felt funny with our long white arms and legs and old-fashioned bathers. The sand felt funny between our naked toes, and we thought that everyone was looking at us. We hid ourselves in the water, and the water was good. Most of our mob didn't know what to do when they got in front of a 'dumper', but I could still manage them, though it made me breathless. I played about for a while and then I went out past the breakers for a swim.

There was a kid with a flash stroke just ahead setting out for a buoy too. I felt good, and decided I'd see how I went against him. I put my head down and started the crawl that used to win races for me. When I looked up he was still ahead. He was looking over his shoulder, laughing. I sucked some air with a bit of unexpected wave mixed up in it, and did everything I could, until my lungs were bursting. I got another glance, and he was further ahead. The buoy was still a long way off, and my heart was hammering. My head was spinning, and I could taste sickness and beer not far from my mouth. I gave up in disgust and paddled back to the shore, where the rest of the bunch were already out and stretched on the sand.

'What a hell of a place to want to *live*!' said someone as I flopped down in the middle of them. 'Golly, I'm thirsty!'

The glare from the sand was horrible, and I could feel now that there was water in my ears. We all had salt in our mouths. We all felt thirsty. The heels of kids sprinting about the beach spurned sand into our faces. When anyone looked at us we felt silly because we were too white. The water had made us tired and thirsty. We went up and dressed, and after we'd had a drink at the car we went back to town.

I felt angry with myself and disappointed. The chaps poked mullock at me, but it wasn't that that hurt. I didn't want to go near the beach again. I was quite content to be heading for the pub.

We stayed at the pub near the station with the rest for our remaining week. We saw a couple of picture shows, and every day we tramped about, bowling into a bar whenever the pavements tired our feet. We spent a lot of money, and we all used to get back to our rooms late and make a good deal of noise. It was surprising the number of other fellows from the fields we met, and we had a good time. But I wasn't sorry when the time arrived for us to get on the train again.

We took plenty of bottles, and after we'd drunk some and piled into the sleepers I lay wondering again about the length of each section of rail. Every *clankety-clank*, I thought, was carrying me a little closer to a place where I was some good, a place where there was work to be done, where I could hold my own with other men and where I didn't look funny and old-fashioned or a colour different from that of my neighbours.

'WESTWARD HO!'

HARRY 'BREAKER' MORANT
(EXCERPT)

We may not camp to-morrow, for we've many a mile to go,
Ere we turn our horses' heads round to make tracks for down below.
There's many a water-course to cross, and many a black-soil plain,
And many a mile of mulga ridge ere we get back again.

That time five moons shall wax and wane we'll finish up the work,
Have the bullocks o'er the border and truck 'em down from Bourke,
And when they're sold at Homebush, and the agents settle up,
Sing hey! A spell in Sydney town and Melbourne for the 'Cup'.

Part 6

BENEFIT OF CLERGY

The influences of religion on the lives of bush dwellers are many and varied in scope.

When freely interpreted, the 'gospel' can become something quite distant from strict doctrine, as observed in 'The Reign of Eugene Ham'. On the other hand, the independent attitude and practicality of some bushmen can lead to a whole new, supposedly more relevant, doctrine, as illustrated in 'Bill's Religion'.

Religion is often an odd thing in any social framework, but especially so in a bush town. Spirituality is of no importance at all to some rural dwellers, as demonstrated in 'First Confession' and the story which gives this section its name, 'Benefit of Clergy'.

On the other hand, to many living in the bush, especially in times gone by, religion was the very basis of their lives, quite often for all the wrong reasons, as observed in 'A Sabbath Morn At Waddy'.

Those bush dwellers without religion, or 'benefit of clergy', fall into two categories in these stories, often depending on who is doing the observing and making the judgments.

There are those, like the characters in 'Benefit of Clergy' and 'The Parson's Blackboy', whose lack of religious sensibility leads them into a more practical, brutish and prosaic lifestyle. Then there are those, like Father Connolly, who make a pretty good fist of sound moral judgments based on compassion and common sense, or the protagonist in 'Bill's Religion', who uses 'bushman's morality' rather than deferring to any particular denomination.

There is a certain 'bush cynicism' evident in the tone and theme of the majority of these stories; whether it is a healthy cynicism or not I am really not in a position to say.

'GOD AND POETS'

JACK SORENSEN

I think God values spinifex as highly as the rose,
He even may like poetry that reads like rancid prose.
The reason I suppose
Is that He feels responsible for all He sows and grows
And so gives equal marks for song to nightingales and crows,
Though why, God only knows.

I USED TO READ THE COMICS FIRST

JIM HAYNES

I USED TO READ the comics first, and then go to Sunday school, that was the real cause of the problem.

I crammed the entire contents of the comic sections of the Sunday papers into my head just before the Anglican Church made its weekly attempt to develop my spirituality.

I'd pedal down to the newsagent on my bike about 7 a.m. every Sunday and wait for the truck to bring the papers from Cooper's Junction. Then I'd dash home for breakfast and read all the comics before dressing in my 'Sunday best' to go to Sunday school at St Matthew's Church of England hall at 10 o'clock.

So, when Miss Everett was attempting to improve my mind and character with Bible stories, my head was already overloaded with the comic sections of the Sunday papers. She thought she was fighting the good fight against the devil in my soul while she was actually up against Ginger Meggs, Fatty Finn and Uncle Joe's Horse Radish.

This has had a profound influence on my life. I tend to be a bit vague about the scriptures because Miss Everett's Bible stories came just after my wide-eyed reading of the adventures of Prince Valiant, Mandrake the Magician and The Phantom.

Mind you, some of those Old Testament stories were pretty good.

The pictures that Miss Everett showed us of Noah's Ark, King David fighting Goliath and Moses coming down the mountain carrying the Ten Commandments were almost as good as Prince Valiant fighting the Black Knight or Mandrake when he 'gestured hypnotically' to create an illusion so that he and Lothar and Princess Narda could escape some awful danger.

Mandrake's tricks were just like Jesus' miracles when you thought about it, and Mandrake's offsider Lothar, in his leopard-skin costume, looked just like Miss Everett's picture of Samson. No wonder I was confused.

I had trouble with scripture stories when the plot was a little weak. I didn't understand that with religion the plot wasn't as important as the moral of the story. I'd find myself asking Miss Everett, 'What happened next, Miss?'

Miss Everett would sigh her special junior Sunday school sigh and reply, 'Nothing happened next, they gave thanks and followed Moses,' or 'Nothing happened next, it just proves that Jesus loves us and forgives our sins.'

My simple desire for a strong plot line led me into a lot of trouble at Sunday school. Miss Everett didn't seem to appreciate my suggestions, even when they were made in response to her own enquiries.

'Why did Lazarus rise from the dead?' she asked.

'Maybe Jesus gestured hypnotically like Mandrake and the crowd were all tricked into believing it,' I suggested, helpfully.

'Why was David able to slay Goliath?'

'Well Miss, Prince Valiant built a big catapult and beat the Vikings a few weeks ago, maybe David and his brothers had a really big slingshot hidden behind the hill in the picture and . . .'

I was only trying to help, but she didn't even let me finish.

'Just be quiet and let me tell you what the Bible says.'

This was said through gritted teeth, which was not easy for Miss Everett. The poor girl had an undershot lower jaw, which meant that her bottom lip protruded about an inch beyond the top lip. This gave her a rather stern appearance and led to the nickname 'Ashtray' being bestowed upon her by my cousin Gerald and myself. She was a local farmer's daughter who, now that I think about it in retrospect, seemed to find Sunday school teaching quite demanding. She probably thought that teaching junior Sunday school at St Matthew's was a punishment for her sins.

Miss Everett's life was so sheltered she probably had no sins to be punished for, except losing her temper with me in Sunday school. My mother described her as 'a trifle gormless'. Though that was said in my defence after the trouble I caused at Sunday school.

Over the years Miss Everett had tolerated many of my attempts to explain the scriptures and improve the plot lines of Bible stories. She had tolerated my theory that the disciples caught no fish on Lake Galilee before the Messiah's intervention because they used the wrong bait. She lived through my supposition that the Hill of Golgotha and the Phantom's skull-shaped mountain were one and the same, which explained the miracle on Easter Sunday. She had even managed to deal with my quite valid argument that we could have had a lot more than ten commandments if there had been paper to write them on, instead of that really heavy stone Moses had to carry down the mountain.

What Miss Everett could not tolerate, apparently, was my disruptive behaviour around the age of ten.

Until then my disruption of her lessons had mostly been a result of misguided enthusiasm and total ignorance of the whole point of religion, but around the time I turned ten I really did become quite naughty. I put some of the problem down to the fact that Miss Everett wasn't particularly worldly enough or well trained enough to handle naughty ten-year-old boys.

Another part of the problem was that I found the Church of England style of religion rather boring. Not that I knew a lot about the others, but they all seemed much more exotic, mysterious and interesting than the Church of England.

For example, the Salvation Army people all wore uniforms, played instruments and sang in public. This didn't happen often in our town because there were only two or three families of 'Salvationists', as Mum called them, and they mostly went to worship in Cooper's Junction where there were lots of them.

A couple of times a year, however, the 'Salvos', as Dad called them, would all come and play and sing in Anzac Park and march down the main street.

And then there were the Catholics.

The Catholics were a strange lot. They had lots of names, like 'tykes', 'RCs' and 'rock choppers', and they called themselves 'Roman Catholics', even though they lived in Australia.

My best mate, Brian Stafford, was a Catholic because his mother had been a Hogan. The Hogans had owned the general store for generations and Brian's mother, Marge Hogan, had married Gill Stafford, whose family owned the hardware and produce store.

The Staffords were not Catholic, but the Hogans were.

It caused a 'bit of a fuss' at the time, according to Mum. They were married in the Catholic church and the kids were 'raised as Catholics'. A lot of people in town (by which Mum meant the eighty per cent or so who were Church of England) grumbled that 'the tykes had got another one'.

This meant that Brian had to go to Catholic Scripture at school with all the O'Sheas and listen to Father Connolly telling jokes in that strange accent of his. He also got to be confirmed at an early age and eat wafers in church and go to confession in a little booth.

It all seemed much more exciting to me than listening to Ashtray Everett's stories with their unsatisfactory endings.

When we were older Brian had me in stitches telling me that he had finally worked out what Father Connolly was talking about when he took special classes for the boys and told them that their 'nocturnal emissions' were not necessarily something they had to confess.

'He's been telling us this for years, in these special lessons,' said Brian, 'and I thought it was something to do with wandering around at night, being a peeping Tom or something. It turns out it's just having wet dreams and apparently we don't have to worry, wet dreams are not a mortal sin.'

Brian was a mine of information about sin and punishment. He seemed to know more about it than Miss Everett. If you asked her if God would make you go to Hell for killing someone in a war she would just mumble about God forgiving everyone, which confused me. I couldn't see the point in having a terrific place like Hell if everyone was forgiven. The good thing about Hell was that you could imagine your enemies there—that would teach them to make your life miserable!

Brian had much better answers. According to him, the Catholics had it all figured out. They solved the problem by having a place called Purgatory, which was like detention at school—it was awful but only lasted a certain time, depending on your sin. That was easy for a ten-year-old to understand. Dropping papers in the playground was worth fifteen minutes' detention. Justifiable homicide might mean fifteen years in Purgatory, but not permanent residence in the fires of Hell.

It sounded like a good system to me, but when I asked Miss Everett why it wasn't available to those of us who were C of E, she became quite agitated. Apparently the idea was just 'superstitious nonsense and mediaeval mumbo-jumbo' and I was getting 'more wicked by the day'.

I don't know if Ashtray Everett's first assertion is true or not, but she was quite right in her second assertion. I was getting naughtier and was badly behaved at Sunday school around that time.

Eventually, of course, I went too far.

I must have been around eleven when it happened and I'm not sure that I even understood the sexual connotation of what I said, but when the class was asked why the disciples went to Mount Olive I simply replied that I didn't know, but Popeye would be very cranky about it.

Whether I was simply guilty of silliness or something far worse is really immaterial. The effect on Miss Everett was immediate, astonishing and spectacular. She had had enough, and she exploded.

'Get out! Get out!' she screamed. 'Go straight to Reverend Bennett at once, you wicked boy!'

Her undershot jaw was quivering and her eyes were wide and wild-looking. It is a sight I will never forget. The shock of her anger hit me like a thunderbolt. As my cousin Gerald later put it, 'Old Ashtray just went crackers!'

There are moments in life, especially in childhood, when the realisation that things have changed forever is instantaneous. Miss Everett going crackers was one such moment.

A total and deafening silence filled every square inch of the church hall as I made my way to the parish office where Rev. Bennett was conducting senior Sunday school. Even the little kids colouring in pictures of Jesus on a donkey were frozen into a motionless and silent tableau as I made my way past them on my long pilgrimage across the bare wooden floor of St Matthew's church hall.

Reverend Bennett seemed more stunned by Ashtray Everett's outburst than by my wickedness. He 'ummed and arrghed' a bit and asked what I'd done.

I said I'd been cheeky to Miss Everett, and he sent me home. Later that week, no doubt after conferring with the poor girl, he came around home and talked to Mum.

Mum was furious. What would people think?!

Didn't I remember that Uncle Cyril was on the Parish Council? Didn't I know that Auntie Val, Auntie Maude and Mum herself were on the Ladies' Auxiliary and did the flowers once a month at St Matthew's? How could I do such a thing?

It was one of the rare occasions when Dad really hit me. Not just a 'clip round the earhole', but a couple of real whacks with a leather belt across the bum as I stood behind a chair in the kitchen. The pain was minimal but our mutual male embarrassment was excruciating.

There was some compensation to the whole affair. It hastened my departure from the bosom of the Church. I didn't have to put up with Miss Everett anymore and she, poor girl, no longer had to put up with me. Perhaps it was better, Mum decided, if I finished with Sunday school for a while after Easter prize-giving. It was still a few months until I could progress to the senior class, so maybe I should have a break and come back later when I'd 'grown up a bit'.

Needless to say, I never completed Sunday school, and thus became the first in my family to miss confirmation and the full embrace of the Church of England.

I've thought about it a lot since then and I understand perfectly why Miss Everett, and the Rev. Bennett too, wanted to see the back of me. I'm sure they were happy for me to find my own spiritual path in life because there were a lot of souls to look after and they could do the most good for the most people if I wasn't around to hinder the process. They could achieve a lot more each Sunday if they remained relatively sane and calm.

On the other hand, it does seem strange to me that the lost sheep was encouraged to find a pasture of his own and stop annoying the shepherd. If I was as wicked as everyone said at the time, didn't I need special attention and religious direction?

I wonder what Jesus would have done to remedy the situation. From what I'd heard about him from Miss Everett, I don't think he'd have given me away quite so easily.

Mandrake, of course, would simply have 'gestured hypnotically' and kept me completely under control.

I returned briefly in order to apologise to Miss Everett and sit silently through the one or two lessons leading up to Easter.

At the Sunday school presentation service I received a small book for 'attendance', while the rest of the class received large books for all sorts of achievements like 'excellent manners' and 'Bible knowledge'. And that was it; the church and I parted company by mutual agreement.

I don't know where I'll end up; it might be Heaven, or Purgatory, or Hell, or Limbo—or just a plot in the cemetery. Brian Stafford assured me that I couldn't go to Purgatory because only Catholics believed in it, and I couldn't go to Heaven because only Catholics went there for believing in the Pope.

It's rather odd to think that wherever I end up, it will all be due to the fact that I used to read the comics first.

THE REIGN OF EUGENE HAM

'BRIAN JAMES'
(JOHN TIERNEY)

WHEN, BY HAPPY CHANCE, Mr Foster the schoolteacher at the Grey Box fell down a shaft and broke both his legs, there was a little hypocritical sympathy and much sincere rejoicing among the small fry along the Cookabundy. The Department of Education stayed its hand for one glorious but far too brief fortnight, then sent along a relieving teacher.

His name was Ham—Eugene Ham. He was young, enthusiastic, unmarried, and wore a straw hat with an extraordinarily narrow brim. He had an enormous head—very bumpy at the back; hair of no describable shade of cream clipped short all over; white eyebrows; a mouth that wouldn't shut properly anywhere, and a pair of blue eyes that were eternally lit up in surprise. He had no shoulders worth noticing—he just tapered off like a pilsener bottle till he came to that enormous head. He was about six foot high, though the tapering effect made him look seven at least. In addition to all these things he had a lisp.

The children found him good to look upon, and forgot their grievance over the curtailment of their holiday. And not in appearance only did he find favour; in methods he was refreshing, and in simplicity a pure delight.

He introduced himself: 'Good morning, boyth and girlth. I'm Ham, Eugene Ham, Eugene Thethil Ham, Mithter Ham.'

The children were gladdened to hear it and wondered somewhat where the department had stored such a treasure, and why they hadn't known of him before. As a result of an early spelling lesson in which he had some trouble with the word 'thistle' he was nicknamed 'Thithle'.

There was such an enthusiasm, such a vim in all he did, such a desire to make interesting and visual all he told them—and the additional treasure of his lisp—that his treatment of scripture made that often dry subject a new world indeed, and something to be entirely disassociated from the boring dissertations so many of them knew and dreaded in sermons and Sunday school.

His presentation of the story of Adam and Eve was a masterpiece.

'God thed to Adam, "Look Adam at that ortyard." And Adam looked at rowth and rowth of fruit-treeth, peacheth, plumth, cherrieth, pineappleth, pumpkinth and Ithabella grapeth. And Adam cried "My word!" and Gawd thed, "They are all yourth, Adam, the whole blinking lot." And Adam thed, "Thank you Gawd."

'You thee, Adam wath very polite. And then he thed, "I thay, Gawd, what'th that tree over there by itself?" and Gawd thed, "Adam, you can't eat any of the fruit from that tree." And Adam thed, "Oh Gawd, why can't I?" And Gawd thed, "You jutht can't, Adam."

'But Adam was very perthithtent and kept nagging Gawd about that tree; tho Gawd thed at latht, to shut Adam up, "I tell you, Adam, I want the fruit from that tree for jam."'

That story was an undoubted success, the more so no doubt because Mr Ham dramatised it as he told it with much gesticulation, the Deity speaking in a low rumbling voice and Adam in a rather squeaky one. And the colloquial tone and homely touches were certainly appreciated. Those children thoroughly understood the story.

But when the children got home and repeated the story there was not such marked appreciation shown by their elders. In other ways, too, Mr Ham appeared altogether too modern, though at first the other ways weren't so obtrusive. The first two Sundays of his sojourn at the Grey Box he attended Father Moran's church;

then for three weeks he became a sturdy Methodist; and then he appeared in the Church of England.

Then Mr Ham transferred for a Sunday or two to the Presbyterian Kirk, and the Reverend Dobbie told two old ladies that he found it hard to stifle the impulse to throw him out. Mr Dobbie had played third-grade rugby somewhere or other in his youth, and from that circumstance retained—and added to—a reputation for muscular Christianity.

After that assortment of worship, Mr Ham didn't go to any church at all, and spent Sundays fishing or shooting. But each religious body felt that it had been unpardonably slighted and mocked.

Clearly such a fellow was not fit to train the young. People talked of keeping their children at home, or sending them to the school at Two Rocks, or driving into Summerlea every day with them, and 'putting them to the convent' or 'the public', as the case might be. But the children found Mr Ham too entertaining to desert him without a protest.

Since Mrs Foster was away there were no sewing lessons for the girls, but Mr Ham had very practical ideas on sewing. He set some of the big girls to washing his socks and linen; others to ironing or darning or sewing on buttons. Good, practical training, but it wasn't understood.

And later, when definite complaint was made—in writing, to the inspector of schools—the sewing came in for very unfavourable notice: 'He persuaded the girls to sew buttons on the most intimate parts of his garments.'

As much as anything, perhaps, Mr Ham's delightful rendering of the story of Abraham and Isaac led to his undoing. These estimable ancients appeared refreshingly and familiarly as Abe and Ikey.

"'Bleth it all, Ikey, don't arthk tho many questionth—Gawd'll thee uth through . . .'"

'And when poor little Ikey wathn't looking, old Abe grabbed him jutht like thith.' And Mr Ham seized on Georgie Ryan suddenly and expertly, by way of illustration. Georgie yelled in surprise and the rest in sheer delight.

'Then he thruthed up Ikey and put him on a heap of wood. Ikey kept rolling hith eyeth, when Abe got the butcher'th knife, and felt the edge of it with hith thumb. Then Abe raithed hith eyeth to Heaven and thed, "Gawd, it'th awful!" But Gawd thed nothing. Then Abe took little Ikey'th throat in one hand and the knife came nearer and nearer to Ikey'th throat. Little Ikey wriggled and wriggled to keep his throat out of the way, and the look in hith eyeth brought a big lump to Abe'th throat.

'And jutht ath the knife touched Ikey'th throat, Gawd shouted out, "Thtop it, Abe! That will be enough thith time!"'

The children cheered, as much out of relief as anything else at this moving climax.

Mr Ham went on. 'Abe wiped the thweat from hith forehead with hith thleeve, and swallowed the lump in hith throat. Then he cut the rope around Ikey. And he kithed Ikey, and thed, "My word, Ikey, that wath a clothe shave!"

'Jutht then they heard a big row, and looking round they thaw an enormouth ram tangled up in thome vineth. The ram wath bellowing, jutht like a bull, and Abe thed, "That ith a miracle, Ikey."

'And Gawd thed to Abe, in a nithe mild voithe, "Uthe that, Abe."

'Tho Abe and Ikey laid hold of that ram, and wathn't Abe pleathed when he thaw by the ear markth that it wathn't one of hith ramth either, but belonged to a neighbour he didn't like very much.'

Just as remarkable, in its way, was the finding of Moses in the bulrushes. In Mr Ham's rendering the daughter of Pharaoh didn't appear in a good light, if one judged her by modern moral standards. And, further, she shamefully deceived her trusting father, who was made to appear as a man of extraordinary innocence and simplicity.

There was much resentful talk among the parents, assisted by the activity of Mr Joshua Bisley of Tipperary and Mr Benjamin Hopper of Summerlea. These two famous lay preachers and stout upholders of religion and morality took Mr Ham's treatment of the scriptures as an insult to the Deity and a reflection upon themselves. And though Grey Box was, strictly speaking, outside the territory of their ministrations, they were ready to ally themselves with the forces of right-thinking. These gentlemen were in their way just as interesting and picturesque as Mr Ham, but they had Heaven's licence to be so, and Mr Ham hadn't.

So Mr Bisley drove in his buggy to Summerlea, and went to the home of Mr Hopper.

It was near the end of the day and Mr Hopper, who was a carpenter and builder, was sharpening and setting a handsaw in his workshed. Mr Bisley was just in time to hear the exclamation, 'Blast the saw—that's another bloody tooth broken!'

Mr Hopper looked up to see Mr Bisley framed in the doorway.

'Benjamin! Brother! You have said that which is an abomination—an appalling abomination—an annoyance in the sight of the Lord!'

Mr Hopper was all contrition, some of it due to being heard by Mr Bisley.

'Brother, let us pray that our lips be pure,' and Mr Bisley's fingers came together before him, and his venerable head was bowed. His white beard vibrated slightly in whispered communing with his Maker. And the prayer was not for himself, but for a brother who had erred—that made Mr Bisley a grand figure, indeed.

Mr Hopper also bowed his head and felt keenly enough the disgrace of being prayed for; but absent-mindedly held the saw-set in his hand and, even as he prayed he squinted in sidelong fashion at the saw on the bench.

When Mr Bisley deemed that Mr Hopper might reasonably be considered forgiven, he raised his head. In a solemn voice he began, 'Brother Benjamin, Sin is stalking among our people, there is corruption and mockery of God's word in our midst.'

Mr Hopper took his glance from the guilty saw and trembled.

'I mean,' said Mr Bisley, 'a young man who distorts and twists the sacred scriptures.'

'Ah!' Mr Hopper was relieved greatly. 'Brother Bisley, you wouldn't be thinking of that there young Mr Ram at the Grey Box? I tell you what, Brother, he's a bit of a goer, I do believe.'

Mr Bisley held up his right hand. 'Brother Hopper, we must put our shoulders to God's wheel and hurl this unclean mocker into the darkness!'

'Amen!' groaned Mr Hopper.

Mr Bisley wrinkled his nose; half closed his eyes, and concentrated on a scarce audible sniff. In a tone half of tender sorrow and half of honest anger, he said, 'Brother Benjamin!' Then he sniffed quite audibly.

Mr Hopper understood. 'It was for the cold. Nothing else cures a cold for me.'

'Nothing else? Not even your faith in the Lord!'

'Of course, of course, but the two together just fixes them real bad colds.'

'Jerusalem must be searched!'

It was a voice of judgment and doom, and Mr Bisley advanced further into the shed. In a back corner was a large box with a curved top. It was closed. Ostensibly it was for holding tools as several similar boxes, with lids open, were thus employed.

Mr Bisley found that the box was locked. He held out the long fingers of his right hand. 'The key, Brother.'

Mr Hopper took a key from the dusty top of the low wall plate and passed it over.

No more was said. Golden shafts from the level sun lit up the interior of the shed and showed Mr Hopper looking somewhat rebelliously at the bent form of the righteous Bisley opening the box. The sounds were awful, the grating of the key, the unsnapping of the lock, the squeak of the hasp and the creak of the lid.

Each sound was magnified tenfold and said as clearly as could be, 'Guilty'.

In the box was a jumbled collection of bottles—dozens and dozens of them. Some of the labels were right side round and allowed W. Rosen, F. Rosen, O. Reimer, Summerlea Brewing Company, modestly to rub their shoulders with the more famous distillers of joy from Scotland and Holland.

Mr Bisley rubbed the dust from his fingers and stood erect. He faced Mr Hopper.

'Brother Benjamin Hopper, you stand revealed. May God in His goodness and His sweet mercy send His light into the places that are dark within you!'

He looked as if he was going to pray again.

Mr Hopper hardened into a kind of defiance. He was damned if he was going to be prayed for again.

'I takes it for the cold.'

'Brother Benjamin, it is said by the sinful and the unworthy who rejoice in their sins, that you collected enough money at Kilmarnock to buy ten Bibles for our dear dark brothers in Fiji, and you bought nine bottles of wine with it at Otto Reimer's.'

There was enough truth in this to hurt—as a matter of fact it was only six bottles—and Mr Hopper was so stung as to forget his saintly character and calling.

'Look here, Bisley, you bloody tight-lipped, white-bearded old humbug, I'll be telling you a few things what *is* said, if it comes to that!'

Mr Bisley held up a calming hand. 'Brother Benjamin!'

But Mr Hopper was properly aroused. 'You've stolen cattle, you've stolen sheep, you've stolen turkeys. You've stolen grass and lucerne from your neighbours. You carried on fine with that girl of Sinclair's before she became Mrs Whittle. And you're going to preach at me because you find a few bottles in a box.'

Mr Bisley wasn't angered for himself, though he was for Mr Hopper's sake. But Mr Bisley's anger was the low-temperature kind, a placid anger that was calculated to drive others mad. It would have driven Mr Hopper mad perhaps if his attractive daughter hadn't intervened.

'That's enough, now, you two! I've heard the lot of it, and very interesting, too. But tea's ready. So come along.'

Mr Hopper kicked shut the damnable box, but didn't lock it. He still muttered things under his breath, and in all seemed likely to undo all the good of his conversion of nearly twenty years ago.

But under the soothing influence of food the men of wrath relented towards each other and the conversation came back to the proper subject for condemnation—Mr Ham.

It was revealed by Mr Hopper's daughter that, besides giving his curious interpretations of the scriptures, Mr Ham 'got Gracie Nott to put a stitch in his pants when he tore them on the barbed wire'.

'Hi!' said Mr Bisley, 'Gracie is a comely maiden and must be protected!'

'*And* he had the pants on when Gracie mended them!'

After tea the two famous lay preachers decided to see Mr Hart, the Inspector of Schools—just informally—and take counsel with him.

Mr Hart was at home. No, he wasn't too busy at all, and he was pleased, he said, to see the two gentlemen.

Mr Hart was a peppery-looking, important-looking man, of indeterminate age.

After pious preliminaries, Mr Hopper asked after Mr Foster's two broken legs.

'I regret,' said Mr Hart crisply, 'that I can report no immediately promising progress.'

'So he won't be likely to be back at that there school at the Grey Box yet?'

'One of Mr Foster's legs needed breaking and re-setting.'

'So that young man, that very indiscreet young man, that most irreverent young man, will continue to as . . . as . . . as the . . . as a . . .'

'We mean that there young Ram at the Grey Box,' said Mr Hopper.

'Ham,' said Mr Hart.

'Well, we want him shifted, he's no good.'

'Really, really, gentlemen,' replied the official Mr Hart, which wasn't the real Mr Hart at all, 'there are certain strict formalities in these matters, and there are certain well-defined regulations governing them.'

'Which goes to mean you are going to do nothing about it.' There was a man of action in Mr Hopper.

'No! But there are very salutary cautions and precautions. Are you ready to lay substantial charges against Mr Ham that will make his dismissal necessary or his transfer desirable?'

In his best style Mr Hopper got off his tale of complaint—the wicked scripture stories, the implications of intimate buttons and patches, the growing rumours of visits to a disreputable family named Twine.

Mr Hart decided to pay an unannounced call on Mr Ham.

In due course Mr Hart did go out to the Grey Box on his exploratory tour.

There were sounds to reach his ears long before he reached the schoolhouse. Strange sounds, not to be diagnosed as recess, for Mr Hart looked at his watch to verify the time. There were laughing and wailing and shouting and yelling and singing sounds that children never make or do when authority is near, even in their play.

Closer view showed children, mostly girls, at every window on the outside, and struggling for a view within; several boys on the roof and a small crowd yelling encouragement to them; certain enterprising youths trying to get a butt out of the nanny goat with a millet broom; another group hanging a 'bushranger' on an acacia tree. On the verandah a fairly big girl, Nancy Stibbert, it turned out eventually, was wringing out a handkerchief or small towel.

Mr Hart walked up from the road, after commandeering a boy to hold his horse, with his most official tread. The children recognised him even before his sulky stopped.

Word went around quickly, 'Here's Mr Hart!'

It acted like an extinguisher on a candle. Everyone put on looks of concerned innocence—and succeeded in 'guilt writ large'.

'Where,' said Mr Hart, looking around accusingly, 'where is Mr Ham?'

Only Nancy Stibbert had presence of mind. 'He's inside, Mr Hart. And he's very ill.'

'Ill!' repeated Mr Hart. 'Ill, did you say?'

Nancy nodded, very nicely and seriously.

'What is the matter?'

'I don't know, Mr Hart. He fainted about half an hour ago, and we're trying to bring him around.'

Mr Hart went in, followed by Nancy. The faces disappeared from the window and retired to a distance where what was happening inside might still be seen without undue recognition of those looking.

Mr Ham was lying on his back in the middle of the floor. He was quite unconscious, though the announcement of Mr Hart's arrival had sent a violent shiver through him. But only a temporary shiver. He relapsed into complete immobility again.

A grey blanket had been improvised as a pillow for his head. Gracie Nott was in charge. She was dabbing Mr Ham's forehead with a damp rag. Gracie was a very self-possessed young miss, and was not overawed by the presence of Mr Hart. She kept on with her ministrations.

'What happened?' Mr Hart almost deferred to the managerial Gracie.

'Fainted,' she replied as to a bystander of no consequence. 'Ah, his eyes are flickering, have the brandy ready!'

'Do you give brandy for a faint?' Mr Hart asked uncertainly and tentatively.

'Always!'

'Always!' repeated Mr Hart in some wonder.

'Well, it always brings Mr Ham round. Vic, like a good girl, you had better get a new collar for Mr Ham. There are the two I ironed yesterday on the dressing table in his bedroom.'

Then, looking at his shirt, opened as far as it would go, Gracie added, regretfully, 'He'll have to keep his shirt on, there isn't a clean one to give him.'

Mr Hart felt more hopeless, but he thought he'd better do something to assert himself. With some distaste he took Mr Ham's wrist to feel his pulse. He was not sure what he could do about the pulse when he had felt it.

'No need to,' said Gracie, 'I felt it just now. Low—very low. It only disturbs him to feel it.'

Mr Hart put the wrist down.

Mr Ham opened his eyes, slowly flickering, and closed them again.

'He's coming to, thank goodness!' said Gracie.

The others breathed relief.

'Give him air,' said Gracie, and waved the others back, including Mr Hart.

'Ith that Mithter Hart I thee?' and Mr Ham raised his head a little.

'Don't worry Thithle, you'll be alright.' Gracie's tones were almost motherly.

'Thank you Grathie, I'm better now.'

Mr Ham waved the brandy aside, perhaps in deference to Mr Hart. Gracie gave orders for the disposal of the brandy and other items used in bringing Mr Ham round. The blanket and brandy went back to the bedroom, the vinegar and basin back to the kitchen and the washers, towels, rags and handkerchiefs to the clothes line.

Word got around the now subdued groups that Mr Ham was better. But Mr Hart at last decided to act. He had the school lined up and addressed the small gathering. He had decided, he said, in view of Mr Ham's indisposition, to send them home for the rest of the day.

Gracie and Vic didn't want to go.

'Are you sure, Thithle, that you're alright?'

'Thank you Grathie, right ath rain.'

Gracie and Vic left reluctantly.

'Queer turn that wath, Mithter Hart.'

Mr Hart thought it and many attendant circumstances decidedly queer, but he didn't say much. He was feeling official strength and confidence beginning to surge through him.

'I came out,' he said, in a level official voice, 'to inspect the school.'

Mr Ham's eyes lit up with even greater surprise than usual.

'To Inthpect the thcool?'

'But I find that impossible—it will have to wait. Are you often indisposed, like that?'

'Indithpothed?'

'Please, don't repeat. I said 'indisposed'. Do you often faint?'

'Yeth, Mithter Hart, often. I get quite dithy.'

'Dithy!'

'Yeth—dithy.'

Mr Hart pondered over that, and a few other things—prominent among them was 'Thithle'. But he was a diplomat too, of a heavy kind.

'Perhaps, Mr Ham, it's the climate that doesn't agree with you.' His official eye was coldly glancing around the room. It was in a fine disarray, and on the small blackboard was a primitive sort of sketch with 'That's Thithle' attached.

But Mr Ham didn't think the climate made any difference. And the liked the Grey Box, he said.

Mr Hart left it at that. He didn't probe, for he was afraid of what he might find. But his mind was made up, and he wondered how far the faints were genuine.

In less than a week the department moved Mr Ham to a far corner of the state. It removed at the same time the bright spot in the lives of the Grey Box children. Gracie and Vic were wild about it, and blamed each other for something, and didn't speak to each other for a long time.

In its wisdom the department sent along a maiden lady of an age no man could calculate, who seemed all made up of vinegar and chastity. She set that school in order. There was no nonsense about Miss Gorm—and there never had been. She was born a teacher and would die a teacher—and in the great beyond she would be a teacher for all eternity.

It was the end of the Ham regime, and only the pleasant memory was left.

Mr Bisley and Mr Hopper were pleased; they rejoiced, in fact, in their hearts that they had 'shifted' Ham and the dangers of him. There was no danger, potential or otherwise, in Miss Gorm.

Even Venus would have been a different and a broken character entirely after a week of Miss Gorm.

BENEFIT OF CLERGY

ALEXANDER ALLEN

As THE PRIEST REACHED the door of the Squatters' Rest a dozen arms were stretched out to hold his horse and help him alight.

'It's a hot ride you've had, for sure, Father,' said the buxom proprietress.

'Faith, hot's no name for it Mrs Dargan. Is there anything left in my bottle?'

'Well, it's close on four months since you was 'ere, your reverence, but I've got some good old Irish tack ye're welcome to.'

'That's right, Mother. Let's have some, an' a bite too, for I'm off again immediately.'

'Yer won't be stayin' the night, then?'

'No, I've a sick call at Bulbul Station, and I must start again at once to get there tonight.'

'I'm sorry for yer hurry, Father, for there's some business for yer here.'

'Indade! And what moight it be?'

'Well, Father, there's Mary. She's near her toime to Ted Hogan, at Howlong; an' they wants joinin'.'

'Call 'em in, Mother.'

Mrs Dargan went out of the parlour, and soon came back followed by Mary and her lover, a hard-faced young boundary rider, who, fortunately for himself and the object of his affection, had ridden over to the Squatters' Rest that morning.

'So,' said the priest, sternly, 'so, you've not had the dacency to wait my comin'?'

The young couple made no reply.

'How do you expect to obtain a blessin'?' continued the priest, 'when you stole the joys of matrimony widout God's leave? Kneel down, the pair of you. Now, say the words after me. Mrs Dargan, call all hands in as witnesses.'

For some minutes the ceremony proceeded; then the priest asked, 'Mary O'Niell, do you take this man for your husband?'

'You ain't asked him if he'll 'ave me first, Father.'

'Silence, you hussy. Will you have *him*? He is going to marry you.'

'Yes, yer Riverince.'

'That's right. There now, you are man and wife, and God bless you.'

'Whiskey all round, mother!' cried Ted Hogan and all joined in the toast which followed.

'Is there anything else now, Mrs Dargan?' asked the priest.

'Yis, yer Riverince, there's a baptism.'

'Whose is the child?'

'It's Jane's, Father.'

'Jane! She's not married!'

'Ah! Poor thing, Father, she's in a bad way an' her man won't be here this side o' Christmas.'

'Who is he?'

'Alick MacIntyre, the bullocky.'

'Heavens! The sin, the sin of it all! Fetch the mother and child in at once.'

A pale young woman was brought in, bearing in her arms a fine young boy one or two months old.

'Ah! Jane, you've been in a devil of a hurry,' said the priest, not unkindly. 'Who stands sponsors for this child? God bless him! He's a beauty, too.'

A toothless old rabbiter in for a spree, and a young fellow from a neighbouring selection, stepped forward, and the ceremony was soon over.

'There, Jane, my girl, the little one is as pure as the snow now. But what's all these tears for, Mrs Dargan? What's wrong?'

The women folk, as if by magic, had all begun to sob; and the men stood here and there conversing in whispers and looking very glum.

'Come now, Mother, what's the meaning of it all?' asked the priest again, and impatiently this time.

'Ah! Father, there's Pretty Nellie yet.'

'And what, in Heaven's name, is wrong with her—The angel of the flock? The pride of the Big Gum Plain. The flower among so many weeds.'

There was a ring of alarm in the old man's tones, and he looked anxiously from one to the other.

'Faith, Father, it's buryin' she wants.'

'Burying? Nellie dead! No, no. So bright, so fair. The queen of you all! Not dead?'

'Indade, Father.'

'Take me to her.'

'She's all nicely laid out, wid a pretty coffin, too, made by Ted, here. The poor lamb died yester-morn.'

Mrs Dargan led the priest into an adjoining room where, on a stretcher, lay the body of poor Nellie. She had been a very beautiful girl, and even death could not rob her perfect features of their charm. The long golden hair had been carefully brushed and trained down each side of the reclining figure. On her breast was a bunch of wild flowers.

'She'd been ailin' since yer last visit, Father. The young gentleman from Mooraboo run was after her, and Nellie was very fond of him. But the damn blackguard, savin' yer presence, Father, wint away and got spliced to a lady in Adelaide, an' our girl here broke her poor heart an' died.'

Mrs Dargan told her tale with many sobs.

'And she was . . . *innocent*, do you think, Mother?' asked the priest anxiously.

'More's the pity, no, Father. She was . . .'

'Oh God! The sin, the sin! Poor lamb, to be wrecked by that son of the devil. Wait until I meet him, which, please Heaven, will be soon! Now bring all hands in, Mrs Dargan, and I'll say prayers.'

When it was over he spoke to them about the savage way they were living, and said that the back-blocks should be called the *black*-blocks because there was no light there.

An hour later, after poor Nellie's body had been placed in the rough grave prepared for it, the priest took his leave of the shanty and its inmates, blessing them all from his seat in the saddle.

As he rode away a tear trickled down his face. 'Lord,' he whispered, 'when will women know men?'

A SABBATH MORN AT WADDY

EDWARD DYSON

SUNDAY SCHOOL WAS 'IN' at Waddy Wesleyan Church.

The classes were all in place, and of the teachers only Brother Spence was absent, strange to say. This was the first Sunday of the new superintendent's term, always an evil time for grace, and a season of sulkiness, and bickering, and bad blood.

Each beloved brother coveted the dignity of the office, and those who failed to get it were consumed with envy and all uncharitableness for many Sabbaths after. Some deserted the little wooden chapel on the hill till the natural emotions of prayerful men pent in their bosoms could no longer be borne, and then they stole back, one by one, and condoned in hurricanes of exhortation with rain and thunder.

Brother Nehemiah Best occupied the seat of office behind a deal table on the small platform, under faded floral decorations left since last anniversary. Rumour declared that Brother Best was unable to write his own name, and whispered that he spent laborious nights learning the hymns by heart before he could give them out on Sunday, as witness the fact that he 'read' with equal facility whether the book was straight, or endways, or upside down.

Brother Best was thin-voiced, weak in wind, and resourceless and unconvincing in prayer. No wonder Brother Spence was disgusted. Brother Spence could write his own name with scarcely more effort than it cost him to swing the trucks at the Phoenix

Mine; his voice raised in prayer set the loose shingles fairly dancing on the old roof; and his recitation of 'The Drunkard's Doom' had been the chief attraction on Band of Hope nights for years past. Ernest Spence had not hesitated to express himself freely at Friday evening's meeting: 'Ay, they Brother Best, he no more fit for pourin' out the spirit, you, than a blin' kitten. Look at the chest of en!'

'True for en, Ernie!' cried Brother Tresize. 'They old devil, you, he laugh at Best's prayin', surelie, Brother Spence some tuss, you.'

But Brother Spence had left the meeting in a state of righteous indignation. Yet here were Brothers Tresize, and Tregaskis, and Prator, and Pearce, and Eddy. True, they all looked grim and unchastened, and there was an uneasy, shifty feeling in the chapel that inspired boys and girls, young men and young women, teachers and choir, with great expectations.

Brother Best, in his favourite attitude, with one arm behind him under his coat tails, his right hand holding the book a yard from his eyes, his right foot thrust well out, the toe touching the floor daintily, made his first official announcement: 'We will open they service this mornin' by singing hymn won, nought, won.' Then, in a nasal sing-song, swinging with a long sweep from toe to heel and heel to toe, he gave out the first verse and the chorus, ending unctuously with a smack of the lips at the line:

'Thou beautiful, beautiful Poley Star!'

Nehemiah was a dairyman, and had a fixed conviction that the poley star and a poley cow had much in common. The hymn being sung, the superintendent engaged in prayer, speaking weakly, with a wearisome repetition of stock phrases, eked out with laboured groans and random cries. Brother Tresize could not disguise his cynical disgust, and remained mute.

A prayer to be successful amongst the Wesleyans of Waddy must make the hearers squirm and wriggle upon their knees, and cry aloud. Brothers and sisters were all happy when moved to wild sobbing, to the utterance of moans, and groans, and hysterical appeals to heaven, and when impelled to sustain a sonorous volley by the vigorous use of pocket handkerchiefs; but that was a spiritual treat that came only once in a while, with the visit of a specialist, or when the spirit moved Brother Spence or Brother Tresize to unusual fervour.

The superintendent's prayer did not raise a single qualm; and the boys of Class II straggled openly over the forms, pinched each other, and passed such rubbish as they could collect to Dicky Haddon, the pale, saintly, ginger-headed boy at the top of the class, who was in honour bound to drop everything so sent him in amongst the mysteries of the old, yellow, guttural harmonium, through a convenient crack in the back.

Throughout the service Brother Best, proud of his new office, watched the scholars diligently, visiting little boys and girls with sudden sharp raps or twitches of the ear if they dared even to sneeze, but judiciously overlooking much that was injurious and unbecoming in the bigger boys of Class II, who had a vicious habit of sullenly kicking elderly shins when cuffed or wigged for their misdeeds.

The Bible reading, with wonderful, original expositions of the obscure passages by horny-handed miners, occupied about half an hour, and then the superintendent stilled the racket and clatter of stowing away the tattered books with an authoritative hand, and invited Brother Tresize to pray. If he was great he could be merciful.

Brother Tresize made his preparations with great deliberation, spreading a handkerchief large enough for a bedcover to save the knees of his sacred black-cloth trousers, hitching up the latter to prevent bagging, and finally loosening his paper collar from the button in front to give free vent to his emotions—and preserve the collar. Then, the rattling of feet, the pushing and shoving, the coughing and whispering and sniffing having subsided, and all being on their knees, Brother Tresize began his prayer in a soft, low, reverent voice that speedily rose to a reverberant roar.

'Oh, Gwad, ah! look down upon we here, ah; let the light of Thy countenance ahluminate, ah, this little corner of Thy vineyard, ah. Oh, Gwad, ah! be merciful to they sinners what be assembled here, ah; pour down Thy speerit upon they, ah, make they whole, ah. Oh, Gwad, ah! Thoo knowest they be some here, ah, that be wallerin' in sin, ah, some that be hippycrits, ah, some that be cheats, ah, some that be scoffers, an' misbelievers, an' heathens, oh, Gwad, ah! Have mercy on they people, oh, Gwad, ah! Show they Thy fires, ah, an' turn they from the wrath, oh, Loord Gwad, ah!'

Brother Tresize was evidently in fine form this morning; already the windows were vibrating before the concussions of his tremendous voice, and the floor bounded under the great blows that punctuated his sentences. As he went on, the air became electrical, and the spirit moved amongst the flock. The women felt it first.

'Oh, Gwad, ah!' interjected Mrs Eddy from her corner. 'Throw up the windies, an' let the speerit in!' sobbed Mrs Eddy.

Brother Prator blew his nose with a loud report, a touching and helpful manifestation. Brother Tresize prayed with every atom of energy he possessed. His opinion was on record: 'A good prayer Sunday mornin', you, takes it out of en more'n a hard shift in a hot drive, you.' When his proper momentum was attained he oscillated to and fro between the floor and the form, swaying back over his heels till his head almost touched the boards—a gymnastic feat that was the envy of all the brethren—he shook his clenched fist at the rafters and reached his highest note.

The plunge forward was accompanied by falling tones, and ended with a blow on the form that made every article of furniture in the building jump. The perspiration ran in streams down his face and neck; dry sobs broke from his labouring chest; long strands of his moist, well-oiled, red hair separated themselves from the flattened mass and stood out like feelers, to the wild, ungodly delight of Class II; and whilst he prayed the brethren and 'sistern' kept up a continuous fire of interjections and heart-rending groans.

'They be people here, ah! what is careless of Thy grace; chasten 'em with fire an' brimstone—chasten 'em, oh, Lord, ah! They be those of uz what go to be Thy servants, oh, Gwad, ah! an' to do Thy work here below, ah, what is tried an' found wantin', ah—some do water they milk, oh, Gwad, ah! an' some do be misleadin' they neighbours' hens to lay away. Smite they people for Thy glory, oh, Loord, ah!'

A great moaning filled the chapel, and all heads turned towards Brother Nehemiah Best, kneeling at his chair, with his face buried in his hands, trembling violently. Nehemiah, two years earlier, had been fined for watering the milk sold to his town customers; quite recently he had been thrown into the Phoenix slurry by an unregenerate trucker, who accused him of beguiling his hens to lay from home.

Brother Tresize was wrestling with the superintendent in prayer, and the excitement rose instantly to fever heat. 'They what do not as they wad be done by, pursue 'em, ah; smite they with Thy right hand, oh, Lord Gwad, ah! so they may be turned from they wickedness, ah. They what have better food to they table for theyselves than for they children or they wives, ah, they what be filled with vanity, ah, they what havin' no book-learnin' do deceive Thy people, an' fill the seats o' the learned, ah, deal with such, oh, Gwad, ah!'

Brother Tresize was now almost frantic with the ecstasy of his zeal. His exhortation was continued in this strain, and every word was a lance to prick the cowering superintendent. The women sniffed and sobbed, the men groaned and cried 'Ahmen, ah!'

It was a great time for grace. But suddenly a new voice broke in—a shrill, thin voice, splitting into that of Brother Tresize like a steam whistle. Brother Best had assumed the defensive. 'Oh, Lord, ah!' he cried, 'give no ear to they what bears false witness against they neighbours, to they what backbite, ah, an' slander, ah, an' bear malice, ah; heed they not, oh, Lord, ah!'

Abel Tresize rose to the occasion. It was a battle. His voice swelled till it rivalled the roar of the ravening lion; he no longer selected his words or cared to make himself understood of the people; it was necessary only to smother Brother Best, to pray him down, and Abel prayed as no man had ever prayed before at Waddy.

A curious crowd—the Irish children, Dan the Drover, an old shepherd, and a few cattlemen from the Red Cow—attracted by the great commotion, had assembled in the porch, and were gazing in open-mouthed, delighted. Tresize persevered, but Best's shrill, penetrating voice rang out distinctly above all. Brother Best was transformed, inspired; under the influence of his great wrath he had waxed eloquent; he smote his enemy hip and thigh, he heaped coals of fire upon his head, and marshalled St Peter and all the angels against him.

The severity of his exertions was telling heavily upon Abel Tresize; he was dreadfully hoarse, his great hands fell upon the form without emphasis, he was almost winded, and his legs wobbled under him. He pulled himself together for another effort, and the cry that he uttered thrilled every heart, but it quite exhausted him, and he went over backwards, striking his head upon the floor, and lay in the aisle convulsed in a fit.

Instantly the chapel became a babel. The teachers ran to Brother Tresize, and bore him into the open air, the wondering children crowding after, and left the new superintendent sobbing on his table like a broken-hearted boy.

BILL'S RELIGION

WILLIAM BAYLEBRIDGE

AMONG THOSE QUESTIONS PUT to men before we let them into our armed forces, the one that most troubles them is the question that bears upon their creed or religion.

To many men the beliefs of the various church conclaves and synods are dead things of which they know nothing. These men have their own creed, often kept well hidden and containing some strange articles. Some of these articles many a priest, perhaps, would set little store by.

This creed, the creed proper to Australians, we have not yet written down in books, thus, men are at times hard-put to answer questions that bear upon their creed or religious beliefs.

There was a young bushman called Bill. He went early to join up for the Light Horse. Having passed the riding test, he was told, with others, to get stripped, and stand in a tent, and wait there till the tape-sergeant called on him. This he did. Seeing him there in his skin only, you could have marked that he was a lengthy lean fellow, broad of bone, with muscle sitting along it like bunched wire. The bush had done that.

Someone said: 'Step forward!' And he stepped up and onto the scale.

'Twelve seven,' said the sergeant.

He then stood up to have the tape run across him.

'Five eleven and a half—forty—forty four,' said the sergeant again.

Then, when they were done with his age, his eyes, the colour of his hair, and the quaint marks, an officer said, looking up:

'What religion?'

Now, this man, because of the reason I have spoken of, could not well answer this.

'My kind,' he said, 'give little thought to that.'

The officer said, 'But, you must tell me this. We require an answer. What belief does your father hold to?'

'He kept it always inside his shirt,' said Bill, slowly, 'no one rightly knew.'

'How, then, was he buried?' asked the officer again, sharply. He did not care much for this man's manners. 'That will clear this thing up.'

'Well,' said Bill, 'the old man had the laugh on them there too, for he put that job through himself.'

'Himself! How so?'

'He dropped down a shaft,' Bill answered, 'and it fell in upon him. This we found out later and, as he was a dead man then, there was nothing left to do but to put the stone up.'

'A poor funeral!' the officer remarked.

'Well, he always said,' answered Bill, 'that he'd care most for a funeral that had little fuss about it.'

The officer, plainly, was losing his patience. 'Have you never heard tell of such things as the Thirty-nine Articles?' he asked, 'the Sermon on the Mount, and the Ten Commandments? Look, my man, don't you know what a Catholic is, and a Quaker? What a Wesleyan is, or a Seventh Day Saint? It might be, now, that you're an Anabaptist,' he said, 'or a Jew. But one of these things you must be. Speak up. The Sergeant has to fill this form in.'

'One of those things I might be,' Bill answered. 'But I can't tell that. I'm a plain man.'

The officer looked at him squarely and then said, with a hard lip:

'Tell me this—have you any religion in you at all?'

'That I can't swear to,' said Bill. 'But an old fellow up our way, who looked after us well as children and often chatted with us around the campfire, said he reckoned so.'

The officer smiled tartly, 'And this bushman had some articles of faith for this religion?'

'He did,' replied Bill.

'This ought to be looked into,' said the officer, 'it may be that he made up the decalogue for it, too.'

'In a manner of speaking he did,' answered Bill again.

'Indeed! And what, then, was that?'

Bill, taking his time about it, said: 'I got this off by heart. To give it in his own words it ran like this:

Honour your country; put no fealty before this.
Honour those who serve it.
Honour yourself, for this is the beginning of all honour.
A mean heart is the starting place of evil.
A clean heart is the dignity of life; keep your heart clean.
Think first; then labour.
Lay to, so that your seed will stand up thick on the earth.
Possess your own soul.
Thou shalt live . . . and
Thou shalt lay down thy life for more life.

'I think that was it,' he said. 'I can't go much into that swagger; but I guess that's about right. Now, if you'll put that question again, I think I could fix it.'

'What, then, is your religion?' asked the officer.

Glad at heart to have found his answer, Bill said, quickly, 'Australian, that's my religion.'

'Well,' said the officer, with a sour smile, 'that will do. Pass on to the doctor.'

On Bill's form, then, in the space against religion, he wrote this word—'None'.

EVERYONE LIKED FATHER CONNOLLY

JIM HAYNES

EVERYONE LIKED FATHER CONNOLLY, even Dad and Auntie Maude.

Back in those days, when you were either 'Catholic' or 'Protestant', our town had very few 'tykes', or 'rock choppers'. Still, nearly everyone in Weelabarabak liked the local Catholic priest.

Dad liked Father Connolly partly to annoy Mum.

'That Father Connolly's a nice bloke,' he would say to Mum. 'He came into the pub and had a yarn this arvo. You have to admire that, don't you? Our C of E bloke never comes near the pub, too busy with the Ladies' Auxiliary.

'Why don't we switch to being Catholic? My grandmother was a good Irish Catholic, you know. I'm sure they'd have us back. It might straighten out that bloody kid of ours. What do you reckon, Joyce?'

This was guaranteed to get Mum going, which was exactly what Dad intended, of course. He loved to 'stir' Mum when he thought she was putting on 'airs and graces', but only up to a point. He wasn't silly enough to go too far.

Still, Dad *did* like Father Connolly.

Even Auntie Maude had a soft spot for our local Catholic priest, and she was on the Ladies' Auxiliary of the C of E and did the flowers at St Matthew's!

Auntie Maude liked Father Connolly because he was an educated man who always found the same mistakes in the *Weelabarabak Bugle* that she found herself.

This was not exactly true. What Father Connolly did was to sympathise with Auntie Maude when she showed him the mistakes at the newsagent.

'Oh, that shouldn't be a possessive, now should it?' he'd say, 'and the spelling is very wayward, but the poor man does his best.'

Mum always reckoned that Auntie Maude was 'taken in' by Father Connolly's lovely Irish lilt.

'I am taken in by nothing of the kind,' Maude would say, 'but he has a lovely manner and his voice is very educated and pleasant on the ear, I must admit. He's an educated man, and very civil for a Catholic. And he's very kind to the less fortunate.'

This was true, Father Connolly had time for everyone it seemed.

Even our town drunk, Dipso Dan, liked Father Connolly.

Dipso used to make little jokes whenever he ran into the priest downtown. The jokes were based on a scant knowledge of Catholicism similar to my own and seemed to consist of fragments collected from films starring Bing Crosby and Spencer Tracy.

'G'day, Father, are you goin' my way?' he'd ask.

If the priest was wearing his black smock, as he often did when he was on official church business or making house calls, Dipso would always say, 'G'day Father, got any dirty habits you wanna get rid of?'

Father Connolly liked Dan, too. He'd always stop for a yarn and take the jibes in good humour.

But then, Father Connolly liked everyone.

He was always friendly and would ask after everyone's family by name, even though the vast majority of the town's population was not Catholic.

Much of Father Connolly's time was spent ministering to the needs of one particular family.

The O'Sheas were the town's largest Catholic family, although their faith wasn't what you'd call rock solid, or even consistent. In fact the O'Sheas were generally considered to be the biggest bunch of rogues around the district.

Whereas the C of E minister seemed to spend all his time ministering to his regular and committed churchgoers, the Catholic priest spent a lot of time with the local sinners.

Father Connolly walked a very thin line between attempting to keep the O'Sheas on the straight and narrow, and attempting to keep them out of trouble with the authorities. When he failed to do the latter he gave character references to the local Magistrates Court and, when that failed, he made prison visits to keep the family members in touch with one another.

People in our town often debated the priest's commitment to the O'Sheas. They were not good Catholics in any sense of the term, and some people wondered why they got so much attention when they made no attempt to be good members of the flock.

'Their Irish name is the only bloody Catholic thing about them,' Dad would say, 'and that poor bloody priest spends most of his time trying to help them.'

I actually brought the subject up with Father Connolly when I was old enough to be interested in such things.

I was home from college and finally had a car of my own, a Ford Prefect that was always in need of some 'tinkering' to keep it mobile. When your car needed a bit of 'tinkering' you usually took it down to Sheedy's Garage and borrowed Nev Sheedy's tools and paid him for any spare parts you used.

Father Connolly was always tinkering with the parish car at Sheedy's on Saturday. For many years the priest had a beautiful old Morris Isis, but it had been replaced by a less glamorous, but equally unreliable, Morris 1800 by the time I had my first car.

So there we were, 'tinkering' together and yarning a bit about college and cars.

I asked the priest the question in a roundabout sort of way.

'Father,' I said, 'you seem to spend a lot of time helping people who aren't very religious. Don't you get depressed after all these years?'

'Heavens, me boy!' he replied. 'Why would you think such a thing as that?'

'I don't know,' I replied. 'At our Sunday school they always told us you had to always try to be a proper member of the church.'

'Well now, that may be true,' he said with a generous smile, 'but there's no such thing as a perfect Catholic, didn't you know that?'

I replied that I didn't know that.

'Well, we like everyone to be as near to good as they can be, too,' he mused. 'But in our faith you're either a "practising" or "lapsed"—you're never perfect.'

He seemed to find this amusing and was chuckling to himself as he added, 'The thing is though, me boy, if you're born a Catholic, you're always going to *be* a Catholic, of one kind or another, that's for sure!'

He seemed to find this quite funny and was still chuckling as he asked me what the problem was with my car.

He soon became more interested in helping me get the exhaust system back on the Prefect. This was a process that required a fair amount of fencing wire in lieu of the clamps I'd somehow lost or broken. Nev Sheedy didn't carry a stock of clamps for ten-year-old Ford Prefect exhaust systems.

I was surprised at the way Father Connolly was enthusiastic about things apart from religion. He could chat about cars and even horseracing. Our C of E minister never seemed to be interested in anything but religion and the church.

Father Connolly even dropped by Bindi Williams' stables sometimes when I was there helping out and chatted to Bindi and Old Nugget about horseracing.

Nugget used to tell a story about Father Connolly and an old man who went to confession and said he was having an affair with a young woman.

When the priest gave him his penance, according to Nugget, the old bloke said he couldn't say the 'Hail Marys' as he wasn't a Catholic. When the priest asked why he was telling him about the affair in the confessional if he wasn't Catholic, the old bloke replied, 'Are you kidding? I'm eighty-two, I'm telling everyone!'

We all knew Nugget was lying, though he swore he 'knew the old bloke that did it'.

I was surprised at Nugget's obvious affection for Father Connolly. He had no time for what he called 'sky pirates' and 'God botherers' and was rather enthusiastically atheistic in his beliefs.

Nugget also had a soft spot for the 'Salvos'. He used to say, 'At least the Salvos come to the races to collect money. And they make a bit of music and seem to enjoy themselves in their own way.'

Nugget was always pleased to see Father Connolly and pass on a few tips and yarn away for hours without religion ever being mentioned.

'He might be a rock-chopper but he isn't a Bible-basher like the others,' was Nugget's succinct summation of our local priest.

That was an opinion generally held by most of our town's non-Catholic population.

After all, we were a fairly respectful and tolerant mob in Weelabarabak. We were mostly C of E and Methodists, with a few pagans like Old Nugget thrown in for good measure, but we knew a decent sort of a bloke when we met one.

Everyone liked Father Connolly.

FIRST CONFESSION

FRANK DANIEL

I WAS IN SECOND class at school when Sister announced that we were now old enough to make our First Confession.

Confession?

It seemed that we would be able to 'rid ourselves of all those sins that had tarnished our souls since our baptism, when we were cleansed of Original Sin'.

Original Sin?

One we didn't even commit, evidently.

A bloke named Adam committed this first sin when he disobeyed Our Lord and took too much notice of his wife and ate of the forbidden fruit.

The forbidden fruit was an apple his wife had been talked into eating by a snake; 'tempted' was what Sister said.

Sister said the snake was the Devil.

I used to think that Adam must have been real scared of snakes. He should have kept a twisted wire hanging on his verandah for emergencies. He could have given the snake a couple of good whacks and broken its back a few times. It would have been dead by sundown. Dad always said they died at sundown. We were good snake-killers in our family.

Anyhow, in order to make our first confession we were evidently badly in need of tuition in the correct method of going about it.

Firstly, we had to learn the 'Confiteor', a prayer admitting that we were truly sorry for having done wrong, and that we would never do such things again—something like that!

I used to get the Confiteor and a couple of other prayers tangled up together and made a bit of a mess of it. Still, I reckoned that God would know what I was talking about.

Poor Sister had a few worrying weeks trying to convince our class that all of the things we did wrong during the first seven or eight years of our lives weren't altogether bad sins.

There was such a thing as a venial sin, which was less offensive to God. Then there was that real whoppin' bad one called a 'mortal sin', which was a grievous terrible thing and was most offensive to Our Lord.

Mortal sin must be got rid of as quick as a bloomin' wink in case you died and went to 'flamin' Hell', where you would burn forever and forever in a fire bigger than the one that burnt out Charlie Martin's feed shed a couple of years before.

I heard me father say that it was hotter than flamin' Hell.

My father ought to know, too. I remembered him saying that he went to Hell and back during the war.

My best mate, John Doyle, got in a bit of a fix worrying about 'venerial sins' and Sister had an embarrassed look on her face every time he mentioned it.

Nancy Collins wouldn't admit to having any sins and declared that she would not have committed even the 'simplest little fib' in her whole entire life, but Sister said she must've.

'Struth!' I thought. If Nancy had sins on her soul, us poor silly boys would have to own up to a lot. Most of us used to work in the shearing sheds, taking time off from school for the occasion. Our fathers all said that working with 'stupid mongrel sheep' would make 'any man swear and drive a bloke to drink'.

Cripes! What was I gonna do? I always used shearing time to practise my swearing so that I could get it right when I learned to shear.

'Blimey,' I thought, 'do I have to tell all them swear words to the Priest in confession? Geez, I'm in for it!'

The day before the big event Sister gave us a final run-through on what we were to say when we went into the confessional.

'Bless me Father, for I have sinned. This is my first confession. I have already said the Confiteor and these are my sins.'

'Struth!' I thought, 'If we ain't got it right by now, it ain't ever gonna be right.'

From that point onwards it was up to us as individuals to admit to our own collection of sins, tell the number of times each sin was committed during our young life, and then ask for forgiveness.

To finally have your sins fully and completely forgiven, you had to pay a penalty. This was given to us by the Priest according to the severity of our sins.

It was generally felt by most of us boys that we shouldn't tell him too much in case we dobbed ourselves in for things that he really didn't care about. It wouldn't do to tell him too much—we didn't want the old fellow to think we were real bad eggs.

The penalty was known as 'penance'. Sister said that we were not to tell each other what our penance was.

When we compared notes afterwards, however, it appeared that most of us copped the same fine. Like the rest of my mates, I managed to get away with 'The Lord's Prayer and three Hail Marys'.

It was obvious that we must have all been as sinful as each other.

So we all felt good about that—no one was in any real trouble at all.

Except for me!

You see, I hadn't told him everything and I knew that God knew everything, and that He was everywhere. I knew that God would 'get me' as Mother always used to say. You couldn't keep nothing from Him.

What could I do?

I agonised about it until Second Confession, a month later.

I had no plan at all, right up until the fateful day. Then, as we were waiting our turn, I was sitting nervously in church next to my best mate John Doyle, who was rehearsing his sins in a loud whisper—loud enough for me to hear him practising.

I listened very carefully.

'Eating meat on Fridays—twenty-seven times; missing Mass on Sundays—fifty-two times; swearing—a hundred and twenty times; not saying my prayers—eighty-nine times; back-answering my parents—nineteen times; being lazy in class—seventeen times . . .'

Blimey! Was that a sin?

'Teasing my little brother—nine times; drinking Dad's beer—five times . . .'

Bloody flamin' Hell! Could you get forgiven for *that*!

My mate concluded his rehearsal for confession, 'That is all I can remember, Father, and I am very sorry for my sins.'

I was a new man after hearing all that. No longer would I be afraid to tell my sins in confession. From now on I would let it all out. I would get rid of all those that I didn't admit to and get forgiven for the first time around. I would be a sure candidate for Heaven if I should cark it on the way home from school.

My mate didn't seem to be in there very long with his great long list of misdemeanours. Then it was my turn.

My patter went something like this, 'Bless me Father for I have sinned. It is four weeks since my first confession and these are my sins: missing Mass on Sundays—ninety-seven times; eating meat on Fridays—fifty-two times; not saying my prayers . . .'

Here the priest erupted in a kind of suppressed fashion!

In an angry whisper he pointed out that it was impossible to miss Mass on Sundays ninety-seven times in four weeks, and furthermore he said that I should wake up to myself and come to my senses.

Then he dismissed me from the confessional without any penance.

I didn't ask Doyley how he got on, but I had a sneaking suspicion he was evicted early for the same reason—stockpiling his sins.

We never went back to Confession again.

Doyley's uncle died about that time and we discovered that if someone advised the priest of your impending death, he would administer the last rites to get rid of all your sins, whatever they may be, and you would still go to Heaven.

So, just as long as we kept an eye on each other's health, we figured we'd be all right.

THE PARSON'S BLACKBOY

ERNEST FAVENC

THE REV. JOSEPH SIMMONDSEN had been appointed by his bishop to a cure of souls in the Far North, in the days when Queensland was an ungodly and unsanctified place. Naturally, the Rev. J., who was young, green and zealous, saw a direct mission in front of him. His predecessor had never gone twenty miles outside the little seaport that formed the commercial outlet of the district; but this did not suit Joseph's eager temperament. Once he felt his footing and gained a little experience, he determined on a lengthened tour that should embrace the uttermost limits of his fold.

Now, although beset with the conceit and priggishness inseparable from the early stages of parsonhood, Simmondsen was not a bad fellow, and glimpses of his manly nature would at times peep out in spite of himself. This, without his knowledge, ensured him a decent welcome, and he got a good distance inland under most favourable auspices, for, the weather being fine, everybody was willing to lend him a horse or drive him on to the next station upon his route.

The Rev. Joseph began to think that the roughness of the back country had been much exaggerated.

In due course he arrived at a station which we will call Upton Downs; beyond it there were only a few newly taken-up runs. On Upton Downs they were busy mustering, and when the parson enquired about his way for the next day the manager looked rather puzzled.

'You see,' he said, 'we are rather short-handed, and I can't spare a man to send with you; at the same time the track from here to Gundewarra is not very plain, and I am afraid you might not be able to follow it. However, I will see what I can do.'

Mr Simmondsen was retiring to rest that night when a whispered conversation made itself audible in the next room. No words were distinguishable, but from the sounds of smothered laughter a good joke seemed to be in progress.

'I think I can manage for you,' said the superintendent at breakfast next morning. 'When you leave here you will go to Gundewarra, twenty-five miles. From there it is thirty-five miles to Bilton's Camp and ten onto Blue Grass. From Blue Grass you can come straight back here across the bush, about forty miles. I will lend you a blackboy who knows the country well and will see you round safely.'

The young clergyman thanked his host, and, after breakfast, prepared to leave. The blackboy, a good-looking little fellow arrayed in clean moles and twill shirt, was in attendance with a led pack horse, and the two departed.

For some miles the Reverend Joseph improved the occasion by a little pious talk to the boy, who spoke fairly good English, and showed a white set of teeth when he laughed, as he constantly did at everything the parson said. At midday they camped for an hour on the bank of a lagoon, in which Mr Simmondsen had a refreshing swim. In the evening they arrived at their destination, and received the usual welcome.

'I see you adapt yourself to the customs of the country,' said his host at mealtime, and a slight titter went round the table. The Reverend Joseph joined in, taking it for granted that his somewhat unclerical garb was alluded to. In reply to enquiries he was informed that Bilton's Camp was a rough place, and Blue Grass even worse; and he was pleased to hear it, for up to now his path had been too pleasant altogether; he hadn't had a chance to reprove anybody.

Bilton's Camp proved to be indeed a rough place. The men were civil, however, and as the parson had had another exhilarating bath at the midday camp he appreciated the rude fare set before him, although here, as at the other place, there seemed to be a joke floating about that made everybody snigger.

The next day's journey, to Blue Grass, was but a short stage, and as the reverend gentleman had by this time become very friendly with Charley, the blackboy, the two rode along chatting pleasantly until they came somewhat unexpectedly on the new camp.

A very greasy cook and two or three gins in dilapidated shirts were the only people at home, and they stood open-eyed to greet the stranger.

Although Mr Simmondsen had suited his attire to his surroundings, he still retained enough of the clerical garb to signify his profession. The cook, therefore, at once took in the situation, and invited the parson under the tarpaulin which did temporary duty as a hut.

He informed his visitor, at whom he looked rather curiously, that 'everyone' was away, camped out, and that no one would return for a couple of days; that he was alone, excepting for two men who were at work in a yard a short distance off, and who would be in to dinner; in fact, they came up while he was speaking. Mr Simmondsen took great interest in this, the first real 'outside' camp he had seen, and as the two bushmen had gone down to the creek for a wash, and the cook was busy preparing a meal, he called Charley to ask him a few questions.

'What are these black women doing about the place, Charley?'

'O! All about missus belongah whitefellow,' was the astonishing reply.

It was some moments before Joseph could grasp the full sense of this communication; then he considered it his duty to read these sinners a severe lecture, and prepared one accordingly.

'Do you not understand,' he said, when the three men were together, 'the trespass you are committing against both social and Divine laws? If you do not respect one, perhaps you will the other.'

The cook stared at the bushmen in blank amazement, and the bushmen at the cook.

'I allude to these unfortunate and misled beings,' said the parson, waving his hand towards the half-clad gins.

A roar of laughter was the reply. 'Blessed if that doesn't come well from you!' said the cook, when he could speak. The others chuckled in acquiescence.

'What do you mean?' said the indignant Joseph; 'I speak by right of my office.'

'Sit down and have some tucker,' said the cook. 'You're not a bad sort, I can see, but don't come the blooming innercent.'

The indignant pastor refused. He saw that his words were treated lightly, that no one would listen to him, and he left in high dudgeon. Charley had told him that there was a good lagoon about twelve miles on the road back to Upton Downs; he would go on there and camp—they had plenty of provisions on the pack horse—and taking his bridle and calling the boy he went to catch his horse.

As he came back he overheard the fag-end of a remark the cook was making to the others. 'They came round the end of the scrub chatting as thick as thieves, and when I seed who it was—Lord! You could have wiped me out with one hand.'

This was worse than Greek to the Reverend. Greek he might have understood. In spite of a clumsy apology from the delinquent, he departed, and near sundown arrived at the lagoon Charley had spoken of. It was a lovely spot. One end was thick with broad-leaved water lilies, but there was a clear patch at the other end promising the swim the good parson enjoyed so much.

When the tent was pitched he stood in Nature's garb about to enter the water, when Charley called to him. Pointing towards the lilies he told Mr Simmondsen that he would get him some seed pods which the blacks thought splendid eating.

The clergyman had only got up to his waist before he heard a plunge behind him and saw Charley's dark form half-splashing, half-swimming towards the lilies. Presently his head emerged from a dive, and he beckoned towards the clergyman to come over and taste the Aboriginal luxury. The Reverend paddled lazily over and investigated. The seed pods proved of very pleasant flavour, and as the sun was nearly down, Mr Simmondsen wended his way to the bank and emerged in the shallow water, with Charley a few paces behind him.

For some reason he looked back.

Shocking predicament! There was no shirking the fact: all the quiet laughter about 'the customs of the country', the unexplained allusions, the ribald manner of the cook, were evident at a flash.

Charley was a woman!

The wicked superintendent of Upton Downs had started him on his travels with ('after the customs of the country') a black gin dressed in boy's clothes as a valet, and that gin had evidently been recognised by everyone on the road. Mr Simmondsen thought of the past and blushed. That night was spent in fervent prayer.

'My dear sir,' said Davis, the super. of Upton Downs, 'I did the best I could for you. Charlotte is as good as any blackboy and knows all the country round here. Now, own up, did not she look after you well?'

'You forget the scandal that may arise,' said the Reverend Mr Simmondsen.

'Lord, man! Who cares about what is done out here? Nobody will ever hear of it.'

Davis was wrong. Everybody did hear of it. The Reverend Mr Simmondsen received indignant letters from his Bishop, his churchwardens, the Reverend Mr Wriggle, the Western Australian Missionary, several missionary societies, and, last and worst, a letter of eternal farewell from the young lady to whom he was engaged.

Fortunately he inherited some money at the time; so he did the best thing possible—threw up the church, went into squatting, and is now one of the most popular men in the district.

'THE PARSON AND THE PRELATE'

'CREEVE ROE'
(VICTOR DALEY)

I saw a parson on a bike—
A parody on things—
His coat-tails flapped behind him like
A pair of caudal wings.

His coat was of the shiny green,
His hat was rusty brown;
He was a weird, wild sight, I ween,
Careering through the town.

What perched him on a wheel at all,
And made him race and rip?
Had he, perchance, a sudden call
To some rich rectorship?

He'd no such call; he raced and ran
To kneel and pray beside
The bedside of a dying man,
Who poor as Peter died.

I saw a prelate, plump and fine,
Who gleamed with sanctity;

He was the finest-groomed divine
That you could wish to see.

His smile was bland; his air was grand;
His coat was black, and shone
As did the tents of Kedar and
The robes of Solomon.

And in a carriage fine and fair
He lounged in lordly ease—
It was a carriage and a pair—
And nursed his gaitered knees.

And whither went he, and went for,
With all this pomp and show?
He went to see the governor,
And that is all I know.

But in a vision of the night,
When deep dreams come to men,
I saw a strange and curious sight—
The prelate once again.

He sat ungaitered, and undone,
A picture of dismay—
His carriage was too broad to run
Along the Narrow Way!

But, with his coat-tails flapping like
Black caudal wings in wrath,
I saw the parson on the bike
Sprint up the Shining Path.

Part 7
THE CONQUERING BUSH

Isolation, loneliness, drought, despair, melancholy and madness—
the bush has always been a cruel and hostile environment for
European settlers.

All the stories here are sad ones.

The Aboriginal legend of the coming of bush fires, however, has
a different tone to the European tales; the sadness in the legend
has a sacrificial element—suffering and tragedy on an epic scale
provide a gift for the land and its people.

Henry Lawson was, of course, the poet laureate of desperation
and despair in the bush. The saving graces in his more bleak
stories are stoicism and the enduring power of the human spirit.
These are well demonstrated here in 'The Drover's Wife' while the
horror observed in the very short story, 'Rats', is leavened with a
kind of black humour.

The more melodramatic styles of Edward Dyson and Royal
Bridges add a different perspective to the study of suffering in the
bush, whereas the very quirky, almost whimsical, approach to 'bush
madness' in Adam McCay's story, 'An Error In Administration',
has a very modern feel.

There is also a difference in style in the two poems which top
and tail this section. Jim Grahame's stark, Victorian tone is more
obviously dramatic than the gentler, haunting approach of that
great Western Australian writer Jack Sorensen.

This collection of stories might be rather harrowing if read all in one go. Perhaps the reader might like to roam to less lugubrious sections of the anthology in between.

'SPINIFEX'

JACK SORENSEN

It doesn't seem like forty years, but time has hastened on,
Since I came down the river and selected 'Avillon'.
Then I was young, now I am old, my hair has long been grey;
And here among the spinifex I've passed my life away.
They say I'm not the man I was, well, that might easy be,
This life among the spinifex has not agreed with me.

The time I brought the wire up to fence the 'Twenty-mile',
I'd thought I'd have a holiday and stay in Perth awhile;
But I was pleased to hurry back for I'm ashamed to say
I was stepping over spinifex along the pavement way.
They say I walk a trifle queer; I do without a doubt;
I'm stepping over spinifex when there is none about.

Today a little land wind sets the spinifex asway,
And blue with haze the Lost-Star Range seems vague and far away,
The desert gums are white with bloom, galahs are on the wing,
And in the thicket by the creek the sleepy bellbirds sing.
No dreamer I, my temperament is restless like the sea;
But riding through the spinifex contentment comes to me.

I never was a pious man; the prayers I've said are few,
In building up a station I've found other things to do.
But, when I come to judgment, in my own defence I'll say,
'I pioneered the country round the Lost-Star Ranges way.'

I know I have but little faith. Its loss was caused no doubt,
Through watching young stock perish, in the hellish years of
drought.

Now does the silver spinifex reach to the hazy range,
And men will live, and men will die, but this will never change.
The big Ashburton hurries down flood waters to the sea;
And hills, and skies, and spinifex, bound in the world to me.
They say I talk a trifle queer, there's truth in what they say:
It's living in the spinifex that makes a man that way.

THE FIRST BUSH FIRE

C.W. PECK

THERE WAS A TIME when the Australian bush was different from what it is today. Trees were bigger and their wood softer. There were more and bigger and brighter flowers. And the land—especially the mountains—was far more densely clothed with verdure. But some change came, and it was not good for the land.

Seeds failed to germinate, and where fertile tracts had been now desert appeared. Somewhere away in the south, perhaps away over in Victoria, there lived a great chief. His people were very numerous, for he had imposed his will upon other tribes since he was first made leader, and he had succeeded in welding them all together into one harmonious group. They revered him and all sorts of presents were laid by them at his feet.

Yet he never shirked work, and he took a place amongst the hunters just the same as if he were not a great leader. He must have come as far north as the Burragorang—if, indeed, he had not come further—for the Hunter River people have a story just like this.

Living in a valley between two mountains was a very small tribe of unusually docile people. They were an offshoot of that tribe who owned the country at the head of Cox's River. The powerful chief heard of them, and he determined to find out what they were like and add them to his growing tribe. So he set out by stealth.

Wrapping himself about with a wombat skin he came to their camping place. He was a very big man and he could not well conceal himself in so small a skin as that of a wombat—even the biggest of them. Therefore when he was within sight of the camp he hid behind a rock.

He saw that the tribe were very busy just at the time cooking game by heating stones and placing them one after another around and upon the carcasses. The handling of the stones was made easy by the wrapping of waratah stems about the fingers.

This practice of wrapping of waratah stems to make a person immune from burns was so believed in by the first Australians that, when white people arrived and settled, they came to the first blacksmiths that they saw and offered them the twigs, indicating that if they would wear them no flying sparks could injure them.

Now amongst the people was one maiden of exceptional beauty. Some say that the reason for these people separating themselves from all others was that many years before a beautiful woman wished her pretty baby to be called Krubi, the waratah, and there was another Krubi, who was not yet old. So the mother gathered her children about her and went away, and the family increased and increased, and always there were those quite beautiful enough to be called by the coveted name of Krubi—the beautiful red waratah.

Anyhow, when the great chief saw this maiden he lost all his cunning, so entrancing was she, and jumping up without reserve he ran towards the people. They started up in fear and scattered in many directions. He called to them not to fear him, but they did not understand his speech. The beautiful maiden soon found that the stranger pursued her, and her alone. She was very fleet of foot and very cunning, and by dodging and crouching she eluded him. Sometimes she was so close and so still, standing beside a tree, that he ran past her, and only by not hearing her crashing through the bushes and stamping on the twigs and leaves did he know that he had gone too far. No sooner did he turn than she bounded off again.

There was a stream clattering down a gully and falling over boulders and ledges into pure cold pools, and towards that stream the girl now ran. She knew of some footholds close to a waterfall, and, indeed, sometimes even behind it, that led to a very large and deep pool, and outstripping the now panting man she reached it. Never hesitating she clambered and swung herself down, and reaching the bottom she swung over the last ledge and slipped into the water.

Her pursuer reached the top of the fall, and believing that his quarry could not have gone down there he retraced his steps. He went right back to the camping place and found it, of course, silent and deserted. So he returned to the people he had left and told nothing of where he had been and what he had seen.

As often as he could he went back, and though sometimes he saw some of the people, never did he catch sight of the girl. He went so often that the others grew not to fear him. They guessed his desire, and they aided the girl at all times to hide from him.

One day he spied on the people from a hilltop; they were unaware of the fact that he could see them from a neighbouring ridge. They had grown so careless that they did not think of pitching their mia-mias where no one could see them from a distance, and he caught a sight of the maiden of his desires. But she saw him and once more she had to run as if for her life.

He did not hurry after her. Instead he got two dry sticks, and sharpening one on a stone he placed the flatter of the two on the earth before him, and putting the point of the other on it he rubbed and twisted it round and back between his palms until he had caused a fire to glow. He had dry ferns and grass ready, and placing them on the glowing spot he gently blew until the flame burst out. He added more fuel until he had a big blaze. The wind blew in the direction of the little tribe, and soon a great roaring fire was leaping and leaping and shooting out curling masses of consuming flame.

The girl saw it coming. The tribe saw it also. Away they all ran, bounding and crashing, but the fire came faster. It overtook some of them and they perished. On the blackened cleared ground the now wicked chief followed. But he could not go fast. The smouldering sticks and rubbish were still hot. There were no waratahs growing just here for the waratah does not grow as profusely as the gums, but in patches far apart. Hot as he was and suffering burns as he was still, he examined every body he came across, but they were none of them the one he sought.

At last he came to two little heaps of clay. What was this? These heaps told to him a story. They were fresh. They were composed of the clay that the tribal doctor used to make the mystic markings, and the tribal priest used for the same purpose when he wished to invoke the aid of a Great Spirit. Who had used it? Not once had he seen anyone who looked like one who had been initiated into the doubly-hidden mysteries of the rite that gave power to invoke the Spirit. Surely the girl had not seen that corroboree. If she had, then not only could he never capture her, but he was himself lost.

And lost he surely was. For on looking behind him he found that almost as the fallen seeds of the trees were being consumed by fast or slow smouldering, they were bursting with new life, and plants were springing up in such profusion as to block his view. In what direction had he come? Which way would he turn to go back? The smoke was so dense that he could not see the sun. The trees that lay over from the prevailing winds and gave some idea of direction were burning, and their small branches were gone.

Surely, he thought, this is the work of the maiden and she knew more than any woman was allowed to know. He wandered on and on, the bush growing denser. He stayed sometimes to pick up something to eat, for burned and roasted game lay in his path, and succulent roots were cooked. He wandered for many days quite lost.

The girl had visited at night the tribe from which her family was an offshoot, and had come across the corroboree that taught her how to paint herself, and this she had done, and the charm was hers.

A new camping place was chosen by the few who escaped that terrible fire, and the year rolled away. The young plants flowered and their seeds fell, but the next year no new plants came up. This was noticed and talked about by all the people. Even on the river where a few of her people were now living no seeds sent out the little plumule nor their little radicle, and no new plants grew to grace the world with fresh flowers, nor to produce the roots nor fruits for food.

Again the maiden thought of beseeching the Spirit. She went back to the old ground all alone and she found the clay. She painted herself and awaited results. She heard the Spirit and she talked with it. Then she noticed that just before her a little smoke wreath curled up into the air. Then a flame burst, and in a very little while a fierce bush fire was raging. The girl was satisfied that a fire was what was needed and she sent word to the river to say that all would soon be well with the world. That the seeds would germinate and new plants would grow up and flower and all would be good as before.

Since that time bush fires do not need any mystic markings or special communing with spirits by special people. Limbs of trees rub themselves hot on dry days and make flame. The hot sun shining on the mica in the rocks set fire to the tiny mosses that are dried there.

And so without human agency the fires come that are necessary to make our Australian seeds burst into the life of a new and growing plant.

THE DROVER'S WIFE

HENRY LAWSON

THE TWO-ROOMED HOUSE IS built of round timber, slabs, and stringybark, and floored with split slabs. A big bark kitchen standing at one end is larger than the house itself, verandah included.

Bush all around, bush with no horizon, for the country is flat. No ranges in the distance. The bush consists of stunted, rotten native apple trees. No undergrowth. Nothing to relieve the eye save the darker green of a few she-oaks which are sighing above the narrow, almost waterless creek. Nineteen miles to the nearest sign of civilisation—a shanty on the main road.

The drover, an ex-squatter, is away with sheep. His wife and children are left here alone.

Four ragged, dried-up-looking children are playing about the house. Suddenly one of them yells: 'Snake! Mother, here's a snake!'

The gaunt, sun-browned bushwoman dashes from the kitchen, snatches her baby from the ground, holds it on her left hip, and reaches for a stick.

'Where is it?'

'Here! Gone into the wood heap!' yells the eldest boy—a sharp-faced urchin of eleven. 'Stop there, Mother! I'll have him. Stand back! I'll have the beggar!'

'Tommy, come here, or you'll be bit. Come here at once when I tell you, you little wretch!'

The youngster comes reluctantly, carrying a stick bigger than himself. Then he yells, triumphantly:

'There it goes—under the house!' and darts away with club uplifted. At the same time the big, black, yellow-eyed dog-of-all-breeds, who has shown the wildest interest in the proceedings, breaks his chain and rushes after that snake. He is a moment late, however, and his nose reaches the crack in the slabs just as the end of its tail disappears. Almost at the same moment the boy's club comes down and skins the aforesaid nose. Alligator takes small notice of this, and proceeds to undermine the building; but he is subdued after a struggle and chained up. They cannot afford to lose him.

The drover's wife makes the children stand together near the dog-house while she watches for the snake. She gets two small dishes of milk and sets them down near the wall to tempt it to come out; but an hour goes by and it does not show itself.

It is near sunset, and a thunderstorm is coming. The children must be brought inside. She will not take them into the house, for she knows the snake is there, and may at any moment come up through a crack in the rough slab floor; so she carries several armfuls of firewood into the kitchen, and then takes the children there. The kitchen has no floor, or, rather, an earthen one, called a 'ground floor' in this part of the bush. There is a large, roughly made table in the centre of the place. She brings the children in, and makes them get on this table. They are two boys and two girls—mere babies. She gives them some supper, and then, before it gets dark, she goes into the house, and snatches up some pillows and bedclothes, expecting to see or lay her hand on the snake any minute. She makes a bed on the kitchen table for the children, and sits down beside it to watch all night.

She has an eye on the corner, and a green sapling club laid in readiness on the dresser by her side; also her sewing basket and a copy of *The Young Ladies' Journal*. She has brought the dog into the room.

Tommy turns in, under protest, but says he'll lie awake all night and smash that blinded snake.

His mother asks him how many times she has told him not to swear.

He has his club with him under the bedclothes, and Jacky protests:

'Mummy! Tommy's skinnin' me alive wif his club. Make him take it out.'

Tommy: 'Shet up, you little . . . ! D'yer want to be bit with the snake?'

Jacky shuts up.

'If yer bit,' says Tommy, after a pause, 'you'll swell up, an' smell, an' turn red an' green an' blue all over till yer bust. Won't he, mother?'

'Now then, don't frighten the child. Go to sleep,' she says.

The two younger children go to sleep, and now and then Jacky complains of being 'skeezed'. More room is made for him. Presently Tommy says: 'Mother! Listen to them (adjective) little possums. I'd like to screw their blanky necks.'

And Jacky protests drowsily:

'But they don't hurt us, the little blanks!'

Mother: 'There, I told you you'd teach Jacky to swear.' But the remark makes her smile. Jacky goes to sleep. Presently Tommy asks:

'Mother! Do you think they'll ever extricate the (adjective) kangaroo?'

'Lord! How am I to know, child? Go to sleep.'

'Will you wake me if the snake comes out?'

'Yes. Go to sleep.'

Near midnight. The children are all asleep and she sits there still, sewing and reading by turns. From time to time she glances round the floor and wallplate, and, whenever she hears a noise, she reaches for the stick. The thunderstorm comes on, and the wind, rushing through the cracks in the slab wall, threatens to blow out her candle. She places it on a sheltered part of the dresser and fixes up a newspaper to protect it. At every flash of lightning, the cracks between the slabs gleam like polished silver. The thunder rolls, and the rain comes down in torrents.

Alligator lies at full length on the floor, with his eyes turned towards the partition. She knows by this that the snake is there.

There are large cracks in that wall opening under the floor of the dwelling-house.

She is not a coward, but recent events have shaken her nerves. A little son of her brother-in-law was lately bitten by a snake, and died. Besides, she has not heard from her husband for six months, and is anxious about him.

He was a drover, and started squatting here when they were married. The drought ruined him. He had to sacrifice the remnant of his flock and go droving again. He intends to move his family into the nearest town when he comes back, and, in the meantime, his brother, who keeps a shanty on the main road, comes over about once a month with provisions. The wife has still a couple of cows, one horse, and a few sheep. The brother-in-law kills one of the latter occasionally, gives her what she needs of it, and takes the rest in return for other provisions. She is used to being left alone. She once lived like this for eighteen months. As a girl she built the usual castles in the air; but all her girlish hopes and aspirations have long been dead. She finds all the excitement and recreation she needs in *The Young Ladies' Journal*, and Heaven help her! takes a pleasure in the fashion-plates.

Her husband is an Australian, and so is she. He is careless, but a good enough husband. If he had the means he would take her to the city and keep her there like a princess. They are used to being apart, or at least she is. 'No use fretting,' she says. He may forget sometimes that he is married; but if he has a good cheque when he comes back he will give most of it to her. When he had money he took her to the city several times, hired a railway sleeping compartment, and put up at the best hotels. He also bought her a buggy, but they had to sacrifice that along with the rest.

The last two children were born in the bush—one while her husband was bringing a drunken doctor, by force, to attend to her. She was alone on this occasion, and very weak. She had been ill with a fever. She prayed to God to send her assistance. God sent Black Mary, the 'whitest' gin in all the land. Or, at least, God sent King Jimmy first, and he sent Black Mary. He put his black face round the door post, took in the situation at a glance, and said cheerfully: 'All right, missus, I bring my old woman, she down alonga creek.'

One of the children died while she was here alone. She rode nineteen miles for assistance, carrying the dead child.

It must be near one or two o'clock. The fire is burning low. Alligator lies with his head resting on his paws, and watches the wall. He is not a very beautiful dog, and the light shows numerous old wounds where the hair will not grow. He is afraid of nothing on the face of the earth or under it. He will tackle a bullock as readily as he will tackle a flea. He hates all other dogs—except kangaroo-dogs—and has a marked dislike to friends or relations of the family. They seldom call, however. He sometimes makes friends with strangers. He hates snakes and has killed many, but he will be bitten some day and die; most snake-dogs end that way.

Now and then the bushwoman lays down her work and watches, and listens, and thinks. She thinks of things in her own life, for there is little else to think about.

The rain will make the grass grow, and this reminds her how she fought a bush fire once while her husband was away. The grass was long, and very dry, and the fire threatened to burn her out. She put on an old pair of her husband's trousers and beat out the flames with a green bough, till great drops of sooty perspiration stood out on her forehead and ran in streaks down her blackened arms. The sight of his mother in trousers greatly amused Tommy, who worked like a little hero by her side, but the terrified baby howled lustily for his 'mummy'. The fire would have mastered her but for four excited bushmen who arrived in the nick of time. It was a mixed-up affair all round; when she went to take up the baby he screamed and struggled convulsively, thinking it was a 'blackman;' and Alligator, trusting more to the child's sense than his own instinct, charged furiously, and (being old and slightly deaf) did not in his excitement at first recognise his mistress's voice, but continued to hang on to the moleskins until choked off by Tommy with a saddle-strap. The dog's sorrow for his blunder, and his anxiety to let it be known that it was all a mistake, was as evident as his ragged tail and a twelve-inch grin could make it. It was a glorious time for the boys; a day to look back to, and talk about, and laugh over for many years.

She thinks how she fought a flood during her husband's absence. She stood for hours in the drenching downpour, and dug an overflow gutter to save the dam across the creek. But she could not save it. There are things that a bushwoman cannot do. Next morning the dam was broken, and her heart was nearly broken too, for she thought how her husband would feel when he came home and saw the result of years of labour swept away. She cried then.

She also fought the pleuro-pneumonia, dosed and bled the few remaining cattle, and wept again when her two best cows died.

Again, she fought a mad bullock that besieged the house for a day. She made bullets and fired at him through cracks in the slabs with an old shotgun. He was dead in the morning. She skinned him and got seventeen-and-sixpence for the hide.

She also fights the crows and eagles that have designs on her chickens. Her plan of campaign is very original. The children cry, 'Crows, Mother!' and she rushes out and aims a broomstick at the birds as though it were a gun, and says 'Bung!' The crows leave in a hurry; they are cunning, but a woman's cunning is greater.

Occasionally a bushman in the horrors, or a villainous-looking sundowner, comes and nearly scares the life out of her. She generally tells the suspicious-looking stranger that her husband and two sons are at work below the dam, or over at the yard, for he always cunningly inquires for the boss.

Only last week a gallows-faced swagman, having satisfied himself that there were no men on the place, threw his swag down on the verandah, and demanded tucker. She gave him something to eat; then he expressed his intention of staying for the night. It was sundown then. She got a batten from the sofa, loosened the dog, and confronted the stranger, holding the batten in one hand and the dog's collar with the other. 'Now you go!' she said. He looked at her and at the dog, said, 'All right, mum,' in a cringing tone, and left. She was a determined-looking woman, and Alligator's yellow eyes glared unpleasantly; besides, the dog's chawing-up apparatus greatly resembled that of the reptile he was named after.

She has few pleasures to think of as she sits here alone by the fire, on guard against a snake. All days are much the same to her; but on Sunday afternoon she dresses herself, tidies the children, smartens up baby, and goes for a lonely walk along the bush track, pushing an old perambulator in front of her. She does this every Sunday. She takes as much care to make herself and the children look smart as she would if she were going to do the block in the city. There is nothing to see, however, and not a soul to meet. You might walk for twenty miles along this track without being able to fix a point in your mind, unless you are a bushman. This is because of the everlasting, maddening sameness of the stunted trees, that monotony which makes a man long to break away and travel as far as trains can go, and sail as far as ship can sail, and farther.

But this bushwoman is used to the loneliness of it. As a girl-wife she hated it, but now she would feel strange away from it.

She is glad when her husband returns, but she does not gush or make a fuss about it. She gets him something good to eat, and tidies up the children.

She seems contented with her lot. She loves her children, but has no time to show it. She seems harsh to them. Her surroundings are not favourable to the development of the 'womanly' or sentimental side of nature.

It must be near morning now; but the clock is in the dwelling-house. Her candle is nearly done; she forgot that she was out of candles. Some more wood must be got to keep the fire up, and so she shuts the dog inside and hurries round to the wood heap. The rain has cleared off. She seizes a stick, pulls it out, and, crash! The whole pile collapses.

Yesterday she bargained with a stray blackfellow to bring her some wood, and while he was at work she went in search of a missing cow. She was absent an hour or so, and the native black made good use of his time. On her return she was so astonished to see a good heap of wood by the chimney, that she gave him an extra fig of tobacco, and praised him for not being lazy. He thanked her, and left with head erect and chest well out. He was the last of his tribe and a King; but he had built that wood heap hollow.

She is hurt now, and tears spring to her eyes as she sits down again by the table. She takes up a handkerchief to wipe the tears away, but pokes her eyes with her bare fingers instead. The handkerchief is full of holes, and she finds that she has put her thumb through one, and her forefinger through another. This makes her laugh, to the surprise of the dog. She has a keen, very keen, sense of the ridiculous; and some time or other she will amuse bushmen with the story.

She had been amused before like that. One day she sat down 'to have a good cry', as she said, and the old cat rubbed against her dress and 'cried too'. Then she had to laugh.

It must be near daylight now. The room is very close and hot because of the fire. Alligator still watches the wall from time to time. Suddenly he becomes greatly interested; he draws himself a few inches nearer the partition, and a thrill runs through his body. The hair on the back of his neck begins to bristle, and the battle-light is in his yellow eyes. She knows what this means, and lays her hand on the stick. The lower end of one of the partition slabs has a large crack on both sides. An evil pair of small, bright bead-like eyes glisten at one of these holes. The snake, a black one, comes slowly out, about a foot, and moves its head up and down. The dog lies still, and the woman sits as one fascinated.

The snake comes out a foot farther. She lifts her stick, and the reptile, as though suddenly aware of danger, sticks his head in through the crack on the other side of the slab, and hurries to get his tail round after him. Alligator springs, and his jaws come together with a snap. He misses, for his nose is large, and the snake's body close down in the angle formed by the slabs and the floor. He snaps again as the tail comes round. He has the snake now, and tugs it out eighteen inches. Thud, thud comes the woman's club on the ground. Alligator pulls again. Thud, thud. Alligator gives another pull and he has the snake out, a black brute, five feet long. The head rises to dart about, but the dog has the enemy close to the neck. He is a big, heavy dog, but quick as a terrier. He shakes the snake as though he felt the original curse in common with mankind. The eldest boy wakes up, seizes his stick, and tries to get out of bed, but his mother forces him back with a grip of iron. Thud, thud, the snake's back is broken in several places. Thud, thud, its head is crushed, and Alligator's nose skinned again.

She lifts the mangled reptile on the point of her stick, carries it to the fire, and throws it in; then piles on the wood and watches the snake burn. The boy and dog watch too. She lays her hand on the dog's head, and all the fierce, angry light dies out of his yellow eyes. The younger children are quieted, and presently go to sleep. The dirty-legged boy stands for a moment in his shirt, watching the fire. Presently he looks up at her, sees the tears in her eyes, and, throwing his arms round her neck exclaims:

'Mother, I won't never go drovin'; blarst me if I do!' And she hugs him to her worn-out breast and kisses him; and they sit thus together while the sickly daylight breaks over the bush.

MALLEE

ROYAL BRIDGES

HE RODE THE LEAN mare up the sandy track. The sun burnt his eyes and the black flies clouded about him. The sand clogged the mare's hooves as she bore him up the ridge; and to give her breath he paused upon the top.

The road went down the ridge like a ribbon of fire. The sandy paddocks, where the wheat had died in the spring, rolled mile beyond mile brick-red to the black pine clumps against the sky. At every swirl of hot wind the sand was blown up in yellow spirals merging into one ochre-coloured cloud, which crept down into the road.

But he saw none of this, taking in the mere impression of the Mallee around him, for his mind was elsewhere, visualising the lettering on the poster he had inspected back in town. Men needed for service overseas. Twenty thousand promised by the Commonwealth Government to England.

In a good spring the wheat should have rolled miles out as a sea of green and gold under the sun. On the Mallee fringe the sheep would have cropped the grass. Now sand, shaped like the oncoming waves of the sea, made great banks where it met the scrub. The sand leaked through wire fences into the tracks like iron-coloured water. When the wind died the mirage appeared, a flickering fantasy to right and left with lagoons of silver merging into the grey smudges of pine and eucalypt, shadowy and mystical.

He was thinking of fellows he knew, excited, gathered in knots at the railway station, at the post office, before the pub. Recalling the khaki-clad figure of one chap on leave from Broadmeadows—the popular hero, one who had been previously known through the district as a waster, now straight and clean, slouching no longer. The same chap telling him he ought to go!

And he was going. He was sick of the Mallee. Only he knew the Old Man would not let him go; and he couldn't stand up to the Old Man. Never had been able to; couldn't now. He'd stop him from enlisting if he could. There was something about the Old Man!

He spurred the mare on down the track. He passed the old Cocky's shack. Mud brick and a shingle roof. The chap had got some straw left still; but his dam was drying. He was reduced to dipping the water into a bucket, and carrying it up to a rusty pot where a few fowls drank. Full of news of the war, he would have pulled in for a yarn.

The Cocky's son was in khaki; and he wanted to know what his Old Man had thought, maybe get a hint from him how to deal with his own Old Man. But the black flies swarmed and a stinger shimmered, silver-winged, and the mare wouldn't stand, so he rode on.

Mum might work it; but then Mum wouldn't want him to go.

He pulled in by the gate a mile down. Leaning from the saddle, he pulled up the wire loop from the post, and dragged back the gate, two props and a few strands of barbed wire. He rode through and down the track between the dwarf gums and myall. Not a blade of grass, not a cicada piping, not a parrot chattering. Only the hard trees, a green mass above the brick-red sand.

The house lay a quarter of a mile back from the road. In 1911, the last good year, the Old Man had put up a new place, a weatherboard cottage, the paint now blistering pink upon it, iron roofs, with a couple of tanks under the chimney.

The black mud-brick house, where they had lived before, stood a bit to the left. A few sugar-gums shaded the yard. The garden had burnt up for want of water. The dam was holding out; but it was all wanted for the stock. Dead sticks and sand now—sand that drifted to the doors, and leaked inside.

Mum was standing out the front in the sun in her old blue print gown, print sunbonnet, and white apron. He pulled up by the gate as she came down to meet him, smiling to her smile. Mum might work it for him; but it would be horribly rough on her. She wouldn't want him to go any more than she had wanted him to go to town for a job. Though she had tried her hardest with the Old Man, and failed.

'Any mail?' she asked, smiling up at him.

'Only the paper,' he answered. 'Them Germans have cut the British up a bit—and Antwerp's gone. There weren't any letters. Where's Dad?'

'Cutting chaff,' she said, taking the paper. 'Put the mare in, and come for a cup of tea. Tell Dad! See anyone in the township?'

'Young Banks, that's all. Fancies himself no end! He's in khaki—up on leave.'

She caught the bitter inflection; she gave him a look of apprehension, noting the discontent black on his face. She ventured: 'It'll make a man of him.'

'It's more'n I can stand,' he muttered, flicking off flies. 'To see that chap. War news is pretty bad, Mum . . .' breaking off.

She said nothing for a while, her keen blue eyes estimating him—realising. Her eyes dimmed a little—the sun on the sand was glaring.

'You want to go?' she said at last.

'Of course I want to go, I want to get out of this God-forsaken hole.'

'Is that why?' she asked, her voice trembling a little.

He hesitated and would not meet her look. 'No—that isn't why! I don't want to leave you, Mum, stuck here!'

She said, 'I'm glad that's not the reason.'

'Only Dad won't ever let me go,' he muttered savagely. 'He wouldn't let me go to town to work. He wants me here to slave for him. Mum, if he won't . . .' he paused, staring across the yard.

'You'll go? You'll go still?' she sighed, 'I shouldn't like you to go—that way.'

'Mum, can't you work it?'

She did not meet his eyes, but looked down on the sand.

'D'ye think you can work it with Dad? Think you can? Will you have a shot?'

She was scraping a semicircle with the toe of her shoe. 'Go and put the mare up,' she said at last. 'I'll see . . .'

After tea he lounged against the gate post, smoking a fag.

The Old Man was sitting on the bench by the back door—the paper before him, puffing his clay pipe. He'd been grumpy at tea, wanting to know why his son had been loafing in town all the day when the sand needed scooping from the track.

The sun had dropped into the sand like a great live coal, another burning day tomorrow. Mosquitoes buzzed and he turned and slouched towards the door. He'd tell the Old Man straight out that he was going; and if he didn't like it, he could lump it.

Staying here; and the Germans burning through Belgium, murdering women and little kids! He would tell him straight—now! Mum had been yarning to him after tea: but the old chap said nothing, only sat down with his pipe and paper. His son slouched towards him, scowled and hesitated.

'Mum was sayin',' the Old Man suddenly growled, knocking the ashes from his pipe, and breaking off to blow though the stem. "Mum was sayin', you wanted to go to the war."

His son did not meet his eyes. 'Got to go, Dad.'

'Got to! Well, you got to do something. Ain't work on the place for two—not this year! Not a drop o' rain—nor a blade o'grass. I can't keep you. May as well be there as 'ere! Earnin' a bit for yourself . . . doin' a bit for . . . you know . . .'

He blew hard into his pipe, and his son nodded and went past him.

Mum was sniffing a little to herself and putting away the dishes.

'Mum,' he asked a little huskily, 'how did you work it?'

'I didn't,' she sniffed, her back turned to him, 'I just started to tell him that he couldn't get along without you and he shouldn't let you go. Only . . . only . . . he said . . . he said you should go . . . every young chap should . . . though he didn't want you to . . . any more than me.'

A saucer slipped from her fingers and smashed on the floor. She put her apron to her eyes.

*   *   *

And the rain did not come through the spring, when the sun was a white fire in the sky of blue glass and the springing wheat grew yellow and withered away.

Through the summer, when the sun burnt like a scarlet ball in the smoke of the bush fires and the north winds bore blackened gum leaves and scraps of fern down into the paddocks and whirled up the sand, the stock died.

Through the autumn, when the plains were a brick-field; and the sand storms whirled up over them and the sun burnt yellow from its rising to blood-red at its going, paddocks burnt up, dams dried and water was carted from the railway station to supply the house.

All this while, the boy was in Egypt, writing home cheery letters filled, as his mind was filled, with the wonders of the country.

And then the last letter came from him, written before they sailed from Egypt for the Dardanelles.

After that no more letters.

Perhaps he wasn't allowed to write.

No promise of rain.

'It's to be hoped it rains, before he gets back,' his father said. 'Otherwise he won't know the place. Scarcely a thing left on it.'

He'd laugh mirthlessly to the mother, trying to cheer her up and realising all the while that the boy's absence was more to him than the drought—the loss of all things.

He wanted him back badly, he admitted to himself, wandering out to the stable to fling a few handfuls of chaff to the horse. All the time hoping to himself that the rain would come before the boy came back. Not wanting him to come home to find everything burnt up by the drought.

He had read in the local papers that when bad news came through it was always broken to the family by their minister. He should be afraid, if he saw the minister even coming to call. He hoped that he would not chance to come any time while he was away from the house, because the mother knew; she read the papers too.

*   *   *

The year drifted into May and still the rain had not come. Days were warm and still now, evenings too, in a muggy, clammy sort of way, as if baked plains sent out the heat of the dead summer day.

It was looking very black to the north in the mornings and the wind was getting up now and then. It might rain.

For almost a week the cloud built up and broke up in the evenings and mornings.

Then the day came when the blackness kept growing over the day and the wind sighed drearily.

The leaves from the blackened gum trees fell on the stable like drops of rain.

He fed the horse and, going out to the stack-yard, stood peering out at the growing blackness. The sand was whirling across the wastes and a sudden shining fork of light flashed from the profundity to the north—like the tongue of the snake.

Thunder afar.

'It must rain,' he said aloud to himself.

He noticed a shovel that he'd left out against the fence. He walked over, picked it up, walked with it into the stable and hung it up in its place.

He felt the wind buffet the tin shed and something pattered on the roof. 'Just leaves perhaps,' he thought.

As he walked to the house cool wind gusts caught at his clothes.

He walked through the house to the kitchen as the first drops hit the roof.

She was there.

'It's here,' he said.

And then it was raining!

At first it pattered in big drops upon the roof, a broken pattern, then it picked up quickly into a roar of noise.

Conversation was not possible. They sat and listened until it settled into a steady drumming.

Though it was only midday, it was dark almost as night, until the lightning burnt in blue flames out of the blackness.

They were sitting together in silence, the mother and he— listening to the steady din on the tin roof. And the regular thunder—the guns at the Dardanelles must sound like this thunder.

They sat, understanding that the drought was broken and what it meant to them. Understanding what it meant to the boy when he came back . . . listening to the drumming and the thunder . . . or was it all the drumming and the thunder?

Then they realised at once that someone was rapping hard at the front door, shut against the pelting rain.

AN ERROR IN ADMINISTRATION

ADAM McCAY

SMITH WAS BROUGHT UP in the city, though his fathers before him had been men of the forest and sea; and he naturally became a clerk. But the blood asserted itself, and he threw away his billet to go up-country, and finally got a job on a Gippsland selection, where he spent his days and nights in the 'cleared country' with the sheep.

In Gippsland the country is thoroughly cleared when most of the undergrowth has been hacked or burned away, and the trees ring-barked so that they all stand dead.

Such a country is bad for the nerves, especially for those of a man like Smith, whose father had not been particularly virtuous. It consists of an interminable stretch of gaunt grey timber, and in the morning and evening twilight the dead trees seem to wobble their crooked arms towards one another, and join their skeleton hands in a ghastly, jerky minuet, which makes your flesh creep.

They begin to do this when you have known them for about a week; and very soon, if you have a steady head and an adequate supply of tobacco, they stop, and turn into inanimate timber again. But an ex-clerk who has been addicted to inhaling cheap-cigarette smoke, and finds a pipe too much for him, sees their antics for a good while longer. When the darkness has put a stop to this entertainment, the sheep sometimes get restless, and an unquiet

296

flock of sheep at midnight makes a most dispiriting noise, which is a shade worse than the dead stillness.

Sometimes, too, a tree falls without any apparent reason just as you are dropping off to sleep; and when a Gippsland tree comes down it shakes a whole hillside and sounds louder than a cannon. Altogether, a cleared selection in South Gippsland is a cheerless home for a solitary neurotic man.

So it came to pass that Smith contracted many little peculiarities in his behaviour. He would spend hours on his back, looking up towards the sky and trying to fix the outline of a tree on his mind, and it always vexed him that he forgot one limb as soon as he set himself to master the next.

He began to talk to the sheep like human beings, for he had no dog; and he swore at them because they did not answer him in English and he had forgotten the French and Latin he had learnt at school. He got tired of the trees being so grey, and he took to staining them with grass, and watering their bases in the hope of making them sprout again. He was conscious that there was something wrong in his being out there all alone, and he came to the conclusion that he had a deadly enemy somewhere, but he couldn't quite settle who it was. It wasn't the sheep, for they seemed as frightened as himself; and it wasn't the trees, for two of them had fallen within a chain of his hut without doing any damage. After this event he regarded them as his especial friends, and he laughed and clapped his hands when the dance got more than usually mixed—in the mazurka, for instance.

At other than twilight hours he sat still and brooded over his wrongs.

One day the boss rode out himself instead of sending a man with Smith's rations, and explained that he intended to build new yards where the hut stood, because the railway was going to pass right there. The shepherd smiled as if he didn't quite understand, and said that the railway would find it rather lonely, and he hoped it wouldn't hurt his trees.

'They're just learning the quadrilles,' he said.

The boss stared at him and went away. Soon after, a couple of men came and told Smith to take his sheep out of the road, and he drew off and watched them for the rest of the afternoon.

When it dawned on him what they were going to do, and he saw the destruction of all his hopes of the grand chain in the evening, he went up and asked them who had ordered it. Then he sat down and thought a great deal about the boss, until at last he came to a decision.

Now it is very clear that the Government of Victoria has much to answer for. If it had not decided to build that railway, Smith's trees would have been left untouched, and he might have gone on quite harmlessly until it was discovered that big timber was bad for his brain. The sheep would not have been left alone that night while a man with a sharpened knife made his way to the homestead. The kitchen-maid would not have been driven screaming along the passage, three men would have been without a very exciting experience of ten minutes' duration, and one of them would not walk lame. Also, the boss's only son would be two months younger and a good deal stronger, and his wife would be able to give an intelligent answer to a simple question—which, as matters stand, she cannot do.

Smith came out, probably, better than anyone else. He was supported for six months in an asylum, and then sent to a situation up Yackandandah way, where he will not see a stretch of big timber in a lifetime.

If he ever happens to get into different country, most probably someone will be murdered.

THE FEUD

D'ARCY NILAND

A MAN CALLED FINGAL lived with his family in a house in the shade of a great tree. The tree and Fingal were enemies. Every time he came out of the small paddock, where his potato bags stood, or when he came from the bush with his shirt open and the axe on his shoulder, he saw the tree and he sneered.

He could see it a mile off, from a peaky hillock, and when he came down along the windbreak, with the sky as a backdrop behind it, in red and russet. It was a thick, massy monster, a hundred feet high, and wide as the shadow of a mountain. With the evening dying out in quiet colours, it went sable and ominous. There was a menacing witchery about it, as it towered over his little house.

And there was never a good air about it, but always evil, a cunning, waiting, patient evil. In the moonlight it was like a black cloud suspended by his dwelling, threatening to float into it and engulf it. When the dusk was well down, the light yellowing from the window gave no cheer, because he could see the horrible, stifling giant, standing without a movement. And in the morning, when the sun expanded through the trees in filtering radii, creating a golden haze like sunlight in the western dust, that tree was evil, and no sun crept into its dark bosom.

When the storm came with a helter-skelter flurry, it unlimbered itself with a dreadful patience, like a calm but terrible man rolling up his sleeves. It threshed and creaked, growing more powerful, howling and sighing in thunderous fury, all the other trees were as sighing echoes of it.

It swung hard with a semi-gyration. It laboured terrifically. And then, when the storm was gone, after its typhooning, after its invigorating bath and gymnastics, it moved gently, tired and exhilarated. To Fingal it looked more terrible.

His face, cracked like a walnut, came to glower naturally, and he even thought of the tree before he saw it. Its appalling personality gave him no rest. His senses gripped it and rolled it in the hate of his mind. One day, when he and his son were husking corn, the boy asked:

'When are we going to cut down the tree, Dad?'

'Soon.'

'You've been going to cut it down for a long time.'

'Yes. But it is a big job. I will destroy it soon.'

'Mum doesn't like you putting it off. She said she thought you were afraid of it, too.'

'Ah, your mother is a foolish woman,' he snapped. 'Afraid? That's likely! Me—afraid of a tree?' he scoffed. 'It's her that's put the fear of it into you all. She sets a fine example with her ideas. She is only trying to work up excuses to get away to the city. I know how she hankers after the grimy dump.'

The boy was about to remark again, but the father told him sharply to get on with his work. His wife was always nagging. If it wasn't one thing it was another. He resented her quality of determination that jarred with her spirit of submissiveness. She accused him of putting matters off; she detested the scrimping and scraping that made management a travail.

She often came into Fingal's mind; a pale mouth working in the pale face, set into a frame of wispy hair. Always there was an exhausted air about her, as though she had walked a long, long way against a heavy wind. But he never pitied her, never sympathised with her. He just appreciated her as a utility that put a steaming meal before him. He would sooner watch ants steering down pencil tracks, and hate the tree.

He realised his inconsistencies, and he blamed the tree. He blamed it with a hatred that violated sense and reason. It had sucked out of him the very energy that had once made him industrious, and had left only indecisive remnants. And these remnants merely gave him, when necessity impelled, the spurts that caused him to plant corn, and sow potatoes and garden vegetables—enough to keep alive.

*   *   *

Two years ago he had come into the bush to make money and buy himself a farm. He had stood in the sun and seen the land, the wilding grass, bent and silver under the tameless wind, the trees straggling, and the great monster that drank their sappy blood. But then, at that time, he had not realised.

He had hewn the timber and built a house by the great tree, and, achievement filling his heart, had set out to clear the earth and make it arable.

Then, he saw broken stumps all about the monster, and the withered grass, monuments to the gorging appetite of the brute; dumb witness to the striving strength and power, the lushness and greenness for which they had died. And out further it was reaching, with a vampire lust, to other trees. The mark of death showed in their drying leaves, and their stripping bark and stunted growth.

Long ago it had sprouted up through the earth with others. They had all fought to live. They basked in the sun, they breathed in the air, the wind strengthened them, the frosts made them hardy. But not all.

This one, this rapacious giant, took much of what belonged to the others. It fought them. It dug its hold deeper, spread its roots and multiplied them, and clawed into the earth with a callous tenacity.

It grew, full of might that terrified the others. They struggled madly to reach up to the sun; the earth groaned with their straining. And then it weakened them. Slowly, and with a horrible sureness, it drained away all their life. They suffocated. It spread over them, a darkening, enlarging shadow. Its sinewy legs bulged out of the earth, and gnarled themselves together. And the others died. For long years, this selfish murderer had killed to feed itself, encroaching on space even, and claiming an enormous gap.

Fingal cleared away the stumps. He cleared away the other trees; and always it howled in self-mourning. It ranted and dirged. It would grow no more. It could thieve no more. Then it was quiet, like a man done wrong, who schemes vengeance.

Fingal's crops were poor. He made little. He took an axe and gashed and severed its great toes. He ring-barked it, and waited, smiling grimly.

The tree apparently never noticed this disfigurement. It went on in awful, relentless calm. Fingal cursed. There was domestic trouble. His mind changed until he came near to psychosis.

He cleaned all the silt and leaves out of the guttering. The tank was choked up and the water polluted. Water had to be drawn from the creek until he had cleaned the tank. His wife complained. The garden was always sombre; only wilting things grew. The roots of the tree burst up under the house, and moved it slightly on its foundations.

And in his bed at night Fingal heard the sonorous sound of the tree. He heard its repining satisfaction, and a horrible gloating. He thought of ruin. He thought of his schemes gone astray; the trouble and the worry.

Well, he was not finished with it yet. He had done a lot to it; things that nothing else had done. Ferociously and tenaciously though it had killed and eaten, it could not domineer him. It could not break him. It could not oust his little house from its monarchal domain. But the tree was not done with him.

*   *   *

When he came in home that evening from the cornfield, thinking of supper, his wife, on edge, told him straight she was sick of everything and was going away. He knew she was not fooling or bluffing.

'Where will you go?'

'I'll get work in the city,' she said. 'There's plenty of it. They're calling out for factory workers.'

He was thinking who'd look after him; who'd cook his meals.

'And what's more, Jimmy will get a job . . . a decent job,' she went on, determined. 'If you had any sense you'd come, too. Do you good to get into a different job, anyway.'

Fingal protested and persuaded, but there was no stopping her. The next day she left, the boy and the three-year-old baby with her. She had stood enough of that loneliness, and struggling and semi-starvation.

After that Fingal did nothing. He let his beard grow. He ate any time and any thing. The house was eerie, even in the daytime. At night it was full of creaks and winds. The bed was cold. He missed his children.

In an agony of hatred he cursed and swore at the tree. Always it was there, leaning over him in that goblin dwelling, sinister at night, glaring at him when he got out in the morning. His eyes squinted his hatred. His mouth showed bitter abomination, his clenched fists violence, his whole demeanour an aching revenge. He would kill it. He would chop it down if it took him years. He would spend every penny he had and dynamite it to bits. He would wipe the foul thing away forever.

That night he was awakened into consciousness of the storm. He lay listening. He saw a blue flood of lightning, again and again. And he heard before the crash of thunder, a sizzling crackle and a terrible creak.

Quickly, he ran outside. In the flashes of lightning he saw the tree riven in two. He shouted with relief of affrighted surprise, with joy, with triumph; his enemy at last destroyed.

Then his eyes stretched. The tree trembled, toppled, and fell crashing across the house, smashing it flat.

When they found Fingal his glazed eyes were still turned in terror, in numb fear and despair.

THE CONQUERING BUSH

EDWARD DYSON

NED 'PICKED UP' HIS wife in Sydney. He had come down for a spell in town, and to relieve himself of the distress of riches—to melt the cheque accumulated slowly in toil and loneliness on a big station in the North.

He was a stockrider, a slow, still man naturally, but easily moved by drink. When he first reached town he seemed to have with him some of the atmosphere of silence and desolation that surrounded him during the long months back there on the run. Ned was about thirty-four, and looked forty. He was tall and raw-boned, and that air of settled melancholy, which is the certain result of a solitary bush life, suggested some romantic sorrow to Mrs Black's sentimental daughter.

Darton, taught wisdom by experience, had on this occasion taken lodgings in a suburban private house. Mrs Black's home was very small, but her daughter was her only child, and they found room for a 'gentleman boarder'.

Janet Black was a pleasant-faced, happy-hearted girl of twenty. She liked the new boarder from the start, she acknowledged to herself afterwards, but when by some fortunate chance he happened to be on hand to drag a half-blind and half-witted old woman from beneath the very hoofs of a runaway horse, somewhat at the risk of his own neck, she was enraptured, and in the enthusiasm of the moment she kissed the hand of the abashed hero, and left a tear glittering on the hard brown knuckles.

This was a week after Ned Darton's arrival in Sydney.

Ned went straight to his room and sat perfectly still, and with even more than his usual gravity watched the tear fade away from the back of his hand. Either Janet's little demonstration of artless feeling had awakened suggestions of some glorious possibility in Ned's heart, or he desired to exercise economy for a change; he suddenly became very judicious in the selection of his drinks, and only took enough whisky to dispel his native moodiness and taciturnity and make him rather a pleasant acquisition to Mrs Black's limited family circle.

When Ned Darton returned to his pastoral duties in the murmuring wilds, he took Janet Black with him as his wife. That was their honeymoon.

Darton did not pause to consider the possible results of the change he was introducing into the life of his bride—few men would. Janet was vivacious, and her heart yearned towards humanity. She was bright, cheerful and impressionable. The bush is sad, heavy, despairing; delightful for a month, perhaps, but terrible for a year.

As she travelled towards her new home the young wife was effervescent with joy, aglow with health, childishly jubilant over numberless plans and projects; she returned to Sydney before the expiration of a year, a stranger to her mother in appearance and in spirit. She seemed taller now, her cheeks were thin, and her face had a new expression. She brought with her some of the brooding desolation of the bush—even in the turmoil of the city she seemed lost in the immensity of the wilderness. She answered her mother's every question without a smile. She had nothing to complain of: Ned was a very good husband and very kind. She found the bush lonesome at first, but soon got used to it, and she didn't mind now. She was quite sure she was used to it, and she never objected to returning.

A baby was born, and Mrs Darton went back with her husband to their hut by the creek on the great run, to the companionship of bears, birds, 'possums, kangaroos, and the eternal trees. She hugged her baby on her breast, and rejoiced that the little mite would give her something more to do and something to think of that would keep the awful ring of the myriad locusts out of her ears.

Man and wife settled down to their choking existence again as before, without comment. Ned was used to the bush—he had lived in it all his life—and though its influence was powerful upon him he knew it not. He was necessarily away from home a good deal, and when at home he was not companionable, in the sense that city dwellers know. Two bushmen will sit together by the fire for hours, smoking and mute, enjoying each other's society; 'in mute discourse' two bushmen will ride for twenty miles through the most desolate or the most fruitful region.

People who have lived in crowds want talk, laughter and song. Ned loved his wife, but he neither talked, laughed, nor sang.

Summer came. The babe at Mrs Darton's breast looked out on the world of trees with wide, unblinking, solemn eyes, and never smiled.

'Ned,' said Janet, one bright, moonlit night, 'do you know that that 'possum in the big blue gum is crazy? She has two joeys, and she has gone mad.'

Janet spent a lot of her time sitting in the shade of the hut on a candle-box, gazing into her baby's large, still eyes, listening to the noises of the bush, and the babe too seemed to listen, and the mother fancied that their senses blended, and they both would some day hear something awful above the crooning of the insects and the chattering of the parrots. Sometimes she would start out of these humours with a shriek, feeling that the relentless trees which had been bending over and pressing down so long were crushing her at last beneath their weight.

Presently she became satisfied that the laughing jackasses were mad. She had long suspected it. Why else should they flock together in the dim evening and fill the bush with their crazy laughter? Why else should they sit so grave and still at other times, thinking and grieving?

Yes, she was soon quite convinced that the animals and birds, even the insects that surrounded her, were mad, hopelessly mad, all of them.

The country was now burnt brown, and the hills ached in the great heat, and the ghostly mirage floated in the hollows. In the daytime the birds and beasts merely chummered and muttered querulously from the deepest shades, but in the dusk of evening they raved and shrieked, and filled the ominous bush with mad laughter and fantastic wailings.

It was at this time that Darton became impressed by the peculiar manner of his wife, and a great awe stole over him as he watched her gazing into her baby's eyes with that strange look of frightened conjecture. He suddenly became very communicative; he talked a lot, and laughed, and strove to be merry, with an indefinable chill at his heart. He failed to interest his wife; she was absorbed in a terrible thought.

The bush was peopled with mad things—the wide wilderness of trees, and the dull, dead grass, and the cowering hills instilled into every living thing that came under the influence of their ineffable gloom a madness of melancholy. The bears were mad, the 'possums, the shrieking cockatoos, the dull grey laughing jackasses with their devilish cackling, and the ugly yellow-throated lizards that panted at her from the rocks—all were mad. How, then, could her babe hope to escape the influence of the mighty bush and the great white plains beyond, with their heavy atmosphere of despair pressing down upon his defenceless head?

Would he not presently escape from her arms, and turn and hiss at her from the grass like a vicious snake; or climb the trees, and, like a bear, cling in day-long torpor from a limb; or, worst of all, join the grey birds on the big dead gum, and mock at her sorrow with empty, joyless laughter?

These were the fears that oppressed Janet as she watched her sad, silent baby at her breast. They grew upon her and strengthened day by day, and one afternoon they became an agonising conviction. She had been alone with the dumb child for two days, and she sat beside the hut door and watched the evening shadows thicken, with a shadow in her eyes that was more terrible than blackest night, and when a solitary mopoke began calling from the Bald Hill, and the jackasses set up a weird chorus of laughter, she rose, and clasping her baby tighter to her breast, and leaning over it to shield it from the surrounding evils, she hurried towards the creek.

Janet was not in the hut when Ned returned home half an hour later. Attracted by the howling of his dog, he hastened to the waterhole under the great rock, and there in the shallow water he found the bodies of his wife and child and the dull grey birds were laughing insanely overhead.

RATS

HENRY LAWSON

'Why, there's two of them, and they're having a fight! Come on.'

It seemed a strange place for a fight, that hot, lonely cottonbush plain. And yet not more than half a mile ahead there were apparently two men struggling together on the track.

The three travellers postponed their smoko and hurried on.

They were shearers—a little man and a big man, known respectively as 'Sunlight' and 'Macquarie', and a tall, thin, young jackaroo whom they called 'Milky'.

'I wonder where the other man sprang from? I didn't see him before,' said Sunlight.

'He muster bin layin' down in the bushes,' said Macquarie.

'They're goin' at it proper, too. Come on! Hurry up and see the fun!'

They hurried on.

'It's a funny-lookin' feller, the other feller,' panted Milky.

'He don't seem to have no head. Look! He's down, they're both down! They must ha' clinched on the ground. No! They're up an' at it again . . . Why, good Lord! I think the other's a woman!'

'My oath! So it is!' yelled Sunlight. 'Look! The brute's got her down again! He's kickin' her! Come on, chaps; come on, or he'll do for her!'

They dropped swags, waterbags and all, and raced forward; but presently Sunlight, who had the best eyes, slackened his pace and dropped behind. His mates glanced back at his face, saw a peculiar expression there, looked ahead again, and then dropped into a walk.

They reached the scene of the trouble and there stood a little withered old man by the track, with his arms folded close up under his chin; he was dressed mostly in calico patches and half a dozen corks, suspended on bits of string from the brim of his hat, dangled before his bleared optics to scare away the flies. He was scowling malignantly at a stout, dumpy swag which lay in the middle of the track.

'Well, old Rats, what's the trouble?' asked Sunlight.

'Oh, nothing, nothing,' answered the old man, without looking round. 'I fell out with my swag, that's all. He knocked me down, but I've settled him.'

'But look here,' said Sunlight, winking at his mates, 'we saw you jump on him when he was down. That ain't fair, you know.'

'But you didn't see it all,' cried Rats, getting excited. 'He hit *me* down first! And, look here, I'll fight him again for nothing, and you can see fair play.'

They talked a while, then Sunlight proposed to second the swag, while his mate supported the old man, and after some persuasion Milky agreed, for the sake of the lark, to act as timekeeper and referee.

Rats entered into the spirit of the thing; he stripped to the waist, and while he was getting ready the travellers pretended to bet on the result.

Macquarie took his place behind the old man, and Sunlight upended the swag. Rats shaped and danced round; then he rushed, feinted, ducked, retreated, darted in once more and suddenly went down like a shot on the broad of his back. No actor could have done it better; he went down from that imaginary blow as if a cannonball had struck him in the forehead.

Milky called time, and the old man came up, looking shaky. However, he got in a tremendous blow which knocked the swag into the bushes.

Several rounds followed with varying success.

The men pretended to get more and more excited and betted freely, and Rats did his best. At last they got tired of the fun.

Sunlight let the swag lie after Milky called time, and the jackaroo awarded the fight to Rats. They pretended to hand over the stakes, and then went back for their swags, while the old man put on his shirt.

Then he calmed down, carried his swag to the side of the track, sat down on it and talked rationally about bush matters for a while; but presently he grew silent and began to feel his muscles and smile idiotically.

'Can you len' us a bit o' meat?' said he suddenly.

They spared him half a pound; but he said he didn't want it all, and cut off about an ounce, which he laid on the end of his swag. Then he took the lid off his billy and produced a fishing line. He baited the hook, threw the line across the track and waited for a bite.

Soon he got deeply interested in the line, jerked it once or twice, and drew it in rapidly. The bait had been rubbed off in the grass. The old man regarded the hook disgustedly.

'Look at that!' he cried. 'I had him, only I was in such a hurry. I should ha' played him a little more.'

Next time he was more careful; he drew the line in warily, grabbed an imaginary fish and laid it down on the grass. Sunlight and Co. were greatly interested by this time.

'Wot yer think o' that?' asked Rats. 'It weighs thirty pound if it weighs an ounce! Wot yer think o' that for a cod? The hook's halfway down his blessed gullet.'

He caught several cod and bream while they were there, and invited them to camp and have tea with him. But they wished to reach a certain shed next day, so, after the ancient had borrowed about a pound of meat for bait, they went on, and left him fishing contentedly.

But first Sunlight went down into his pocket and came up with half a crown, which he gave to the old man, along with some tucker.

'You'd best push on to the water before dark, old chap,' he said, kindly.

When they turned their heads again Rats was still fishing: but when they looked back for the last time before entering the timber, he was having another row with his swag; and Sunlight reckoned that the trouble arose out of some lies the swag had been telling about the bigger fish it caught.

'THE WIND THAT BURIES THE DEAD'

'J.W. GORDON'
(JIM GRAHAME)

I spring from the land of the drifting sand,
The wind that buries the dead;
I cover the roads like a rippled beach
Where the feet of the lost men tread;
Old is the night when I take my rest;
I sleep till the flaming noon.
I ride to the height of the clouds at night
As they're scurrying past the moon.

Famine and drought are my henchmen stout,
My lover the wild bush fire;
I will never shirk full share of work,
And my lover he will not tire,
As he's soaring high where the grass is dry,
With his wings, like a vulture's, spread,
The great trees fall at the crashing call
Of the wind that buries the dead.

He will strip the limbs of the tallest pine
And gnaw through the knotted bole;
Then he bites at the brush like a monster starved
And snarls at a fallen pole.

But the bones of the perished birds and beasts,
When the grassless plains are red,
Will be hidden deep by the restless sweep
Of the wind that buries the dead.

Half crazed with fears a woman peers
For the sight of a child that strayed;
The father has tramped and called all night
While she cared for the rest and prayed.
Two crusted furrows are on her cheeks—
Dry salt of the tears she shed.
Her tears may flow as the seasons go
For the wind will bury the dead.

The bushmen come in a mounted troop
And they scatter on hill and plain;
They follow the gullies and mulga ridge,
But their search will be in vain.
(There's a creeping army of small black ants
That twist like a winding thread
Round and round and across the mound
Where the wind has buried the dead.)

When the rivers rise to the red soil's edge
And the billabongs overflow,
The land turns green in a single night
Where the creeping waters go;
The wild swamp lilies bedeck the ground,
Like a golden mantle spread—
By the rich spring dress may the bush-birds guess
Where the wind has buried the dead.

Part 8

THE NIGHT WE WATCHED FOR WALLABIES

This is a collection of stories about 'coming of age' in the bush. Mostly these stories have a positive feel to them, with the possible exception of the Miles Franklin story, which revolves around a bush girl coming to an honest realisation of her parents' situation and how it has affected her life and her possibilities.

'Old Heinrich and the Lambing Ewe' is the story of a happy outcome in the face of impending doom, as a young farmer's spirit is lifted when nature is blindly beneficent. This is a story in which farm life is accurately and beautifully observed. No writer has ever captured the behaviour of sheep dogs as well as E.O. Schlunke.

Frank Daniel's well-told tale of two young men being inadvertently rewarded has a ring of authenticity, as does Henry Handel Richardson's delightful tale of a teenage conversation on the delicate topic of sex and love. In each case the older character is merely a year or so ahead of the curious one in terms of experience. Both stories, so different in style, bring a smile of recognition.

'The Night We Watched for Wallabies' has the same ring of truth about it; here the gentle humour is derived from the mundane events of life on the selection. I think this story is Steele Rudd at his best.

'PICKING LEMONS'

GRAHAM FREDRIKSEN

I rode my bike down to the creek
To pick some lemons for my Dad.
It's just like playing hide-and-seek
When there are lemons to be had.

They hide up in the lemon tree—
With thorny branches everywhere.
They are too hard to get for me—
I think that I will leave them there.

I'll tell my Dad if he should seek
To have some lemons on his shelf,
Then he should go down to the creek
To pick the lemons for himself.

THE NIGHT WE WATCHED FOR WALLABIES

STEELE RUDD

IT HAD BEEN A bleak July day, and as night came on a bitter westerly howled through the trees. Cold! Wasn't it cold! The pigs in the sty, hungry and half-fed (we wanted for ourselves the few pumpkins that had survived the drought), fought savagely with each other for shelter, and squealed all the time like—well, like pigs. The cows and calves left the place to seek shelter away in the mountains; while the draught horses, their hair standing up like barbed wire, leaned sadly over the fence and gazed up at the green lucerne. Joe went about shivering in an old coat of Dad's with only one sleeve to it—a calf had fancied the other one day that Dad hung it on a post as a mark to go by while ploughing.

'My! It'll be a stinger tonight,' Dad remarked to Mrs Brown— who sat, cold-looking, on the sofa—as he staggered inside with an immense log for the fire. A log! Nearer a whole tree! But wood was nothing in Dad's eyes.

Mrs Brown had been at our place five or six days. Old Brown called occasionally to see her, so we knew they couldn't have quarrelled. Sometimes she did a little housework, but more often she didn't.

We talked it over together, but couldn't make it out. Joe asked Mother, but she had no idea—so she said. We were full up, as Dave put it, of Mrs Brown, and wished her out of the place. She

318

had taken to ordering us about, as though she had something to do with us.

After supper we sat round the fire—as near to it as we could without burning ourselves—Mrs Brown and all, and listened to the wind whistling outside. Ah, it was pleasant beside the fire listening to the wind! When Dad had warmed himself back and front he turned to us and said:

'Now, boys, we must go directly and light some fires and keep those wallabies back.'

That was a shock to us, and we looked at him to see if he were really in earnest. He was, and as serious as a judge.

'*Tonight!*' Dave answered, surprisedly. 'Why tonight any more than last night or the night before? Thought you had decided to let them rip?'

'Yes, but we might as well keep them off a bit longer.'

'But there's no wheat there for them to get now. So what's the good of watching them? There's no sense in *that*.'

Dad was immovable.

'Anyway,' whined Joe, '*I'm* not going—not a night like this—not when I ain't got boots.'

That vexed Dad. 'Hold your tongue, sir!' he said, 'You'll do as you're told.'

But Dave hadn't finished. 'I've been following that harrow since sunrise this morning,' he said, 'and now you want me to go chasing wallabies about in the dark, a night like this, and for nothing else but to keep them from eating the ground. It's always the way here, the more one does the more he's wanted to do,' and he commenced to cry.

Mrs Brown had something to say. *She* agreed with Dad and thought we ought to go, as the wheat might spring up again.

'Pshah!' Dave blurted out between his sobs, while we thought of telling her to shut her mouth.

Slowly and reluctantly we left that roaring fireside to accompany Dad that bitter night. It *was* a night!—dark as pitch, silent, forlorn and forbidding, and colder than the busiest morgue. And just to keep wallabies from eating nothing! They *had* eaten all the wheat—every blade of it—and the grass as well. What they would start on next—ourselves or the cart harness—wasn't quite clear.

We stumbled along in the dark one behind the other, with our hands stuffed into our trousers. Dad was in the lead, and poor Joe, bare-shinned and bootless, in the rear. Now and again he tramped on a Bathurst burr, and, in sitting down to extract the prickle, would receive a cluster of them elsewhere. When he escaped the burr it was only to knock his shin against a log or leave a toenail or two clinging to a stone. Joe howled, but the wind howled louder, and blew and blew.

Dave, in pausing to wait on Joe, would mutter:

'To *hell* with everything! Whatever he wants bringing us out on a night like this, I'm *damned* if I know!'

Dad couldn't see very well in the dark, and on this night couldn't see at all, so he walked up against one of the old draught horses that had fallen asleep gazing at the lucerne. And what a fright they both got! The old horse took it worse than Dad—who only tumbled down—for he plunged as though the devil had grabbed him, and fell over the fence, twisting every leg he had in the wires. How the brute struggled! We stood and listened to him. After kicking panels of the fence down and smashing every wire in it, he got loose and made off, taking most of it with him.

'That's one wallaby on the wheat, anyway,' Dave muttered, and we giggled. *We* understood Dave; but Dad didn't open his mouth.

We lost no time lighting the fires. Then we walked through the 'wheat' and wallabies! May Satan reprove me if I exaggerate their number by one solitary pair of ears—but from the row and scatter they made there were a *million*.

Dad told Joe, at last, he could go to sleep if he liked, at the fire. Joe went to sleep—*how*, I don't know. Then Dad sat beside him, and for long intervals would stare silently into the darkness. Sometimes a string of the vermin would hop past close to the fire, and another time a curlew would come near and screech its ghostly wail, but he never noticed them. Yet he seemed to be listening.

We mooched around from fire to fire, hour after hour, and when we wearied of heaving fire-sticks at the enemy we sat on our heels and cursed the wind, and the winter, and the night birds alternately. It was a lonely, wretched occupation.

Now and again Dad would leave his fire to ask us if we could hear a noise. We couldn't, except that of wallabies and mopokes. Then he would go back and listen again. He was restless, and, somehow, his heart wasn't in the wallabies at all. Dave couldn't make him out.

The night wore on. By and by there was a sharp rattle of wires, then a rustling noise, and Sal appeared in the glare of the fire. '*Dad!*' she said. That was all. Without a word, Dad bounced up and went back to the house with her.

'Something's up!' Dave said, and, half-anxious, half-afraid, we gazed into the fire and thought and thought. Then we stared, nervously, into the night, and listened for Dad's return, but heard only the wind and the mopoke.

At dawn he appeared again, with a broad smile on his face, and told us that mother had got another baby—a fine little chap.

Then we knew why Mrs Brown had been staying at our place.

CRUTCHING THE RAMS

FRANK DANIEL

IN HIS EARLY TEENS my brother Jim was a 'learner shearer' and had been coming along quite promisingly working for the local shearing contractor.

My early ambition to become a shearer had, on the other hand, waned in the light of becoming interested in farm machinery and mechanical things.

One day Jim's boss asked him to go out to a nearby station, owned by a former World War I officer, to crutch a hundred and eighty stud merino rams. Jim was told that he would have to find a mate to do the rouseabouting. He was also warned to be very careful with the rams and make sure he didn't cut off any important bits.

Although I had no interest in sheep whatsoever, I was very proud of my brother having his first shed all to himself and I was really pleased when he asked me to go with him to help out.

The station's shearing shed was built on a rise well above ground level, with room to pen sheep underneath.

There were twenty-five stands along one wall.

Jim carried his tools of trade in through the entrance door past the engine room and set himself up at stand number twenty-four. I'm not sure why he chose stand twenty-four. I think it was something to do with less noise from the engine room.

I carried our tucker box in and placed it at stand twenty-four. Jim swiftly laid the boot into it and sent it sliding back another three stands away from his work area.

'There's a place for that!' he said. I couldn't see any obvious 'place' so assumed stand number twenty-one must have been the spot he was talking about.

I was awestruck by the immense size of the building, and even more impressed by the bush carpentry skills that had gone into its construction. They built things to last in those days.

If I was awestruck at the size of the shearing shed, I was totally dumbstruck at the size of the rams that were rattling their feet on the grating of the catching pens.

They were monsters.

Up to that point I hadn't given much thought to my actual duties. I was just prepared to do whatever was necessary—sweep away the crutchings, pen up a few more rams as needed.

I figured I should be able to handle that all right.

Then the station mechanic turned up. He said 'Gidday' to us and asked if I was ready to start the engine up. Too right I was. I was interested in that job, mechanical stuff! No worries about that, at all.

So off we went, twenty-four stands back along that big shed to the top of the steps that led down into the engine room—and there she was.

Bloody hell!

It was a monster. A two-cylinder Lister diesel engine standing over six foot high on a heavy concrete foundation. It had a flywheel about three-and-a-half feet in diameter, brass pipes and taps, other bits and pieces that I knew absolutely nothing about and of course there were heavy leather belts to drive the overhead shearing plant. There was a large tank of water connected to keep the engine running cool.

Jack, the mechanic, showed me how to start the engine.

'First, you turn the fuel on,' and he gave the tap a few turns, 'then you lift this lever here to decompress the valves.'

So far so good.

Then he produced the crank handle. Blimey! It was as big as my leg. It was made of cast steel and it certainly looked heavy!

The old fellow gave the flywheel a few turns with the crank, giving me directions as he went.

'You turn this . . . then you drop this valve lever down and she should go.'

She did.

It kept boppin' and poppin' and going on for a bit till it settled down.

The flywheel was hummin' and drummin' and the belts were slappin' and clappin' and the whole atmosphere was vibratin' and shakin'.

It sounded like the army had arrived on the scene.

With raised voice he told me that I could 'have a go now' to get used to the starting procedure.

'No thanks . . . she'll be right,' I shouted back. 'I know what to do now. She'll be right.'

He looked at me and for a horrible moment I thought he was going to turn it off.

There was no way in the world I was interested in cranking that big old engine.

I'd already had an 'experience' with a smaller Cooper's three-horsepower engine at home, in our own shearing shed.

That engine of ours was shorter in height but longer. It was necessary to hold a decompression valve in the head of the engine with your left hand whilst you cranked the flywheel with your right hand. To do that required my arms to be outstretched as far as I could reach. While the cranking was in progress a magneto let out loud clacking noises and emitted strong sparks of electricity right in front of my face.

On the day I'd had the 'experience' I'd just reached full cranking speed when the crank handle slipped from the crankshaft. Having sufficient momentum, it turned one more revolution in my right hand and gave me a resounding crack in the side of the mouth, leaving one tooth missing.

I vowed I would not be cranking one of those cantankerous old machines ever again if it could be avoided.

'You know what to do, do ya?' asked Jack, with a frown.

I assured him that I was well and truly versed in what to do.

Jack then told me how to shut the engine down for smoko and how to set it up again for a restart. Then he went away happy that all was in order.

For the first two hours Jim struggled with the heavy merino rams. Jim only weighed about ten stone wringing wet and those rams would have been close to fourteen stone each.

They were as strong as bulls and, when they got a grip on the grated floor with their hooves, they were near impossible to turn over and drag from the pen. I gave Jim as much help as I could in that department, but it was really hard yakker.

Nine-thirty was smoko time and Jim said I could 'go and turn that injin orf' while he had a break.

So off I went. Twenty-four stands up that long shearing board. Ten steps down into the engine room and there she was. The flywheel hummin' and drummin', the belts were slappin' and clappin', the tappets were poppin' and boppin', the water was hissin' an' . . . . an' . . . an' . . . well the whole flamin' show looked like it could go on forever.

'Bugger it!' I said aloud, eyeing off that big crank handle.

I left it running and went back to join Jim for a cuppa.

'Ain't you gonna turn it orf?' he asked as I rummaged through our lunchbox looking for a plum-jam sandwich.

'Nah! Dad says it does them good to have a bit of a run,' I said knowingly.

So we left it at that; Jim didn't seem too concerned.

Back we went to dragging those monster rams to the stand. Then I'd stand back and watch as Jim wrestled with each one and got them crutched one at a time.

When lunchtime came Jim was really in need of a rest.

'You better go and turn that injin orf this time!'

So off I went . . . twenty-four stands along that great shed to the top of the stairs at the engine room.

I peered down at that big old Lister.

The flywheel was still hummin' and drummin', the valves were still poppin' and boppin', the belts were still slappin' and clappin' and the water was still hissin' an' . . . hissin' . . . an' I could tell that it was still full of oil because it wasn't making any funny noises, and that crank handle didn't look any smaller.

So I let it run right through dinner, and again Jim didn't seem terribly worried.

The third run for the day was a bit slower for Jim as he was getting knocked about a bit by those rams and I was about as handy as a pocket in a singlet as far as the sheep were concerned. I'd lost all interest in them about half an hour after we started that morning.

Three o'clock was smoko time again.

Jim didn't even ask if I wanted to 'turn that old injin orf' this time. He just settled down for a cuppa and some cake as curiosity drew me along those twenty-four stands where I made another observation from the top of the ten stairs.

Same old story. The flywheel was still hummin' and drummin', the valves were still poppin' and boppin', the belts were still flappin' and clappin', the water was still hissin' . . . and I could tell that it still had plenty of oil in the sump—so I left it alone.

About four-thirty we saw the last of the rams down the chute and into the paddock and Jim cleaned up his gear and I swept the board clean and tidied up the wool.

I made absolutely sure that no rams were left in the shed and then quite confidently I went twenty-four stands up that long shed, and ten steps down into the engine room.

The flywheel was still hummmin' and drummin', the belts were still flappin', the valves were still poppin', the belts still slappin' and flappin'. There was a strong smell of oil and the water was still hissin' away.

'Now!' I thought to myself as I went through the formalities of 'turning that big injin orf.'

'Lift the decompression lever—turn off the fuel tap.'

I did both.

The hummin' and the drummin' of the big flywheel gradually slowed as the belts stopped their slappin' and clappin' and the last of the poppin' an' boppin' faded away.

The water finally hissed its last hiss.

Blimey, it was quiet; I felt as I had been left behind after shearing finished.

As we drove down the track past the homestead we saw the figure of the old Colonel coming towards us. He was waving his walking stick and beckoned us to pull over. I thought we were in some kind of trouble. The old bloke used to worry us kids a lot. He always seemed to be a bit of a cranky old bloke.

'And what would your name be?' he asked abruptly.

'Daniel,' Jim answered.

'And who would your father be?'

'Bill.'

Jim was going real well.

'I know him,' said the old bloke, 'knew his father too. He was the blacksmith wasn't he? Never a better worker in the district.'

We nodded mutely.

'And you boys are just like him,' he said emphatically.

'You worked right through smoko—right through lunch, and right through the afternoon. You never stopped all day—well done!'

And, with that, he gave us a ten-bob note for our troubles.

CONVERSATION IN A PANTRY

HENRY HANDEL RICHARDSON

It was no use, she simply could not sleep. She had tried lying all sorts of ways: with the blanket pulled over her or the blanket off; with her knees doubled up to her chin or stretched so straight that her feet nearly touched the bottom of the bed; on her back with her hands under her neck, or with her face burrowed in the pillow. Nothing helped.

Going on in her she could still feel the bumps and lurches of the coach in which she had ridden most of that day.

Then the log that had been smouldering in the brick fireplace burnt away in the middle, and collapsed with a crash; and the two ends, rolling together, broke into flames again. These threw shadows which ran about the ceiling, and up and down the white walls, like strange animals.

She was spending the night with Alice, and they had had a fire 'just for luxury', and had sat by it for nearly an hour before going to bed. It would be her last chance of anything like that, Alice said: in schools, you never had fires, and all lights went out to the minute.

Their talk had been fearfully interesting. For Alice was in love—she was over seventeen—and had told her about it just as if she was grown up, too; looking into the fire with ever such a funny little smile, and her blue eyes quite small behind their thick, curly lashes.

'Oh, don't you wish we could see into the future, Trix? And what it's going to bring us?'

But though she said yes, she wasn't sure if she did, really; she liked surprises better. Besides, all the last part of the time Alice talked, she had been screwing up her courage to put a question. But she hadn't managed to get it out. And that was one reason why now she couldn't sleep.

With a fresh toss, she sighed gustily. And, where her tumblings and fidgetings had failed, this sound called her companion back from the downy meadows. 'What's the matter, child? Aren't you asleep yet?'

'No, I simply can't.' Alice sat up in bed, and shook her hair back from her face.

'You're over-excited. Try a drink of water.'

'I have. I've drunk it all up.'

'Then you must be hungry.'

'Well, yes, I am perhaps . . . a little.'

'Come on then, let's forage.' And throwing back the sheet, the elder girl slid her feet to the floor.

One tall white figure, one short, they opened the door and stepped out on the verandah. Here it was almost as bright as day; for the moon hung like a round cheese in the sky, and drenched everything with its light. Barefoot they pattered, the joins in the verandah floorboards, which had risen, cutting into their soles.

They had to pass open windows, dark holes in which people lay sleeping; Alice laid a finger on her lips. From one of these came the sound of snores—harsh snores of the chromatic kind, which went up the scale and down, over and over again, without a pause.

Turning a corner, they stepped off the verandah and took a few steps on hard pebbly ground. Inside the pantry, which was a large outhouse, there were sharp contrasts of bluish-white moonlight and black shadows. Swiftly Alice skimmed the familiar shelves.

'Here's lemon cheesecakes . . . and jam tarts . . . and ginger-snaps . . . and pound cake. But I can't start you on these, or you'd be sick.'

And cutting a round off a homemade loaf, she spread it thickly with dairy butter, topped by a layer of quince jelly.

'There, that's more wholesome.'

Oh, had anything ever tasted so delicious as this slice eaten at dead of night? Perched on an empty, upturned kerosene tin, the young girl munched and munched, holding her empty hand outspread below, lest the quivering jelly glide over the crust's edge.

Alice took a cheesecake and sat down on a lidded basket. 'I say, DID you hear Father? Oh, Trix, wouldn't it be positively too awful if one discovered *afterwards*, one had married a man who snored?'

The muncher made no answer: the indelicacy of the question stunned her: all in the dark as she was, she felt her face flame. And yet . . . was this not perhaps the very chance she had been waiting for? If Alice could say such a thing, out loud, without embarrassment . . .

Hastily squeezing down her last titbit—she felt it travel, over-large, the full length of her gullet—she licked her jellied fingers clean and took the plunge. 'Dallie, there's something I . . . I want to ask you something . . . something I want to know.'

'Fire away!' said Alice, and went on nibbling at the pastry edging that trimmed her tartlet.

'Yes. But . . . well, I don't quite . . . I mean I . . .'

'Like that, is it? Wait a tick,' and rather more rapidly than she had intended, Alice bolted her luscious circle of lemon-cheese, picked up her basket and planted it beside the tin. 'Now then.'

Shut away in this outhouse, the young girl might have cried her words aloud. But leaning over till she found the shell of her friend's ear, she deposited them safely inside.

Alice, who was ticklish, gave an involuntary shudder. But as the sense of the question dawned on her, she sat up very stiff and straight, and echoed perturbed: 'HOW? Oh, but kid, I'm not sure—not at all sure—whether you ought to know. At your age!' said seventeen to thirteen.

'But I must, Dallie.'

'But why, my dear?'

'Because of something Ruth said.'

'Oh, Ruth!' said Alice scornfully. 'Trust Ruth for saying the wrong thing. What was it?'

'Why, that . . . now I was growing up . . . was as good as grown up . . . I must take care, for . . . for fear . . . . But, Dallie, how can I . . . if I don't know?'

This last question came out with a rush, and with a kind of click in the throat.

'Well, well! I always have felt sorry for you children, with no mother but only Ruth to bring you up—and she forever prinking before her glass. But you know you'll be perfectly safe at school, Trix. They'll look after you, never fear!'

But there was more to come. It was Ella, it seemed, Ella Morrison, who was two years older than her, who'd begun it. She'd said her mother said now she mustn't let the boys kiss her anymore.

'And you have, eh?' Trixie's nod was so small that it had to be guessed at. Haltingly, word by word, the story came out. It had been at Christmas, at a big party, and they were playing games. And she and some others, all boys, had gone off to hide from the rest, and they'd climbed into the hayloft, Harry MacGillivray among them; and she rather liked Harry, and he liked her, and the other boys knew it and had teased them. And then they said he wasn't game to kiss her and dared him to. And she didn't want him to, not a bit . . . or only a teeny weeny bit . . . and anyhow she wasn't going to let him, there before them all. But the other boys grabbed her, and one held her arms and another her legs and another her neck, so that he could. And he did—three times—hard. She'd been as angry as anything; she'd hit them all round. But only angry. Afterwards, though . . . when Ellie told her what her mother had said . . . and now Ruth. But she got no further; for Alice had thrown back her head and was shaking with ill-repressed laughter.

'Oh, you babe . . . you blessed infant, you! Why, child, there was no more harm in that than . . . well, than in this!' And pulling the girl to her she kissed her soundly, some half-dozen times, with scant pause between. An embarrassing embrace, from which Trixie made uneasy haste to free herself; for Alice was plump, and her nightgown thin.

'No, you can make your little mind easy,' continued the elder girl on recovering her breath. 'Larking's all that was and couldn't hurt a fly. *It's what larking leads to*,' said Alice, and her voice sank, till it was hollow with mystery.

'What does it?'

'Ah!' said Alice in the same sepulchral tone. 'You asked me just now how babies came. Well, *that's how*, my dear.'

'Yes, but . . .'

'Come, you've read your Bible, haven't you? The Garden of Eden, and so on? And male and female created He them?'

'But . . .'

'Well, Trix, in MY opinion, you ought to be content with that . . . in the meanwhile. Time enough for more when . . . well, when you're married, my dear.'

Not for the world would Alice have admitted her own lack of preciser knowledge, or have uncovered to the day her private imaginings of the great unknown.

'But suppose I . . . Not *every* lady gets married, Dallie! And then I'd never know.'

'And wouldn't need to. But I don't think there's much fear of that, Trix! You're not the stuff old maids are made of,' said Alice sturdily, welcoming the side issue.

Affectionately Trixie snuggled up to her friend. This tribute was most consoling. (How awful should nobody want you, you remain unchosen!) All the same she did not yield; a real worm for knowledge gnawed in her. 'Still, I don't quite see . . . truly I don't, Dallie . . . how you *can* "take care", if you don't know how.'

At this outlandish persistence Alice drew a heavy sigh. 'But, child, there's surely something in you . . . at least if there isn't there ought to be . . . that tells you what's skylarking and what isn't? Just you think of undressing. Suppose you began to take your clothes off in front of somebody, somebody who was a stranger to you, wouldn't something in you stop you by saying: it isn't done, it's not NICE?'

'Gracious, yes!' cried Trixie hotly. 'I should think so indeed!' (Though she could not imagine herself *beginning*.) But here, for some reason, what Alice had said about a husband who snored came back to her, and got tangled up with the later question.

'But, Dallie, you have to . . . do that, take your clothes off . . . haven't you? . . . If you . . . sleep in the same bed with somebody,' was what she wanted to say, but the words simply would not come out. Alice understood.

'But *only* if you're married, Trixie! And then, it's different. Then everything's allowed, my dear. Once you're married, it doesn't matter what you do.'

'Oh, doesn't it?' echoed Trixie feebly, and her cheeks turned so hot that they scorched. For at Alice's words horrid things, things she was ashamed even to think, came rushing into her mind, upsetting everything she had been taught or told since she was a little child. But SHE wouldn't be like that, no, never, no matter how much she was married; there would always be something in *her* that would say 'Don't, it's not nice.'

A silence followed, in which she could hear her own heart beating. Then, out of a kind of despair, she asked: 'Oh, *why* are men and women, Dallie? Why have they got to be?'

'Well now, really'!' said Alice, startled and sincerely shocked. 'I hope to goodness you're not going to turn irreligious, and begin criticising what God has done and how He's made us?'

'Of course not! I know everything He does is right,' vowed Trixie, the more hotly because she couldn't down the naughty thought: if He's got all that power, then I don't see why He couldn't have arranged things differently, let them happen without . . . well, without all this bother . . . and so many things you weren't supposed to know . . . and what you were allowed to, so . . . so unpleasant. Yes, it *was* unpleasant, when you thought of undressing . . . and the snores . . . and—and everything. And then quite suddenly and disconcertingly came a memory of Alice sitting looking into the fire, telling about her sweetheart. She had never known before that Alice was so pretty, with dimples round her mouth, and her eyes all shady. Oh, could it mean that . . . yes, it must: Alice simply didn't *mind*.

Almost as if this thought had passed to her, Alice said: 'Just you wait till you fall in love, Trix, and then it'll be different—as different as chalk from cheese. Then you'll be only too glad, my dear, that we're not all the same—all men or all women. Love's something that goes right through you, child. I couldn't even begin to describe it—and you wouldn't understand it if I did—but once you're in love, you can't think of anything else, and it gives you such a strange feeling here that it almost chokes you!' And laying one hand over the other on the place where she believed her heart to be, Alice pressed hard.

'Why, only to be in the same room with him makes you happy, and if you know he's feeling the same, and that he likes to look at you and to hold your hand—oh, Trix, it's just Heaven!'

I do believe she'd even like him snoring, thought Trixie in dismay. (But perhaps it was only *old* men who snored.) Confused and depressed, she could not think of anything to reply.

Alice did not speak again either, and there was a long silence, in which, though it was too dark to see her, Trixie guessed she would have the same funny little smile round her mouth and the same funny half-shut eyes, from thinking about George. Oh dear! What a muddle everything was.

'But come!' cried Alice, starting up from her dreams. 'To bed and to sleep with you, young woman, or we shall never get you up in time for the morning coach. Help yourself to a couple of cheesecakes . . . we can eat them as we go.'

Tartlets in hand, back they stole along the moon-blanched verandah; back past the row of dark windows, past the chromatic snores—to Trixie's ears these had now a strange and sinister significance—guided by a moon which, riding at the top of the sky, had shrunk to the size of a pippin.

POSSUM GULLY

MILES FRANKLIN
(EXCERPT FROM *MY BRILLIANT CAREER*)

I WAS NEARLY NINE summers old when my father conceived the idea that he was wasting his talents by keeping them rolled up in the small napkin of an out-of-the-way place like Bruggabrong and the Bin Bin stations. Therefore he determined to take up his residence in a locality where he would have more scope for his ability. He gave up Bruggabrong, Bin Bin East and Bin Bin West, bought Possum Gully, a small farm of one thousand acres, and brought us all to live near Goulburn.

Here we arrived one autumn afternoon. Father, mother, and children packed in the buggy, myself, and the one servant-girl, who had accompanied us, on horseback. The one man father had retained in his service was awaiting our arrival. He had preceded us with a bullock-drayload of furniture and belongings, which was all father had retained of his household property. Just sufficient for us to get along with, until he had time to settle and purchase more, he said.

That was ten years ago, and that is the only furniture we possess yet—just enough to get along with. My first impression of Possum Gully was bitter disappointment—an impression which time has failed to soften or wipe away. How flat, common, and monotonous the scenery appeared after the rugged peaks of the Timlinbilly Range!

We had been resident in our new quarters nearly a month when my parents received an intimation from the teacher of the public school, two miles distant, to the effect that the law demanded that they should send their children to school. It upset my mother greatly. What was she to do?

'Do! Bundle the nippers off to school as quickly as possible, of course,' said my father.

My mother objected. She proposed a governess now and a good boarding school later on. She had heard such dreadful stories of public schools! It was terrible to be compelled to send her darlings to one; they would be ruined in a week!

'Not they,' said father. 'Run them off for a week or two, or a month at the outside. They can't come to any harm in that time. After that we will get a governess. You are in no state of health to worry about one just now, and it is utterly impossible that I can see about the matter at present. I have several specs on foot that I must attend to. Send the youngsters to school down here for the present.'

We went to school, and in our dainty befrilled pinafores and light shoes were regarded as great swells by the other scholars. They for the most part were the children of very poor farmers, whose farm earnings were augmented by roadwork, wood-carting, or any such labour which came within their grasp. All the boys went barefooted, also a moiety of the girls. The school was situated on a wild scrubby hill, and the teacher boarded with a resident a mile from it. He was a man addicted to drink, and the parents of his scholars lived in daily expectation of seeing his dismissal from the service.

It is nearly ten years since the twins (who came next to me) and I were enrolled as pupils of the Tiger Swamp public school. My education was completed there; so was that of the twins, who are eleven months younger than I. Also my other brothers and sisters are quickly getting finishedwards; but that is the only school any of us have seen or known.

All our neighbours were very friendly; but one in particular, a James Blackshaw, proved himself most desirous of being comradely with us. He was a sort of self-constituted sheik of the community.

It was usual for him to take all newcomers under his wing, and with officious good nature endeavour to make them feel at home.

He called on us daily, tied his horse to the paling fence beneath the shade of a sallie-tree in the backyard, and when mother was unable to see him he was content to yarn for an hour or two with Jane Haizelip, our servant-girl.

Jane disliked Possum Gully as much as I did. Her feeling being much more defined, it was amusing to hear the flat-out opinions she expressed to Mr Blackshaw, whom, by the way, she termed 'a mooching hen of a chap'.

'I suppose, Jane, you like being here near Goulburn, better than that out-of-the-way place you came from,' he said one morning as he comfortably settled himself on an old sofa in the kitchen.

'No jolly fear. Out-of-the-way place! There was more life at Bruggabrong in a day than you crawlers 'ud see here all yer lives,' she retorted with vigour, energetically pommelling a batch of bread which she was mixing.

'Why, at Brugga it was as good as a show every week. On Saturday evening all the coves used to come in for their mail. They'd stay till Sunday evenin'. Splitters, boundary riders, dogtrap-pers—every manjack of 'em. Some of us wuz always good fer a toon on the concertina, and the rest would dance. We had fun to no end. A girl could have a fly round and a lark or two there I tell you; but here,' and she emitted a snort of contempt, 'there ain't one bloomin' feller to do a mash with. I'm full of the place. Only I promised to stick to the missus a while, I'd scoot tomorrer. It's the dead-and-alivest hole I ever seen.'

'You'll git used to it by and by,' said Blackshaw.

'Used to it! A person 'ud hev to be brought up onder a hen to git used to the dullness of this hole.'

'You wasn't brought up under a hen, or it must have been a big Bramer Pooter, if you were,' replied he, noting the liberal proportions of her figure as she hauled a couple of heavy pots off the fire. He did not offer to help her. Etiquette of that sort was beyond his ken.

'You oughter go out more and then you wouldn't find it so dull,' he said, after she had placed the pots on the floor.

'Go out! Where 'ud I go to, pray?'

'Drop in an' see my missus again when you git time. You're always welcome.'

'Thanks, but I had plenty of goin' to see your missus last time.'

'How's that?'

'Why, I wasn't there harf an hour wen she had to strip off her clean duds an' go an' milk. I don't think much of any of the men around here. They let the women work too hard. I never see such a tired wore-out set of women. Why, on Bruggabrong the women never had to do no outside work, only on a great pinch wen all the men were away at a fire or a muster. Down here they do everything. They do all the milkin', and pig-feedin', and poddy-rarin'. It makes me feel fit to retch. I don't know whether it's because the men is crawlers or whether it's dairyin'. I don't think much of dairyin'. It's slavin', an' delvin', an' scrapin' yer eyeballs out from mornin' to night, and nothink to show for your pains; and now you'll oblige me, Mr Blackshaw, if you'll lollop somewhere else for a minute or two. I want to sweep under that sofer.'

This had the effect of making him depart. He said good morning and went off, not sure whether he was most amused or insulted.

* * *

While mother, Jane Haizelip and I found the days long and life slow, father was enjoying himself immensely. He had embarked upon a lively career—that gambling trade known as dealing in stock.

When he was not away in Riverina inspecting a flock of sheep, he was attending the Homebush Fat Stock Sales, rushing away out to Bourke, or tearing off down the Shoalhaven to buy some dairy heifers. He was a familiar figure at the Goulburn saleyards every Wednesday, always going into town the day before and not returning till a day, and often two days, afterwards.

He was in great demand among drovers and auctioneers; and in the stock news his name was always mentioned in connection with all the principal sales in the colony.

It takes an astute, clear-headed man to keep himself off shore in stock dealing. I never yet heard of a dealer who occasionally did not temporarily, if not totally, go to the wall.

He need not necessarily be downright unscrupulous, but if he wishes to profit he must not be overburdened with niceties in the point of honour. That is where he fell through. He was crippled with too many Utopian ideas of honesty, and was too soft ever to come off anything but second-best in a deal. He might as well have attempted to make his fortune by scraping a fiddle up and down Auburn Street, Goulburn.

His dealing career was short and merry. His vanity to be considered a socialistic fellow, who was as ready to take a glass with a swaggie as a swell, and the lavish shouting which this principle incurred, made great inroads on his means. Losing money every time he sold a beast, wasting stamps galore on letters to endless auctioneers, frequently remaining in town half a week at a stretch, and being hail-fellow to all the spongers to be found on the trail of such as he, quickly left him on the verge of bankruptcy. Some of his contemporaries say it was grog that did it all.

Had he kept clear-headed he was a smart fellow, and gave promise of doing well, but his head would not stand alcohol, and by it he was undermined in no time. In considerably less than a twelve-month all the spare capital in his coffers from the disposal of Bruggabrong and the Bin Bins had been squandered. He had become so hard-up that to pay the drovers in his last venture he was forced to sell the calves of the few milch cows retained for household uses.

At this time it came to my father's knowledge that one of our bishops had money held in trust for the Church. On good security he was giving this out for usury, the same as condemned in the big Bible, out of which he took the text of the dry-hash sermons with which he bored his fashionable congregations in his cathedral on Sundays.

Father took advantage of this Reverend's inconsistency and mortgaged Possum Gully. With the money thus obtained he started once more and managed to make a scant livelihood and pay the interest on the bishop's loan. In four or five years he had again reached loggerheads. The price of stock had fallen so that there was nothing to be made out of dealing in them.

He resolved to live as those around him—start a dairy; run it with his family, who would also rear poultry for sale.

As instruments of the dairying trade he procured fifty milch cows, the calves of which had to be 'poddied', and a hand cream-separator. I was in my fifteenth year when we began dairying; the twins Horace and Gertie were, as you already know, eleven months younger. Horace, had there been anyone to train him, contained the makings of a splendid man; but having no one to bring him up in the way he should go, he was a churlish and trying bully, and the issue of his character doubtful.

Gertie milked thirteen cows, and I eighteen, morning and evening. Horace and mother, between them, milked the remaining seventeen.

Among the dairying fraternity little toddlers, ere they are big enough to hold a bucket, learn to milk. Thus their hands become inured to the motion, and it does not affect them. With us it was different. Being almost full grown when we started to milk, and then plunging heavily into the exercise, it had a painful effect upon us. Our hands and arms, as far as the elbows, swelled, so that our sleep at night was often disturbed by pain.

Mother made the butter. She had to rise at two and three o'clock in the morning, in order that it would be cool and firm enough to print for market.

Jane Haizelip had left us a year previously, and we could afford no one to take her place. The heavy work told upon my gentle, refined mother. She grew thin and careworn, and often cross. My father's share of the work was to break in the wild cows, separate the milk, and take the butter into town to the grocer's establishment where we obtained our supplies.

Dick Melvyn of Bruggabrong was not recognisable in Dick Melvyn, dairy farmer and cocky of Possum Gully. The former had been a man worthy of the name. The latter was a slave of drink, careless, even dirty and bedraggled in his personal appearance. He disregarded all manners, and had become far more plebeian and common than the most miserable specimen of humanity around him. The support of his family, yet not, its support. The head of his family, yet failing to fulfil the obligations demanded of one in that capacity. He seemed to lose all love and interest in his family, and grew cross and silent, utterly without pride and pluck. Formerly so kind and gentle with animals, now he was the reverse.

His cruelty to the young cows and want of patience with them I can never forget. It has often brought upon me the threat of immediate extermination for volunteering scathing and undesired opinions on his conduct.

The part of the dairying that he positively gloried in was going to town with the butter. He frequently remained in for two or three days, as often as not spending all the money he got for the butter in a drunken spree. Then he would return to curse his luck because his dairy did not pay as well as those of some of our neighbours.

The curse of Eve being upon my poor mother in those days, she was unable to follow her husband. Pride forbade her appealing to her neighbours, so on me devolved the duty of tracking my father from one pub to another and bringing him home.

Had I done justice to my mother's training I would have honoured my paternal parent in spite of all this, but I am an individual ever doing things I oughtn't at the time I shouldn't.

Coming home, often after midnight, with my drunken father talking maudlin conceited nonsense beside me, I developed curious ideas on the fifth commandment. Those journeys in the spring cart through the soft faint starlight were conducive to thought. My father, like most men when under the influence of liquor, would allow no one but himself to handle the reins, and he was often so incapable that he would keep turning the horse round and round in the one place. It is a marvel we never met with an accident. I was not nervous, but quite content to take whatever came, and

our trusty old horse fulfilled his duty, ever faithfully taking us
home along the gum tree-lined road.

My mother had taught me from the Bible that I should honour
my parents, whether they were deserving of honour or not.

Dick Melvyn being my father did not blind me to the fact that
he was a despicable, selfish, weak creature, and as such I despised
him with the relentlessness of fifteen, which makes no allowance
for human frailty and weakness. Disgust, not honour, was the
feeling which possessed me when I studied the matter.

Towards mother I felt differently. A woman is but the helpless
tool of man—a creature of circumstances. Seeing my father beside
me, and thinking of his infant with its mother, eating her heart
out with anxiety at home, this was the reasoning which took
possession of me.

OLD HEINRICH AND THE LAMBING EWE

E.O. SCHLUNKE

YOUNG OTTO WEISMANN WAS riding over the farm, feeling for the first time since his father's death that it really belonged to him. He had a good horse under him and two sheep dogs following, which caught up to him at each gate, generally dripping from some dam or waterhole they had come across, or panting extravagantly and giving him deceitfully pathetic glances because he was making the going so hard.

At each gate Otto thought to himself, 'Now I can shut this or leave it open, just as I please. I can put the wethers into the Big Grass or the Reefton wheat stubble. I can leave the ewes in the Clay Hill stubble or put them on the oats.'

And then he was on his horse again, letting it have its head across the stubble paddock, while he felt the cool autumn air against his face and round his neck where it blew into his open shirt. He watched underfoot trying to see how the trefoil, ball clover, and self-sown wheat were lasting, feeling the softness of the soil under the horse's hooves as an insurance that they would keep on growing for some weeks without further rain.

Up he went over the gentle, rolling rise where the self-mulching red clay caused the horse to labour so that the dogs gained on him and made a hopeful burst as if they expected to catch him. But they quickly fell behind again when down the other side he galloped hard, shouting and waving his arms because a flock of about twenty crows had gathered round a prostrate ewe.

The crows, which had kept so cautiously out of range yesterday when he had a gun, stayed insolently beside the sheep, walking round it with their long, sharp, black beaks stabbing the air with each step.

One even settled on the sheep's head to make a last attempt to maim it by pecking at its eye before Otto, shouting louder and swearing, arrived among them, then it flew away after the rest and settled in a nearby pine tree to watch, still insolent, as if it were confident that it was only a matter of time and it would have the ewe—first its eyes and tongue, then a hole in its chest to get at the heart and lungs, helping other crows to strip off the wool and skin bit by bit, quarrelling and fighting, and feasting so heavily each day that it would hardly be able to fly home.

Otto dismounted and dropped the reins close to him on the ground, remembering that he'd have to keep half an eye on the horse or walk home.

The sheep, which Otto had feared to be dead, so helplessly it had lain on its side on the ground while the crows were around it, now began to throw itself about violently, beating its head on the ground after each futile attempt to rise, so that it bled from the crow pecks around its eyes, and from its nostrils. Otto put his hand on it to quieten it and noticed that it was just about to lamb. It looked a strong, healthy ewe and Otto cursed the crows that took advantage of its temporary weakness.

He rolled the ewe on her side, knowing that the wool underneath would be wet from lying on the damp ground all night, and so heavy that its weight had prevented the sheep from rising. The sheep seemed relieved and stretched its cramped legs. It made a few grunting noises and the lamb's head appeared.

Just then the two dogs arrived, panting demonstratively. Full of curiosity, they ran to the ewe and sniffed at it. The ewe thrashed about in terror, made a frantic effort, got to its feet and ran totteringly, leaning so far over towards its wet side that it ran in a circle, collapsing again a few yards from Otto.

He swore at the dogs, but they refused to take him seriously and, confident in their virtue, came creeping against his legs, casting placatory glances at him while he walked to the sheep. The ewe began to struggle again as it saw the dogs, so Otto gave each a nicely weighed and measured kick, sufficient to convince them he wanted them out of the way, but not enough to send them home offended. He rolled the sheep over again so that the sun could dry its wet side, and looked at the lamb.

It was still in the same position as before and, though the ewe strained and grunted, there was no progress. Otto began to realise that something was wrong. He hadn't much experience with sheep, his father and old Heinrich attending to them in the few years since he'd been home from school, but he recalled a lecture at his agricultural college.

The presentation should take place front feet foremost, with the head resting upon the legs. Clearly the silly lamb had made a mistake, what old Taylor called 'malpresentation'. Otto watched the ewe's struggles and pondered while his horse nibbled at the grass, trailing the bridle. The sheep dogs sat bolt upright a few yards further away, watching too, very bright of eye and knowing, ears pricked and giving little sideways nods with their heads, glancing at each other as if they were sure they could soon put things to rights if they were allowed to go about it their way. Meanwhile they were being very good, only edging a little bit nearer when Otto wasn't watching, or when it seemed he wouldn't mind.

Otto was recollecting. You washed your hands and arms in disinfectant and smeared them with Vaseline. (But while you were away doing that the crows pecked out the eyes of both the ewe and the half-born lamb.) You returned the lamb's head, fished out the front feet one at a time, allowed the head to advance again, pulled very gently and very carefully, and all would be well.

But the ewe had no intention of allowing the lamb's head to be returned; whatever strength she retained she concentrated on resisting retrogression, grunting most outrageously.

Otto desisted. The thing was obviously hopeless; there was something wrong with either the ewe or his instructions. It was

a messy business, too, and the lamb looked as if it were dead. He
didn't know what he should do.

He looked around, and the two dogs came shuffling up to him
on their behinds, as if they could deceive him into thinking they
were still sitting down.

When he said nothing they leapt up with their paws on his
chest, pushing their heads in front of his face to remind him that
they were more important than a miserable half-dead sheep. When
he pushed them away absent-mindedly they raced away in a wide
circle, to stop suddenly, tails erect, hackles bristling, and bark at
something half a mile away at the other end of the paddock—a
bent old man in a sulky with a slow, quiet pony.

That would be old Heinrich. Otto had told him this morning
to go out and mend that fence.

Otto gave a quick look around for his horse and caught it before
it realised he was after it. He galloped across to the tree where
the nearest crows were sitting and waved and shouted until they
flew away, all except the most insolent one, who wouldn't move
though he shouted until the horse began to rear and the dogs
retreated cowering.

Otto dashed past the dogs, kicking his horse for more speed and
looking back at the crows. The dogs leapt out of his way, looked
at each for a moment wonderingly, decided that it was a lark, and
went bounding after him in great glee.

Old Heinrich was so absorbed in his fencing job that it took
quite a while to make him understand that the morning's order
was being countermanded. He was a tall, thin old man with
shoulders stooped from much hard work, mild, trustful blue
eyes and a long, aquiline nose, that would probably have looked
aristocratic if he'd had the etceteras to go with it. His face was
long and furrowed and he had an Adam's apple and a lot of loose
wrinkled skin about the neck.

When old Heinrich understood about the ewe he looked worried
and began to stare about anxiously for the sheep with his short-
sighted old eyes. Otto said, 'Follow me,' and was off, and after a

few moments of hesitation the old man clambered into the sulky and flicked the pony into a sedate trot.

The crows were flying back. Otto pounded with his heels until he could feel the compulsive effort of the horse's strong muscles with each bound. He began to shout when he was still two hundred yards away, but now he didn't feel so desperately savage with them. He remembered his father saying, 'Old Heinrich's the best man with lambing ewes I ever saw.'

The crows departed reluctantly, and fortunately they hadn't had time to do further damage. Old Heinrich arrived, climbed creakily out of the sulky and stood looking, making some clucking noises with his tongue. The dogs, who had enjoyed themselves chasing the crows away, now returned and made an enthusiastic rush at the men, past the sheep's nose.

The ewe made a desperate plunge, got to its feet and, because it was starting to dry, managed to run off, though rather erratically. Otto chased it but soon realised that he couldn't catch it without what would be a cruelly gruelling race to the ewe in its present condition. He stopped and looked at Heinrich.

Old Heinrich looked aside and rubbed a hand over his face, embarrassed. He didn't know how to behave in the face of his young employer's dreadful faux pas.

'What will we do now?' asked Otto. 'We can't let her run around like that.'

Old Heinrich made an 'ah-rrr' noise in his throat and seemed all at sea. Obviously when he attended to the sheep no distressed ewe was ever sent flying in a panic. But the dogs were sure they knew what to do. Their forepaws were on Otto's thighs and they looked into his face, trying to make him understand. Then they made little runs in the direction of the ewe, only waiting for a word of consent.

Otto said to Heinrich, 'I believe it would be best to let the dogs catch her. Better than letting her stagger about like that.'

The dogs tore off without waiting for more. Otto gave a yell and a whistle, but they pretended not to hear him. They headed off the ewe and, because she wouldn't turn, they got annoyed and tackled her. One grabbed her by the dewlap and the other got a grip on the wool at her flank. She soon toppled and the dogs stood over her, half pleased and half surprised that it had happened so easily.

Otto came up at a run, scolding the dogs whenever one gave a tentative tug at her wool. Heinrich followed, with long strides to make the pace, because he couldn't move his limbs quickly.

Otto sent the dogs away and Heinrich knelt beside the ewe.

'We'll hafter get his legs out,' he said.

'Our veterinary lecturer,' Otto commented, 'said you had to push the head back first.'

Heinrich stopped and a look of acute distress came across his face.

'I always used to just get the legs out,' he confessed, now utterly at a loss, because he was a very humble old fellow.

'You do it your way,' Otto encouraged him. 'Dad always said there wasn't a better man with lambing ewes than you.'

Heinrich turned to the ewe to hide a slow delighted smile, hesitated a moment and half turned back again, then made up his mind and put his hands on the sheep with a sure, confident touch. In a couple of minutes he was pulling gently on the lamb's forelegs and it came away easily.

The ewe gave a great sigh of relief and lay quietly, breathing quickly and deeply, its flanks rising and falling so much that the fleece opened up and closed with each breath.

'Nice work, Heinrich,' said Otto. 'It's a pity the lamb's dead, though.'

He picked up the lamb with his hand under its chest and it hung limply down each side of his hand like a wet dish rag. Old Heinrich looked at it with his wrinkled face puckered up but said nothing.

Then, suddenly, the lamb's legs began to squirm; it stiffened its body and drew in a deep breath, then it gave a sneeze, shook its head and opened its eyes.

Otto and Heinrich looked at each other. And both smiled with wonder and pleasure. Otto set the lamb on its legs and it stood there, swaying precariously, with its head hanging low.

'My word, that was marvellous!' Otto exclaimed. 'Coming to life in my hand like that!'

And old Heinrich grinned away to himself, not saying a word to indicate that he'd known all along that there was a good chance of its being alive.

They stood there for a while, the old man and the young, listening to the ewe's heavy breathing, watching the lamb moving its head slowly, searchingly, from side to side and edging gradually towards the ewe, though it clearly didn't understand how it contrived to walk, impelled by the strong instinct of the young animal seeking its mother.

Presently the ewe's breathing eased. It began to roll its eyes round at the men and the dogs and the horses. It made a sudden attempt to rise, but Heinrich caught it by the wool.

'A, steady there,' he said, and the ewe lay down again. He turned to Otto.

'When they've had trouble like this, they'll often run for their lives and leave the lamb and never come back.' He added after a moment, 'She's been so scared.'

He picked up the lamb and put it where the ewe would see it, but the ewe threw itself about in alarm and tried to get up and run.

'It'll want a lot of watching,' he said.

So they stayed there under the pleasant autumn sun while an aeroplane changed from a tiny spot in the south to roar over them and dwindle to a speck in the north. Heinrich stood the ewe on her legs and held her while she swayed. Whenever he let go she tried to leap away. Otto put the lamb in front of her again but she backed away from it, even though it smelt confidently at her and gave the first feeble little wag of its tail.

Old Heinrich said 'ah-rrr' a couple of times, then remarked apologetically, 'All these people and horses and dogs around it.'

So Otto said, 'I'll go and look over the Kurrajong and Trungley paddocks. I'll leave her to you and call back to see how you get on.'

He jumped on his horse and the dogs raced after him, delighted that all the tedious hanging around was over.

* * *

When Otto returned half an hour later old Heinrich was working at the fence again. He rode over towards the ewe and stopped at the top of the rise as soon as she came into view.

She stood up sturdily now, sniffing at the lamb, which was nuzzling speculatively along her flank, giving little forward butts now and then, in the grip of another strong instinct that was leading it blindly to its mother's udder.

When the ewe saw Otto she became stiff with hostility. She held up her head, walked protectively in front of her lamb and stamped with her front feet.

Otto chuckled to himself. His dogs arrived and looked about wonderingly, standing on their hind legs to get a better view.

Then Otto was off at a gallop, pulling hard on the rein against the strong curve of his horse's neck. He felt extraordinarily uplifted, far more than the mere saving of a ewe and its lamb justified. As he bounded along through the breaking wheat stubble, with the horse's hooves dubbing soundlessly in the soil and his dogs following cunningly in the wake the horse had cleared, he felt that somehow this morning he had caught more than a glimpse of the grandeur of life. He saw old Heinrich looking across at him and he waved an arm in cheerful greeting.

Old Heinrich stared after him for a long time, wondering if he was supposed to do something.

'SUCCESS'

JAMES LISTER CUTHBERTSON

The apple on the topmost tree
That ripens rosy red
Is ever fairer when we see
It hanging overhead.

But when, with many a weary fall,
At length we grasp the prize,
The longed-for treasure loses all
Its beauty in our eyes.

Ah! Could we know our happiness
Is not in what we gain,
But in the struggle and the stress,
The effort to attain.

The patient heart, the steady toil,
Not one triumphant feat,
Alone can lift us from the soil,
And make life's labour sweet.

Part 9

THE LOST SOULS' HOTEL

The bush was, and probably still is, inhabited by many lost souls. In the earliest days of European settlement convict shepherds were forced to live a solitary life in an alien environment, existing on the standard shepherds' monthly rations of 'ten-ten-two-and-a-quarter'. Ten pounds of meat, ten of flour, two of sugar and a quarter pound of tea became the standard ration for boundary riders and other station employees working in isolation away from the company of others.

Often the ration-cart driver was the only living soul these men would talk to in a month.

There are, however, many who endure the isolated life in the bush by choice, for reasons often known only to themselves, like the old man in 'A Letter from Colleen'. The bush can be a refuge from many things.

Isolation is not the only form of loneliness experienced by those who live in the bush. Distance from major cities has always led to a lack of amenities, communication and services in rural Australia. This still exists to an extent today, but was far worse in Lawson's day, as the poignant story of the bushman in 'Going Blind' relates.

The passing of time makes us all 'lost souls' and the wonderful Brian James story 'Bring Your Fiddle, Joe', in which a single, seemingly inconsequential life is endowed with respect, dignity

and sadness, is a moving and nostalgic tribute to the old values
that existed in small-town communities between the wars.

Small-town rivalries and squabbles are part of the sub-plots of
both 'A Letter from Colleen' and 'Bring Your Fiddle, Joe' but the
full-blown consequences of small-town small-mindedness and
partisanship are the main subject of another beautifully observed
story from Brian James, 'The Hagney Affair'.

This section concludes, appropriately, with several of Lawson's
stock characters daydreaming and yarning about the perfect resting
place for the 'lost souls' of the bush. Of course, as we expect from
Lawson, the champion of lost souls and lost causes, mateship
features heavily in the fabian dream of a place where 'lost souls'
might be at peace.

'AFTER MANY YEARS'

HENRY KENDALL
(EXCERPT)

The song that once I dreamed about, the tender, touching thing,
As radiant as the rose without the love of wind and wing—
The perfect verses to the tune of woodland music set,
As beautiful as afternoon, remain unwritten yet.

It is too late to write them now; the ancient fire is cold;
No ardent lights illume the brow as in the days of old.
I cannot dream the dream again; but, when the happy birds
Are singing in the sunny rain, I think I hear its words.

I think I hear the echo still of long-forgotten tones,
When evening winds are on the hill and sunset fires the cones.
But only in the hours supreme with songs of land and sea,
The lyrics of the leaf and stream, this echo comes to me.

There is a river in the range I love to think about:
Perhaps the searching feet of change have never found it out.
Ah! Oftentimes I used to look upon its banks and long
To steal the beauty of that brook and put it in a song.

* * *

Ah! Let me hope that in that place the old familiar things,
To which I turn a wistful face, have never taken wings.

Let me retain the fancy still that, past the lordly range,
There always shines, in folds of hill, one spot secure from change!

No longer doth the earth reveal her gracious green and gold:
I sit where youth was once and feel that I am growing old.
The lustre from the face of things is wearing all away:
Like one who halts with tired wings, I rest and muse today.

* * *

But in the night, and when the rain the troubled torrent fills,
I often think I see again the river in the hills.
And when the day is very near, and birds are on the wing,
My spirit fancies it can hear the song I cannot sing.

'BRING YOUR FIDDLE, JOE'

'BRIAN JAMES'
(JOHN TIERNEY)

'BRING YOUR FIDDLE, JOE! You won't forget your fiddle?' they used to say through many a year, just as if Joe would come and not bring his fiddle.

'Tuesday night, Joe, down at Mason's barn! Great turnout! Bring your fiddle, Joe!'

And Joe's answer was an invariable formula, 'I'll be there at seven o'clock, sharp.'

Or it may have been a 'hop' at The Gap, or a 'shivoo' at Riley's, or a 'ball' in the new School of Arts at Round Swamp. But it was all one, Joe and his fiddle must be there. And at seven o'clock sharp Joe would tie up the quietest and fattest and most contented of mokes to a tree or a stump or a fence, as the case may be, and shuffle into the barn, or shed, or 'big room', or hall, or whatever it was, fiddle in an old green baize bag under his arm, and he'd smile in his quiet, shy fashion and say, 'Goodnight Mr Mason, and are you well? Goodnight Mrs Mason, and are you well? Goodnight, Sid. Goodnight, Tom, and are you all well?'

And everyone was all well and pleased to see Joe, and said, 'You brought the fiddle, Joe?'

Joe Wilmot lived at Two Rocks. At least, on the very vague boundaries of Two Rocks. Some people reckoned he really belonged to Kilmarnock. It didn't matter so much, no doubt, and Joe didn't mind much, only there are people who are fussy about such matters and they were stout in their claim that Joe lived in Kilmarnock. Anyway, he lived on the farm where he had been born and reared. His father and mother had died long ago, and the rest of the family had gone far and wide. Joe just lived there alone and didn't do much with the farm, although it had kept a big family in the old days.

No one seemed to know how old Joe might be. 'Strike me, now that you mention it, I don't rightly know how old Joe is.' That was Flip Riley. As Flip knew practically everything, it seemed to indicate that Joe's age was one of the mysteries—like the terrible 'yahoo' at Barney's Elbow, or the red light that was seen at times over Sandy McLean's grave.

Flip would ponder deeply, and pucker his forehead, and squint with the efforts of memory, and say at last, 'But, dammitall, I *ought* to know! Let me see: Old Perry Wilmot died fifteen years ago, or was it sixteen? Anyhow, the year I got twelve quid for the bullocks, and Joe was the fourth boy, not counting the two older ones that died, and there was two boys and two girls younger than Joe, not counting the baby girl who died on Palm Sunday, though I don't think the Wilmots worried much about Palm Sunday. And there you are, I'm damned if I can tell you exactly how old Joe ought to be.'

Joe didn't have any age, in a way of speaking. He had always looked the same, and it was hard to imagine him looking any different. His big head was covered with a thick, sandy thatch that no one had ever seen properly trimmed; his face was leathery and durable and set with a rusty moustache that curved right over his mouth and could be sucked without undue stress when Joe was so inclined; very blue eyes with brows that drooped and looked like small models of his moustache; big ears with tussocks growing out of them. His head always seemed to be leaning over his right shoulder, his legs were slightly bandy, and he walked with a stoop. His clothes were always baggy, even his 'going out' suit. And his clothes looked like Joe. If you saw Joe's coat among a thousand others you could pick it out every time. His boots, always polished for dances, had the toes turned up as though they were surprised at something, and between the toes and laces were hills and hollows like the folds of fat on an over-nourished baby.

Joe was not really a farmer, and you could hardly call Joe's place a farm anymore. His heart wasn't in farming. He was a better carpenter. He liked carpentering. Not that he was an expert either, in the city sense of the term, but a town carpenter would have been maddened if he had to work with timber Joe mostly had to use; round stuff—cypress poles—for rafters, battens adzed out of similar poles, and where square timber was needed, Joe trued it up as good as any mill could ever do.

Joe could put up a house fit for anyone—unless perhaps for a squatter or an uppity sort. There are some houses still standing that Joe built—good solid houses, too, though perhaps a little shy of architectural adornments. People liked to have Joe building for them, that is, if they weren't in a hurry. He was very slow, but he did a good job, and he was cheap. He liked working for people in his 'go-easy', independent fashion, yarning as much of the day as he worked, and puffing solemnly at his crooked-stemmed briar, and smelling thoughtfully at a curly-adzed chip now and then as he yarned. It was all no good for his farm, of course, and neighbours' cows got in and ate out the orchard till the only trees left were long stems with bunches of leaves on top of them; and the wheat paddocks were covered with briar bushes, giving a pattern much like a slice of pudding with plenty of raisins in it.

Still, a man can't be everything, and Joe was a public character and rendering an important public service. Not that public service went to Joe's head at all, as it often does with public characters whose service is much less than his. He was not a bit conceited, though he was proud enough, with the humble pride of a true giver. Hardly a week went by but he was reminded, 'Bring your fiddle, Joe.'

Sometimes Joe went to two dances in a week, and had he been so minded he might have made a lot of money. He never asked for money for his playing, and he always looked surprised when it was mentioned after a dance. No one was foolish enough to ask beforehand, 'What do you want for it?' Just as no one would have been rude enough to ask after the dance, 'What's the damage, Joe?'

What Joe would have said or done can only be conjectured, but it is pretty certain he wouldn't have fiddled *there* again.

No, it was a far more delicate matter, and far more delicately handled. If it was at Round Swamp, where Curly Jack Ryan was M.C., Joe would see the crowd getting ready in a most indeterminate fashion to depart, for the crispy smell of dawn would be in the air outside. Curly would say, 'Well, Joe, it's been a great night.' And Joe, with the music of his fiddle still softly in him, would look dreamily pleased.

'And you'll be having a small wee taste of schnapps, Joe, before we go, won't you now? There's just a drop left in the bottle.'

The schnapps was an institution. Joe drank only schnapps or brandy, and very particular he was in such things.

'Well, Curly, only a taste then.'

Curly would pour about a half a tumbler. 'It's about a taste and a half, maybe, Joe.'

Joe would drink half of it slowly, stop, suck his moustache and say, 'I'm glad they all had a good time.' Then he would drink the second half at a gulp.

'Oh, by the way, Joe, the boys asked me to make you a little presentation.'

'What is it, Curly?'

'A little mark of appreciation, Joe. Only this.' Curly held out a sovereign or pound note, 'Just a quid, Joe.'

'No, Curly, I couldn't take *that*.'

'That's what I thought, Joe. But it's not as simple as that. You see, if you don't take it the boys will think you're offended or that you don't think it's enough or you don't really want to play anymore, and they'll be afraid to ask you.'

'It's jolly good of them, Curly, I'm sure. But I don't play for money.'

'And don't we all know it!'

'But the way you put it, Curly, it's different. And I'll take it. Just this time, mind.'

Then Curly would put half a taste more of the schnapps in the tumbler. Or perhaps a shade more than a half. And what with the schnapps and a night of fiddling, and everyone having such a good time, and the boys thinking so much of him, and the fresh, clean smell of morning, and his fat moke having a head too many and twice as many legs as usual, Joe found it a kind and gracious world.

Curly would say, 'Give me the fiddle, Joe,' and lead Joe carefully along. 'Look, Joe, Alec Sims says he wants to ride your horse so that you can go along with the Ritchies in their sociable. Tom Ritchie wants to have a yarn with you.'

It was a palpable subterfuge that always worked. And so Joe went to sleep in the Ritchies' sociable, and played the fiddle, no doubt, in his dreams.

It is not to be supposed that Joe was a brilliant musician. No doubt, really, he wasn't. He couldn't read music if he had tried to. He played by ear, as all the true fiddlers did, and he was, if he had known it, about the last of the fiddlers. Like the minstrels of old, the fiddlers are all gone now. A new world doesn't want fiddlers, and is perhaps by that much the poorer. A new age was dawning, and the good, old, easy world was going to pieces. In every way, that was, and not merely as far as a fiddler was concerned: the motor car was being heard of in distant places—fantastical, of course—but 'They're doing such wonderful things these days!'

Into this planned and ordered world came pianos. Many of the old bush homes got pianos, and the girls, and even the boys sometimes, went into town to learn music at the convent. A violin teacher appeared in Summerlea, 'Professor Karl', who taught his pupils to play stuff that no one could properly understand or appreciate.

A sleek-looking fellow was the 'Professor', and with long smooth black hair that glistened behind his white forehead, with great side-levers to make him look foreign and distinguished; and a big mouth, and paper-thin lips, that moved easily into a grin to show rows of regular white teeth in great numbers, and smooth-shaved all the time, and smelling of toothpaste and hair oil and scented soap; and dressed up with long swallowtails and all, as if he was

ready for a wedding or a funeral. Blast him, and his long white
fingers and his thin contempt for fiddlers and such as played by ear!

But pupils went to him in great numbers, and he said so often,
'Ah, but I must unlearn you then.' And he made a refined clicking
noise, 'tch, tch!', which meant that Joe and all his race of fiddlers
were condemned.

Of course, the professor could play, but the dancing feet of all
the ages were not in any of his smart playing. And he banished
the word 'fiddle' as something uncouth, if not indecent. 'Feedle!
Feedle! You call it the feedle! To me!'

The fiddler was doomed, and along with him, among others,
the old midwife. Trained nurses and private hospitals appeared.
The nurses were efficient, uniformed, and intolerant. Said one
of them, 'We will put an end to all the "Sairy Gamps",' and she
specially mentioned Mrs Want, the midwife.

'Fancy that old Mother Want carrying on so long, driving
around, spring cart, umbrella, black gloves and little white coffin!'

And Mother Want *did* go. She wasn't required anymore, so
she died.

There came, too, the 'qualified' vets. They 'set up' just like
doctors and charged big fees, so that horses and cows and famous
rams and infamous bulls could die a lot more expensively. So Joe
wasn't alone in being pushed from the stage.

What Joe thought of it all he didn't say. But fewer and fewer
were the calls to 'Bring your fiddle, Joe!' He saw, too, the waning
of all the old-time dances, the varsovienne (always pronounced
'vasuvienna') with its 'one, two, three, stop!'; the mazurka, the
polka ('my mother said that I never should . . .'); the schottische; the
waltz, and the 'squares' like the Alberts and the Lancers, with the
M.C. chanting, 'Ladies catch hold of the gentlemen—deedle-dum,
deedle-dum, deedle-dum-dee.'

The old dances were pushed back to the rude ages where
they belonged. The new dances, hoydenish and hugging, were as
indecent to Joe as the too-obvious blandishments of a prostitute.

At the Round Swamp School of Arts the committee installed a
piano, and ran a welter of dances to pay for it. Some of the local

girls, pronounced brilliant by the town teachers of music, now played for the dances, and were burning jealous of each other, and hated each other with an intensity that only genius knows. They were wonderful players, but yet, there was something missing.

'We are holding a dance in the School of Arts on Tuesday, Joe.'

'I'm glad to hear it,' rather wistfully.

'You will be along, won't you, Joe?'

There was still some feeling that Joe's presence was a benediction in itself.

'I'm not so sure. I might be.'

'Aw, do come. And bring your violin, Joe.' This was an afterthought.

Violin! So that was it, was it? Violin! And be asked perhaps to play an 'extra' or two! Joe sucked his moustache, and his blue eyes looked farther than the farthest distance. It was young Bill Ritchie talking to him. One of the Ritchies of all people!

'It will give you a kind of spell, Joe, and give you a chance to have a hop yourself.'

'Yes, Bill, that's very thoughtful of you. And I might, too.'

Joe's eyes looked still farther into the distance. He didn't wish to offend young Bill. But he didn't go on Tuesday night.

The Masons were having big dances all the winter in their 'barn'. They were helping to pay off the church debt, a swollen affair being attacked with great vigour just now. The Masons enjoyed the church debt, for it gave the younger Masons a chance to 'perform'. They supplied wonderful music, with two of the girls learning the piano and one of the boys learning the violin. They didn't even bother to send word to Joe anymore. Just as well, perhaps. The Masons, at least *she* and the young folk, had big ideas. They didn't, like other people, have a 'shed'—they had a 'barn'. They always got in the 'harvest', too, while other people had 'crops'. Small things these to notice, maybe, but they went to show, just the same.

No, Joe wasn't wanted anymore. And fancy Joe dancing, even if they did the old-time dances anymore! Joe never had danced. He had been the grand celibate, the very high priest of dancing. Lesser musicians *had* danced, of course: there had once been an

accordion player at Tipperary, a flash fellow he was, who played
and danced at the same time; the girl hung onto him, and he
played over her shoulder and behind her back. And sometimes
he acted as M.C. as well. That was the lowest debasing of art.
A true fiddler, Joe felt, danced all the time in his own heart, and
he took his joy from the rhythmic swaying couples that translated
his music to motion.

So Joe stayed at home mostly on his 'farm'. He didn't do so
much carpentry either. Contractors from town did nearly all the
jobs now, skilled tradesmen, and very expensive. But they did put
a 'finish' to a job. In any case, people were putting up brick houses
(the Masons, of course, set the fashion there) if they could afford
it, and very often when they couldn't afford it at all.

There was once a vague sort of theory that Joe might marry
and 'settle down'. It was thought that he 'had his eye' on one of
the Hayes girls, the oldest one, Mary. Nothing came of it. True,
Joe went over to the Hayes' house on Sunday afternoons for years
and years, and sometimes on week nights, and he built a shed for
the Hayeses, and put a verandah on their house, and played his
fiddle by the fire at night, tapping out the time with his foot, and
though Mary made better honey cakes and plum cakes and scones
than she had ever done, before or since, there was really nothing
in it. It is hard to know what Mary herself thought of it. Anyway,
she never married anyone in the end.

There were certain 'impediments', though it is doubtful that
Mary would have been 'minding them now' over much. The first
of these was the stark fact that Joe was a 'Prodestan', and 'eats meat
on Friday and all that'. Mrs Hayes was very strict and proper in
the matter of religion. She had said to Mary once, 'Do you think
he would "turn" at all?' And Mary had said, 'I think he would
now, for me.'

There was really not much for Joe to turn from, the Wilmots
never having been strong on formal religion, and even their special
brand of it was a matter for conjecture; part, as Mrs Hayes wisely
pointed out, 'Them wid no convictions at all are always the most
contrary in the very convictions they haven't got at all.'

She had even once or twice sounded out Joe in her own way in this important matter, and found him 'deep as the sea, but wid no depth at all neither', which meant probably that Joe had looked mildly at her with his big blue eyes, said nothing, and sucked his moustache in his absent-minded sort of way. Once she had mentioned that there 'would be a grand mission next week in Summerlea', and 'worth anyone's while, so it was'.

But Joe didn't go to the mission. And Mrs Hayes sighed, and said that even if the religion part of it were right now there were other things nearly as bad, and even a lot worse; which meant Joe's family.

Mrs Hayes, with old Daniel concurring, of course, considered the Hayeses were a cut above the Wilmots, and a pretty big cut too. Not that Joe could help what his mother had been, and him as decent a fellow as you like. It seems that Mrs Wilmot had a 'reputation' that stretched right back to the digging days, and she had only improved 'in *that*' when she had attained her seventieth birthday or thereabouts, even though she still had a 'dirty tongue' and indulged in 'rough talk' that betokened no contrition for what she had been, but only regrets that her age was against her. And when the factory began in Summerlea, she took milk to it, and continued to do so right up till she died, with the manager so often complaining of the bullfrogs in her cans.

All this was bred in the bone, as it were, and a big bar to any close association with such a family, Mrs Hayes felt. The Hayeses might have had their own little misfortunes, but these could easily happen anywhere, and were not a matter of family at all.

One of the Hayes boys, because he was a trifle wild, had got into trouble over a horse, outback somewhere it was; and another had trouble at Crisp's store; and the girl Anna had trouble, too, being 'strayed' by a young fellow in town, who cleared out. But all such things did not detract from the deep and solid quality and respectability of the Hayes family. So, if Joe had been inclined at all, he would have found himself up against a pretty solid impediment. At least, Mrs Hayes often said so.

But Joe hadn't been inclined at all.

Joe started to 'ail' in a gradual and uncomplaining way. He got thin, and his brown leathery skin started to turn a nasty tone of yellow, and his cheekbones began to stand out quite prominently.

'I'm all right, just a bit off colour, that's all,' he would answer to enquiries.

But the general verdict was that 'poor old Joe is pretty crook', and a more discriminating verdict was, 'He's got a growth on his liver, you see if he hasn't.'

Joe got worse, and thinner, and yellower, but he stuck it out on his 'farm', and no one could discover if he suffered much or not. People went to see him, and 'took him a few things' for which he was always grateful, and mostly didn't use. His fiddle, long unused, was in its old green baize bag on the table. It was as much an anachronism as Joe.

At last, Joe had to go to hospital in Summerlea. It was the end really, and he didn't last long there, and his passing didn't matter much either, except perhaps as a sort of satisfaction to the wise ones who had correctly diagnosed the state of his liver.

But somewhere, wherever old fiddlers happen to go, someone of proper understanding and a real memory of things gone forever would surely have asked, 'You've brought your fiddle, Joe?'

GOING BLIND

HENRY LAWSON

I MET HIM IN the Full-and-Plenty Dining Rooms.

It was a cheap place in the city, with good beds upstairs let at one shilling per night. 'Board and residence for respectable single men, fifteen shillings per week.'

I was a respectable single man then.

I boarded and resided there.

I boarded at a greasy little table in the greasy little corner under the fluffy little staircase in the hot and greasy little dining room or restaurant downstairs.

They called it dining rooms, but it was only one room, and there wasn't half enough room in it to work your elbows when the seven little tables and forty-nine chairs were occupied.

There was not room for an ordinary-sized steward to pass up and down between the tables; but our waiter was not an ordinary-sized man, he was a living skeleton in miniature.

We handed the soup, and the 'roast beef one', and 'roast lamb one', 'corn beef and cabbage one', 'veal and stuffing one', and the 'veal and pickled pork', one . . . or two, or three, as the case might be . . . and the tea and coffee, and the various kinds of puddings . . . we handed them over each other, and dodged the drops as well as we could.

The very hot and very greasy little kitchen was adjacent, and it contained the bathroom and other conveniences, behind screens of whitewashed boards. I resided upstairs in a room where there were five beds and one wash-stand; one candlestick, with a very

367

short bit of soft yellow candle in it; the back of a hairbrush, with about a dozen bristles in it; and half a comb, the big-tooth end, with nine-and-a-half teeth at irregular distances apart.

He was a typical bushman, not one of those tall, straight, wiry, brown men of the West, but from the old Selection Districts, where many drovers came from, and of the old bush school; one of those slight active little fellows whom we used to see in cabbage-tree hats, Crimean shirts, strapped trousers, and elastic-sided boots, 'larstins' they called them.

They could dance well; sing the old bush songs indifferently, and mostly through their noses; play the concertina horribly; and ride like . . . like . . . well, they *could* ride.

He seemed as if he had forgotten to grow old and die out with this old colonial school to which he belonged.

They had careless and forgetful ways about them.

His name was Jack Gunther, he said, and he'd come to Sydney to try to get something done to his eyes. He had a portmanteau, a carpetbag, some things in a three-bushel bag, and a tin box. I sat beside him on his bed, and struck up an acquaintance, and he told me all about it.

First he asked me would I mind shifting round to the other side, as he was rather deaf in that ear.

He'd been kicked by a horse, he said, and had been a little dull o' hearing on that side ever since.

He was as good as blind.

'I can see the people near me,' he said, 'but I can't make out their faces. I can just make out the pavement and the houses close at hand, and all the rest is a sort of white blur.'

He looked up: 'That ceiling is a kind of white, ain't it? And this,' tapping the wall and putting his nose close to it, 'is a sort of green, ain't it?'

The ceiling might have been whiter.

The prevalent tints of the wallpaper had originally been blue and red, but it was mostly green enough now, a damp, rotten green; but I was ready to swear that the ceiling was snow and that the walls were as green as grass if it would have made him feel more comfortable.

His sight began to get bad about six years before, he said; he didn't take much notice of it at first, and then he saw a quack, who made his eyes worse.

He had already the manner of the blind, the touch of every finger, and even the gentleness in his speech. He had a boy down with him, a 'sorter cousin of his', and the boy saw him round.

'I'll have to be sending that youngster back,' he said. 'I think I'll send him home next week. He'll be picking up and learning too much down here.'

I happened to know the district he came from, and we would sit by the hour and talk about the country, and chaps by the name of this and chaps by the name of that, drovers mostly, whom we had met or had heard of.

He asked me if I'd ever heard of a chap by the name of Joe Scott, a big sandy-complexioned chap, who might be droving; he was his brother, or, at least, his half-brother, but he hadn't heard of him for years; he'd last heard of him at Blackall, in Queensland; he might have gone overland to Western Australia with Tyson's cattle to the new country.

We talked about grubbing and fencing and digging and droving and shearing, all about the bush, and it all came back to me as we talked.

'I can see it all now,' he said once, in an abstracted tone, seeming to fix his helpless eyes on the wall opposite. But he didn't see the dirty blind wall, nor the dingy window, nor the skimpy little bed, nor the greasy wash-stand; he saw the dark blue ridges in the sunlight, the grassy sidings and flats, the creek with clumps of she-oak here and there, the course of the willow-fringed river below, the distant peaks and ranges fading away into a lighter azure, the granite ridge in the middle distance, and the rocky rises, the stringybark and the apple-tree flats, the scrubs, and the sunlit plains . . . and all.

I could see it, too, plainer than ever I did.

He had done a bit of fencing in his time, and we got talking about timber.

He didn't believe in having fencing posts with big butts; he reckoned it was a mistake.

'You see,' he said, 'the top of the butt catches the rain water and makes the post rot quicker. I'd back posts without any butt at all to last as long or longer than posts with 'em, that's if the fence is well put up and well rammed.'

He had supplied fencing stuff, and fenced by contract, and, well, you can get more posts without butts out of a tree than posts with them. He also objected to charring the butts.

He said it only made more work, and wasted time, the butts lasted longer without being charred.

I asked him if he'd ever got stringybark palings or shingles out of mountain ash, and he smiled a smile that did my heart good to see, and said he had.

He had also got them out of various other kinds of trees.

We talked about soil and grass, and gold-digging, and many other things which came back to one like a revelation as we yarned.

He had been to the hospital several times.

'The doctors don't say they can cure me,' he said, 'they say they might be able to improve my sight and hearing, but it would take a long time, anyway, the treatment would improve my general health. They know what's the matter with my eyes,' and he explained it as well as he could.

'I wish I'd seen a good doctor when my eyes first began to get weak; but young chaps are always careless over things. It's harder to get cured of anything when you're done growing.'

He was always hopeful and cheerful.

'If the worst comes to the worst,' he said, 'there's things I can do where I come from. I might do a bit o' wool-sorting, for instance. I'm a pretty fair expert. Or else when they're weeding out I could help. I'd just have to sit down and they'd bring the sheep to me, and I'd feel the wool and tell them what it was, being blind improves the feeling, you know.'

He had a packet of portraits, but he couldn't make them out very well now. They were sort of blurred to him, but I described them and he told me who they were.

'That's a girl o' mine,' he said, with reference to one, a jolly, good-looking bush girl.

'I got a letter from her yesterday. I managed to scribble something, but I'll get you, if you don't mind, to write something more I want to put in on another piece of paper, and address an envelope for me.'

Darkness fell quickly upon him now, or, rather, the 'sort of white blur' increased and closed in. But his hearing was better, he said, and he was glad of that and still cheerful.

I thought it natural that his hearing should improve as he went blind.

One day he said that he did not think he would bother going to the hospital anymore. He reckoned he'd get back to where he was known. He'd stayed down too long already, and the 'stuff' wouldn't stand it. He was expecting a letter that didn't come.

I was away for a couple of days, and when I came back he had been shifted out of the room and had a bed in an angle of the landing on top of the staircase, with the people brushing against him and stumbling over his things all day on their way up and down.

I felt indignant, thinking that, the house being full, the boss had taken advantage of the bushman's helplessness and good nature to put him there. But he said that he was quite comfortable.

'I can get a whiff of air here,' he said.

Going in next day I thought for a moment that I had dropped suddenly back into the past and into a bush dance, for there was a concertina going upstairs.

He was sitting on the bed, with his legs crossed, and a new cheap concertina on his knee, and his eyes turned to the patch of ceiling as if it were a piece of music and he could read it.

'I'm trying to knock a few tunes into my head,' he said, with a brave smile, 'in case the worst comes to the worst.'

He tried to be cheerful, but seemed worried and anxious.

The letter hadn't come.

I thought of the many blind musicians in Sydney, and I thought of the bushman's chance, standing at a corner swanking a cheap concertina, and I felt sorry for him.

I went out with a vague idea of seeing someone about the matter, and getting something done for the bushman, of bringing a little influence to his assistance; but I suddenly remembered that my clothes were worn out, my hat in a shocking state, my boots burst, and that I owed for a week's board and lodging, and was likely to be thrown out at any moment myself; and so I was not in a position to go where there was influence.

When I went back to the restaurant there was a long, gaunt, sandy-complexioned bushman sitting by Jack's side.

Jack introduced him as his brother, who had returned unexpectedly to his native district, and had followed him to Sydney.

The brother was rather short with me at first, and seemed to regard the restaurant people, all of us, in fact, in the light of spielers who wouldn't hesitate to take advantage of Jack's blindness if he left him a moment; and he looked ready to knock down the first man who stumbled against Jack, or over his luggage, but that soon wore off.

Jack was going to stay with Joe at the Coffee Palace for a few weeks, and then go back up-country, he told me.

He was excited and happy. His brother's manner towards him was as if Jack had just lost his wife, or boy or someone very dear to him. He would not allow him to do anything for himself, nor try to, not even lace up his boot.

He seemed to think that he was thoroughly helpless, and when I saw him pack up Jack's things, and help him at the table and fix his tie and collar with his great brown hands, which trembled all the time with grief and gentleness, and make Jack sit down on the bed whilst he got a cab and carried the trap down to it, and take him downstairs as if he were made of thin glass, and settle with the landlord—then I knew that Jack was all right.

We had a drink together, Joe, Jack, the cabman, and I.

Joe was very careful to hand Jack the glass, and Jack made a joke about it for Joe's benefit. He swore he could see a glass yet, and Joe laughed, but looked extra troubled the next moment.

I felt their grips on my hand for five minutes after we parted.

A LETTER FROM COLLEEN

FRANK DALBY DAVISON

OLD MCSHANE'S SELECTION, WHERE he lived quite alone, was in the middle of the Big Scrub, twelve hundred acres of belah and brigalow, forty feet high and as thick as the hair on a heeler's back, fair in the middle of ten thousand acres of the same class of country. 'He'll have a fine place some day—if ever he gets the land cleared.' That's what people said of him, practical people who had selected in open forest country, or, at most, had selections that were part forest and part scrub.

You reached Mac's selection by a foot track the old boy had hacked for himself; seven miles and never a house once our bit of a township was left behind; just the still twilight of the scrub, with the branches meeting overhead and the wind whispering in them.

I never saw his place, but a lot of talk went around from those who had come on his camp when looking for strayed cattle; and from what I knew of scrub land I could imagine it well enough. He had felled and burnt off four or five acres, and there, in that rich absorbent soil, sheltered from drying winds by the walls of scrub around the clearing, he had raised crops of pumpkins, sweet potatoes, corn, sorghum, cotton, and he was experimenting with tobacco. I gathered that his plot was as neat as a Chinese garden and twice as lush; this in the middle of a dryish summer.

People accepted his dramatic if rather unpractical achievement as a bolster to their own hopes. 'It just shows you what the land will do,' they said. Most likely Old Mac would be able to make some sort of a living for himself, what with growing his own vegetables, keeping some fowls and a pig, potting a scrub turkey now and again, and perhaps doing a little wallaby-scalping in the season; but of the vision that must have taken him into the heart of the Big Scrub, a vision of twelve hundred acres felled and sown to grass, there seemed small likelihood of fulfilment; it would have called for twenty years of a strong young life, and a man would need his feet planted in open country while he tackled the thick stuff.

I met Old Mac first when he came to my place for water. He looked like a scarecrow coming through the bush; a gangling figure, youthful in proportions but moving with the rusty agility of spry old age, his flannel and dungarees faded and patched, the dungarees bagged at the knees and showing an inch of bare shank above the top of his blucher boots. Two seven-pound syrup tins dangled from a big brown hand at the end of a skinny brown arm. Hair like silver fluff stood out below the rim of his shapeless old hat. His face, when he came close, was as kind as I have ever seen, features big and bony, but fine in their massive way, and blue-grey eyes that were startlingly clear and liquid for a man of his years; a dreamy Celt, gentle—as I came later to know—with the gentleness of an old horse.

The weather was dry and the little gilgai on which he had been depending for water had failed; could he take what he needed from my tank until rain fell? It wasn't much to ask; my tank was brim-full, two thousand cubic yards. With his two empty syrup tins, his gaunt physique, his comical get-up, his years, his gentle diffidence, he made me feel ashamedly rich.

The reason he hadn't brought larger vessels, kerosene tins, for instance, was that he wouldn't be able to carry them the four miles across bush to his camp. While the dry spell lasted he came every second day, eking out the water for cooking and washing, a syrup tin each twenty-four hours.

If he saw me about he would turn in my direction to exchange civilities and perhaps have a short yarn before going to the tank to dip his water. Sometimes he would bring a scrub turkey that he had shot, pleased, I could see, to have hit on a way to return a kindness for a kindness.

He had been to America in his youth, and back to Ireland, before coming to Australia, and since then had wandered over a good deal of the Commonwealth. He liked to tell me about Ireland, particularly as he recalled it after that voyage to America, when he had seen it with fresh eyes. I gather—squatting there in the scant shade of a box tree—that Ireland was really the Ireland of picture-book and story.

His was a tale of poor living and high spirits. He told me how, at mealtimes, on the farm where he had worked, the potatoes, with their jackets on, would be dumped straight from the pot, in a heap along the centre of the bare board table; then all would seat themselves, men, women and children, each with a little heap of salt and a pot of buttermilk; and that was the meal. They had to work long hours for it, but holidays were strictly observed, fox hunts and fair days, and there would be nights when the scrape of a fiddle would bring all around to jig and dance. When he told me of these things Old Mac laughed in a tenderly reminiscent way. 'I was happy then,' he said. I don't think he meant that there had not been other times when he was happy; only that his return trip to Ireland was bright among the jewels of recollection.

In Australia, where most of his manhood years had been spent, he had followed a number of occupations, all laborious; farm hand, navvy, mill hand, miner. I couldn't help but feel that his gentle manner and dreamily thoughtful eyes sorted badly with the heavy callings he had followed; callings, it seemed, that had been stages in a laborious journey in search of the foot of the rainbow.

He had tried wheat farming in Western Australia, but with insufficient capital to win in the race against the mortgagee, the implement-maker and the storekeeper. He had ventured once into business, a fuel and produce store in a Sydney suburb, but there wasn't the money in it he had thought, not with motorcars coming in and people turning to gas and electricity. He had tried gold prospecting in north Queensland, but had only made tucker, although—he seemed disinterestedly pleased to report—fellows lower down the creek had struck it rich; an event, I dare say, that served to confirm his belief in the pot of gold at rainbow's end.

I understood how he came to follow a vision into the middle of the Big Scrub.

'You never married, Mac?'

Yes, he had married, but his wife had died years ago, while their only child was still an infant. The child had been brought up by friends. Colleen was her name. It was not a right name, Mac told me, but—with a smile—his wife thought it pretty, along with McShane. Colleen was married now, and living in Melbourne. Her man was doing quite well. That their lives had, in the main, been spent apart didn't prevent Colleen's behaving as a daughter to her father.

'She writes to me every week,' Mac said. He said it half to himself, as if he scarcely expected it to interest me, but found it a nice thought to have in his mind and to speak aloud.

Old Mac's daughter, married and living in Melbourne, was certainly very remote from my range of interests, and I might never have thought of her again but for an incident that gave her some imaginative reality.

It was on a Saturday afternoon, when Mac, who had tramped in from his selection for no other purpose, failed to receive from the stationmaster the expected letter. I had driven to the railhead to pick up mail and also a couple of rolls of wire netting I knew to be waiting for me in the goods shed. The up-train from Wilga-town had arrived, discharged mail and passengers, and the engine was fussing about, pushing trucks up to the shed and carriages over onto the shunting tracks. We, the settlers—thirty or forty of us—were grouped around the open door of the station office, where Grimwade, the stationmaster, was calling names as he delved in the mail bag and brought letters and packages to light.

He was a mean customer, this Grimwade, a petty bureaucrat, and a smooger, to boot. When business brought any of the scrub aristocracy to the station he was more than a model of willingness and eagerness to oblige. 'You've an hour until the train goes, Mrs Brigalow Downs. If you come across to the house, Mrs Grimwade will give you a cup of tea.' 'Would you care to have lunch before starting home, Mr Hereford Bullock?' He was fishing for invitations to the cattle stations beyond the settlement. At the same time, I've seen a settler's wife sitting in the boiling sun in a cart outside the goods shed for half an hour waiting for Grimwade to make his leisurely appearance. You'd think it would be easy to catch him out over something like that; plenty of us were just waiting a chance; but he could always produce the Regulations, and the Regulations, it appeared, could always be interpreted to the inconvenience of the public.

When Grimwade was calling the mail you'd think he had written the letters himself and was now regretting his good nature.

He reached the bottom of the bag. Nearly everyone had withdrawn from about the door except young Harry Marchant, who was squatting near the step, his back to the wall; I, who was waiting for Grimwade to go with me to the goods shed; and Old Mac, who was looking in the door of the office like a dog who had seen dinner disappear without being flung so much as a crust. He was still in hope.

'Nothing for you, Mr McShane,' said Grimwade crisply and, it seemed, not without relish.

'No letters,' said Old Mac brightly, evidently playing the part of a man who wasn't really expecting a letter, but had just happened along, in case there should be one; and he turned away briskly.

It was rather pitiful. I wouldn't have thought a man could have been taken aback so hard, or been so self-conscious about a disappointment that only one or two had noticed. He was like a child that has been publicly slapped but is determined not to cry. He went off with a false jauntiness, streaking straight for home, as if something especially pleasurable awaited him there.

When Grimwade was ready he came from the office, glanced down at the top of young Marchant's head, locked the door with a brisk click, and started with me for the goods shed, ostentatiously jingling the keys from the ring. No doubt he was being rightly obedient to the Regulations in locking the door, but he needn't have been so pointed about it.

He was giving Harry Marchant a jolt. The Marchants were reckoned a bad lot. They weren't settlers, but lived in a big straggling camp on the reserve, a couple of hundred yards from the edge of the township. Beside the parents there were the two sons, two daughters and a couple of children who were claimed by the old lady but were said to be the fatherless offspring of the daughters. They lived by scalping—in season and out—thievery, trickery at bush races, sly grog, and a rare spasm of hard work when all else failed. They owned no cattle and bought no meat, yet always had a full beef cask and a plentiful pot. They were the human raw material of another Kelly episode, and were only saved from social ostracism among us by the entertainment of their daring.

Young Harry flaunted a horse with a faked brand right under the noses of the police, knowing he had been a shade too clever for them; and he had fought Douggie Duncan, one of the biggest men on the settlement, with bare fists for half an hour in the railway trucking yards on a Sunday morning for an old grudge and a purse of five pounds, with the sergeant of police present from an official sense of caution to see that one didn't kill the other outright.

When I returned from the goods shed with Grimwade to sign off for my netting everyone had gone but Harry, who was still squatting with his back to the office wall, staring moodily across the plain. He was in one of his friend-of-no-man moods, a mood in which he was contrarily impelled to seek the company—or at least the presence—of others. Now they had drifted homewards and left him.

As soon as the stationmaster opened the door of the office I noticed an envelope lying face downward on the floor. While he was reaching for the paper I had to sign I picked it up and having turned it over, read the name on it aloud, 'Mr Michael McShane.' It must have fallen unnoticed from the bag. I handed it to Grimwade. He glanced at it, expressed no regret in the matter, but shot it into the box where the leftover mail was kept and grunted, 'He can get it next week,' almost as if matters couldn't have arranged themselves more to his liking.

There was a sound of young Marchant rising to his feet. He stood in the doorway. 'Give it here!' he demanded. 'I'll go after him; poor old coot!'

It was Grimwade's chance to be official, offensive to Harry in strict accordance with the Regulations, and mean all round.

He glanced from the letter to the young man, and then at me. I am not very good in a situation that arises suddenly, but I must have met his glance with an unfriendly look. He handed the letter to Harry and turned again to the business of the docket I had to sign.

Harry winked at me, and a minute later he was mounted and clattering off on the track to McShane's. I saw the last of him through the timber as I climbed into the buckboard to drive home. He would overtake Old Mac something less than halfway along the track to his camp.

I could just see Old Mac stumping along his pad through the scrub, one of the props of his days suddenly missing, feeling forlorn, looking forward to a week of wondering. He would be surprised at hearing hooves coming up behind him on that untravelled track. He would be very happy to think that another man thought well enough of him to do him a good turn like that. And then there would be the letter from Colleen. I imagined Old Mac would be light-hearted that evening, in his lonely camp.

THE HAGNEY AFFAIR

'BRIAN JAMES'
(JOHN TIERNEY)

As a young man, fresh from his native Cork, Father Moran had been counted extraordinarily handsome. In those early days he had pioneered the new parish—nearly as big as all Ireland it was—with an energy as great as his ability.

Not so handsome now, but still remarkable—black waves of hair turning to white, big face growing craggy, mouth growing hard, nose losing its shapeliness and more inclined to resemble the beak of an eagle, figure losing its ease and grace. But the blue eyes—despite occasional use of glasses—were bright; as hard and piercing as ever. The mind was as alert, the memory as retentive, the tongue as eloquent. He was more intolerant, more impatient of opposition, more tyrannical.

He ruled his flock with a calculated harshness. His people admired him, respected him, were even proud of his uniqueness among clerics; but they feared him, and some there must have been who hated him. This proud man had had only two human contacts—two concessions to human needs. One of those had been his friendship with Hagney, the solicitor; the other, his affection for his niece.

Hagney, Matthew Hagney, as became a 'family solicitor', was quietly wealthy, of active middle age, always well groomed, always well attired, silver-grey beard clipped to a neat point. In learning and intellectual quality he came near Father Moran himself. Apart from that they were quite unalike.

The niece, Miss Cathleen Moran, had a family resemblance to her uncle, but was like him in nothing else. She had come out from Ireland long ago to keep house for Father Moran. She was not young, but a fine woman still. She advanced gracefully with the years.

When Father Moran went to Ireland on extended leave Mr Hagney and Miss Moran were married—very quietly.

For some reason Mr and Mrs Hagney did not inform Father Moran either of their intention or of the marriage when it had taken place. No doubt they had good and sufficient reasons, or perhaps they thought to give the good cleric a surprise.

If this last was their object, it succeeded admirably. Father Moran, on his return to the Cookabundy, *was* surprised; and fumed and raged in his surprise. All friendly relations with the Hagneys ceased forthwith, though his real anger was for Hagney.

His years, no doubt, were largely responsible for this unreasonable anger, and for what followed when, Sunday after Sunday, he began to preach sermons in which the word 'clandestine' was rather overworked. The word was pointed at Hagney every time, no matter what the subject might have been. Hagney and his wife ignored the thrusts and sat it out, as it were.

Then very suddenly, Mrs Hagney died. There might have been reconciliation at this point. But there wasn't.

After the first pangs of his loss, Father Moran prayed publicly for his niece, said masses and masses for her, exhorted the congregation to offer fervent prayers for her, introduced her into his sermons, more than hinted at the treachery that had robbed him of her. Still Mr Hagney sat it out—he might not have heard a word for all the sign he gave, staring straight before him, as still as though he were carved in stone.

And then at last, one Sunday when a reference to the evil consequences of a 'clandestine' marriage was too personal and too pointed to be borne, Mr Hagney rose from his seat.

In a voice cold, clear, tremorless, he spoke, 'Father Moran, you have seen fit to attack me Sunday after Sunday, in this our house of worship. While I appreciate the depths of your grief, it must stop now.'

Mr Hagney sat down, and stared before him, still as a rock once more.

No one seemed to breathe; there might not have been a living soul in that church. Perhaps some were tensed for the bolt from heaven that must fall to destroy the holy place now so defiled. Father Moran was turned to statue, a statue with living moveless eyes that were focused forever on Mr Hagney.

Two, three seconds at the most but an age in living; then he turned to the pulpit step, walked slowly down, crossed the sanctuary, seeming to grow smaller, older and crushed beneath some unaccountable burden as he proceeded. Then he sat on his chair, on the gospel side of the altar, while the collection was being taken. He stared, still as a rock, over the sanctuary. It might have all been a dream.

The congregation stirred—guiltily it seemed, as though any movement was added profanation. Breaths were released audibly.

Then the very relief of looking in purses and pockets for coins, the tramp of the collectors down the aisles, and the sounds of threepences and sixpences in the brass plates. When the service was over at last Mr Hagney walked as always from the door to his carriage. He stopped nowhere, nodded to friends and acquaintances, never noticed that every eye was upon him and pretending not to be. He drove off.

Of course, during the week, the event was broached and savoured, but there was no full taste to it, only a sort of astringency like a green persimmon.

Certainly Kelly at the Contingent spoke of it, waiting a fit opportunity when the Protestants might not hear, for he said the Protestants were licking their very lips for it.

'I never did see the like of it,' said Kelly.

Pat Casey bored the eternal blacknailed forefinger into his hairy ear: 'Come what might, Kelly, come what might, Father Moran is God's priest.' This was relevant and pertinent, for Casey had deep within him the vague desire for salvation, and the conviction that, with the aid of Father Moran, he would reach heaven at last, shaggy, beery, dirty, and unkempt; but he would get there, and no doubt something would be done about his appearance and the trimming up of him.

Teddy Clark came in. Teddy 'belonged', and he didn't. A 'sport' and a bookmaker, he hadn't been to church for years. 'Just saw Hagney,' he said, easing his superfluous girth against the bar. 'Looking seedy, too.'

'I doubt if he is Irish at all,' said Pat Casey.

'He don't look Irish at all,' Dinny Regan spoke for the first time. In Dinny was a sturdy pride that he himself looked very Irish. The Irish didn't share in this pride.

'Look at his beard!' said Pat. 'Ever see an Irishman wid a beard like that?'

No one could recall such a thing, now that Pat mentioned it.

'But he's up against it now, if you ask me,' said Teddy.

They all had another drink on the strength of that.

Next Sunday the crowd at the ''leven o'clock' was a record.

And Teddy was a part of that record crowd; so was Dinny Regan; and so were scores of others who found, after varying lapses of time, that the 'ould faith' was still strong within them.

Every seat was taken, every available space for standing at the back was filled and packed.

And then came the surprise. The Bishop of the Diocese was to be the celebrant. The Bishop! Unannounced and never even thought of. He preached, too, a very brief sermon for a bishop who had come hundreds of miles to do it. A mild sermon and kindly—just like the Bishop himself.

But there must be some connection between his visit and the happenings of last Sunday. And there was sure enough. The Bishop was really there to bless the church—or to re-bless it.

Up and down the aisles before Mass went the Bishop and Father Moran and the altar boys. Incense and holy water and the solemn intoning of blessing and dedication.

And all the time Hagney in his place, still alive, still not struck down, still like stone.

'I wonder what Hagney will do now?' said Teddy Clark after the service was over.

'What can he do?'

That summed up all the curiosity, and perhaps some of the anticipation. But what could Hagney do? If he wasn't humiliated now all his pride was a hopeless thing. The victory was with Father Moran.

But all victories have the seeds of defeat in them.

The whole town now began to seethe with real excitement. The inevitable sides were taken. And the excitement—and the cleavage—extended to the district for miles around: the Grey Box, Round Swamp, Two Rocks, Tipperary, Kilmarnock.

There seemed to be more afternoon teas than usual, and the row at the church would invariably be introduced, so very casually as if it wasn't the real reason at all for the afternoon teas. And the row was sweeter than any of the nice cakes that were served.

Then Mr Hagney, Farley Gray, and a few others of influence began a movement to have all church matters—not strictly sacerdotal—brought under the management of a church committee. That was taken as a direct retaliatory measure against the re-blessing of the church.

Two big, separate meetings were held on quite a number of Sundays after mass. One was in the long room at the boys' school, and the other in the long room at the girls' school. Hagney ran one, and Teddy Clark, true member of the fold once more, ran the other.

Hagney's meeting was for the purpose of instituting a church committee, and Teddy Clark's to defend Father Moran from the indignity of having such a committee. Father Moran, of course, attended neither meeting. But he had runners provided for him to carry the latest intelligence.

After the excitement of the meetings many found it necessary to adjourn to the pubs to recover. The Clark party went to the Contingent.

Mrs Kelly was all draped in very expensive, lacy black. Above the level of the bar she was mostly bosom, and a big red face that was hard, calculating and sweaty. She was saying, 'And all he's done for this town—what sort of a place would it be if he hadn't lived here and toiled this forty years?'

Kelly came in at the moment, but Mrs Kelly didn't retire. It was almost like a family gathering; even Pat Casey and Paddy Griffin were snarling at each other.

'It's up to us to show what we really think of him,' said Kelly.

That was a popular sentiment. Teddy Clark took it up. 'You're right, Kelly. You're right. Something in a practical way.'

There were more drinks, and more talk, and Paddy Griffin summed up Pat Casey as a 'shanty Irish', and Teddy Clark told the two of them to be quiet, and 'Drink this up, will you?' and Hagney was damned for his 'flashness', and Farley Gray for his meanness, and Regan, the storekeeper, for not taking sides, and a lot of other people for taking sides—the wrong side. But the germ of an idea began to grow out of Teddy Clark's suggestion of 'something practical'.

As the days went by, and a lot more talk with them, the plan emerged of making a presentation to Father Moran—as a mark of appreciation from half the town for what he had done for the whole town. It would have to be done properly and in a big way.

The sympathetic ear of Mr Trist ('our worthy mayor') was tapped. Mr Trist was delighted at the move. 'All denominational considerations apart, Father Moran has been a big, a useful, an ornamental part of the very life and progress of this town.'

Mr Trist said this on the tapping of his ear, and repeated it at a small but influential meeting he convened. Though Mr Hagney's name was not mentioned, his discomfiture was as much the real purpose of the meeting as anything else. It was not to honour St George, but to gloat over the dragon.

The meeting was in the mayor's room—very secret, for whatever was done was to be a complete surprise to Father Moran. There were many suggestions of suitable presentations, ranging from a portrait in oils to a pair of ponies; from a purse of sovereigns to a memorial drinking fountain.

It was Teddy Clark who said, 'If I may make bold to say it there are people who might not favour a drinking fountain.' Everyone saw the point, and everyone smiled, or would have smiled but for Mrs Hawley-Brett, who was not disposed to be amused at anything said by Teddy Clark.

It was decided finally to present the 'grand old priest' (the quotation is from Mrs Thompson-Watts) with a pair of ponies, their purchase to be left in the capable hands of Mr Clark; and a purse of sovereigns and an illuminated address. And all this to take place at a grand banquet in the Town Hall.

The whole plan was to be kept secret so that Father Moran might not be embarrassed by foreknowledge of it. Of course, Father Moran was almost immediately apprised of every smallest detail.

Teddy Clark and Tim Noonan, from the livery stables, went into conference, and secured a beautiful pair of black ponies at Bardoo. The deal was shrouded in mystery, but there were not wanting those who declared that Teddy and Tim made a handsome thing out of those ponies.

An obscure artist was rescued from his obscurity and brandy and commissioned to 'do' the address, which he did in fine style.

The purse was being every day more heavily loaded with golden sovereigns.

And all the while, the great 'secret' being wide open by now, the other half of the town was joyfully supposed to be writhing in futile rage. But that was a very mistaken view. In the excitement it wasn't noticed at first that though the 'committee push', as it was called, had given up its campaign for church management, it was still very active. Now it was evolving a master plan for making a presentation to Mr Hagney.

'Ah,' said Mr Trist, when he heard of the matter, 'a laudable move in every way. What wouldn't I give to bring together two such outstanding citizens of this town?'

Of course, he meant Father Moran and Mr Hagney, and he was speaking to Farley Gray. Although Farley was anxious to run the whole show himself, he saw that he really belonged to the shire—the perimeter, as it were. He needed the mayor for the more essential centre.

'Of course, you're running the Father Moran presentation. A cheap bit of spite that business is, if you ask me.'

'Laudable, too, Farley; laudable and worthy. A remarkable citizen and a giver of illustrious service.'

'What about Hagney?'

'The very embodiment of all that is best. I stand second to none in my admiration of him.'

Farley Gray let it go at that. He was powerless and speechless before this tower of virtue.

So, without seeking, Mr Trist was the guiding spirit of both presentations. The position was a unique one. Only Mr Trist could have filled it. The waves of bitterness that beat on all the shores never reached Mr Trist: he was above group and party.

The banquet was held in the Town Hall on Thursday evening. Turkeys and sucking pigs and young roosters gladly gave up the joys of living to grace the occasion.

Jellies and blancmanges quivered under the lights; trifles by the ton almost, and no stinting of sherry in them. Long bottles of hock; claret-cup in great bowls; even Summerlea Bing for those who couldn't stand alcohol.

Mr Trist brought in the guest of honour, and the assembly burst spontaneously into 'For he's a jolly good fellow'—after Mrs Thompson-Watts began it in her sweet clear voice.

Father Moran somehow looked older; more careworn. But his eye was bright, his gaze steady. He had, too, the comprehensive eye that took in all without looking at anyone.

There were toasts and speeches and replies, and cheers and hear-hears. The right things were said and duly applauded. 'Our guest' had that very day completed forty-three years of strenuous work in Summerlea. He was a great churchman, a great townsman. There was the customary admiration and the wonted hope of many more years, etc, etc.

Father Moran spoke with feeling but without warmth, and he spoke eloquently. He spoke as priest and citizen, but not as a preacher. He said exactly the right thing and the correct thing.

But he was pleased with the ponies—Tim Noonan had driven him down to the Hall with the pair of blacks. He knew horses, no one in the whole district—not even Tim Noonan, shrewd as he was—knew half as much. In the years gone by there was no better horseman in the district, and certainly no one who looked half as well on a horse. Yes, he could speak of those trotting ponies with a warmth of feeling.

There was no barest hint of Hagney in it at all. But perhaps Hagney was there just the same, a Banquo at the feast.

Over at last, Mrs Hawley-Brett and Mrs Thompson-Watts were taking leave of the Trists.

'What a wonderful occasion!'

'Historic, really!'

'So spontaneous!'

'Not one jarring note!'

The stars looked down on the quiet town, iron roofs faintly showing white and silver in the clear starlight. A silence settled down, that was never quite silence, though the lowing of distant and occasional cows blended with it without disturbing it. The big event was over, and now, as Mrs Thompson-Watts had said, a part of history.

Mr Trist and Farley Gray were interviewing Mr Hagney very soon after in Mr Hagney's office, the roomiest and quietest office in town, in the Town Hall buildings.

'Believe me, Mr Trist, I am deeply grateful, deeply moved. But such has been my life in this town that I couldn't accept, I really couldn't. It's good of you, Farley, too, and perhaps you'll understand better than anyone why I can't.' Mr Hagney smiled ever so little, a weary smile, and it made him look older.

But Farley didn't understand. 'Funking it now!' was all he could think of. He was even inclined to argue, to persuade, to cajole.

Mr Trist interposed, without interrupting. He understood, he said, as he respected the feeling and regretfully bowed to the necessity.

The wan smile appeared again. 'Thank you, Mr Trist.'

So that was that, and a triumph vanished.

Sunday after Sunday, Mr Hagney was in his accustomed place, ornate, solid and unbending. A hundred things might never have been for all he showed of them.

Father Moran preached his eloquent sermons, and attacked Saturday night dances, and State education, and mixed marriages, and immorality, and skimpiness in Christmas and Easter dues. He announced the banns of marriage for the second time—or the third time, and perfunctorily invited all to mention the impediments they might be aware of. He prayed for souls—recently departed, or, anniversaries 'about this time of year'. He railed at the young men who *would* stand at the back of the church when there was room in front.

But he never, by hint or sign or gesture, gave the slightest intimation that he remembered the presentation. He never used the word 'clandestine' again. He never noticed the presence of Mr Hagney.

THE LOST SOULS' HOTEL

HENRY LAWSON

HUNGERFORD ROAD, FEBRUARY. ONE hundred and thirty miles of heavy reddish sand, bordered by dry, hot scrubs. Dense cloud of hot dust. Four wool-teams passing through a gate in a 'rabbit-proof' fence which crosses the road. *Clock, clock, clock* of wheels and rattle and clink of chains, etc., crack of whips and explosions of Australian language. Bales and everything else coated with dust. Stink of old axle grease and tarpaulins. Tyres hot enough to fry chops on; bows and chains so hot that it's a wonder they do not burn through the bullocks' hide. Water lukewarm in blistered kegs slung behind the waggons. Bullocks dragging along as only bullocks do. Wheels ploughing through the deep sand, and the load lurching from side to side. Halfway on a dry stretch of seventeen miles. Big 'tank' full of good water through the scrub to the right, but it is a private tank and a boundary rider is shepherding it. Mulga scrub and sparse, spiky undergrowth.

The carriers camp for dinner and boil their billies while the bullocks droop under their yokes in the blazing heat; one or two lie down and the leaders drag and twist themselves round under a dead tree, under the impression that there is shade there. The carriers look like Red Indians, with the masks of red dust 'bound' with sweat on their faces, but there is an unhealthy-looking, whitish space round their eyes, caused by wiping away the blinding dust, sweat and flies. The dry sticks burn with a pale flame and an almost invisible thin pale blue smoke. The sun's heat dancing and dazzling across every white fencepost, sand hill, or light-coloured object in the distance.

One man takes off his boot and sock, empties half a pint of sand out of them, and pulls up his trouser leg. His leg is sheathed to the knee in dust and sweat; he absently scrapes it with his knife, and presently he amuses himself by moistening a strip with his forefinger and shaving it, as if he were vaguely curious to see if he is still a white man.

The Hungerford coach ploughs past in a dense cloud of dust.

The teams drag on again like a 'wounded snake that dies at sundown', if a wounded snake that dies at sundown could revive sufficiently next morning to drag on again until another sun goes down.

Hopeless-looking swagmen are met with during the afternoon, and one carrier, he of the sanded leg, lends them tobacco; his mates contribute bits o' tea, flour, and sugar.

Sundown and the bullocks done up. The teamsters unyoke them and drive them on to the next water, five miles, having previously sent a mate to reconnoitre and see that the boundary rider is not round, otherwise, to make terms with him, for it is a squatter's bore. They hurry the bullocks down to the water and back in the twilight and then, under cover of darkness, turn them into a clearing in the scrub off the road, where a sign of grass might be seen, if you look close. But the bullockies are better off than the horse teamsters, for bad chaff is sold by the pound and corn is worth its weight in gold.

Mitchell and I turned off the track at the rabbit-proof fence and made for the tank in the mulga. We boiled the billy and had some salt mutton and damper. We were making back for Bourke, having failed to get a cut in any of the sheds on the Hungerford track. We sat under a clump of mulga saplings, with our backs to the trunks, and got out our pipes. Usually, when the flies were very bad on the track, we had to keep twigs or wild turkey tail feathers going in front of our faces the whole time to keep the mad flies out of our eyes; and, when we camped, one would keep the feather going while the other lit his pipe, then the smoke would keep them away. But the flies weren't so bad in a good shade or in the darkened hut. Mitchell's pipe would have smoked out Old Nick; it was an ancient string-bound meerschaum, and strong enough to kill a blackfellow. I had one smoke out of it once when I felt bad in my inside and wanted to be sick, and the result was very satisfactory.

Mitchell looked through his old pocketbook, more by force of habit than anything else, and turned up a circular from Tattersall's. And that reminded him.

'Do you know what I'd do, Harry,' he said, 'if I won Tattersall's big sweep, or was to come into fifty or a hundred thousand pounds, or, better still, a million?'

'Nothing, I suppose,' I said, 'except to get away to Sydney or some cooler place than this.'

'I'll tell you what I'd do,' said Mitchell, talking round his pipe. 'I'd build a Swagman's Rest right here.'

'A Swagman's Rest?'

'Yes. Right here on this very God-forsaken spot. I'd build a Swagman's Rest and call it the Lost Souls' Hotel, or the Sundowners' Arms, or the Halfway House to somewhere, or some such name that would take the bushmen's fancy. I'd have it built on the best plans for coolness in a hot country; bricks, and plenty of wide verandahs with brick floors, and balconies, and shingles, in the old Australian style. I wouldn't have a sheet of corrugated iron about the place. And I'd have old-fashioned hinged sashes with small panes and vines round 'em; they look cooler and more homely and romantic than the glaring sort that shove up.

'And I'd dig a tank or reservoir for surface water as big as a lake, and bore for artesian water—and get it, too, if I had to bore right through to England; and I'd irrigate the ground and make it grow horse-feed and fruit, and vegetables too, if I had to cart manure from Bourke. And every teamster's bullock or horse, and every shearer's hack, could burst itself free, but I'd make travelling stock pay, for it belongs to the squatters and capitalists. All carriers could camp for one night only. And I'd . . . no, I wouldn't have any flowers; they might remind some heart-broken, new chum black sheep of the house where he was born, and the mother whose heart he broke, and the father whose grey hairs he brought down in sorrow to the grave, and break him up altogether.'

'But what about the old-fashioned windows and vines?' I asked.

'Oh!' said Mitchell, 'I forgot them. On second thought, I think I would have some flowers; and maybe a bit of ivy green. The new chum might be trying to work out his own salvation, and the sight of the roses and ivy would show him that he hadn't struck such a God-forgotten country after all, and help strengthen the hope for something better that's in the heart of every vagabond till he dies.'

Puff, puff, puff, slowly and reflectively.

'Until he dies,' repeated Mitchell. 'And, maybe,' he said, rousing himself, 'I'd have a little room fixed up like a corner of a swell restaurant with silver and napkins on the table, and I'd fix up a waiter, so that when a broken-down university wreck came along he might feel, for an hour or so, something like the man he used to be.

'All teamsters and travellers could camp there for one night only. I'd have shower baths; but I wouldn't force any man to have a bath against his will. They could sit down to a table and have a feed off a tablecloth, and sleep in sheets, and feel like they did before their old mothers died, or before they ran away from home.'

'Who? The mothers?' I asked.

'Yes, in some cases,' said Mitchell. 'And I'd have a nice, cool little summer house down near the artificial lake, out of earshot of the house, where the bullock drivers could sit with their pipes after tea, and tell yarns, and talk in their own language. And I'd have boats on the lake, too, in case an old Oxford or Cambridge man, or an old sailor came along, it might put years onto his life to have a pull at the oars. You remember that old sailor we saw in charge of the engine back there at the Government tank? You saw how he had the engine? Clean and bright as a new pin, everything spick and span and ship-shape, and his hut fixed up like a ship's cabin. I believe he thinks he's at sea half his time, and shoving her through it, instead of pumping muddy water out of a hole in the baking scrubs for starving stock. Or maybe he reckons he's keeping her afloat.'

'And would you have fish in this lake of yours?' I asked.

'Oh, yes,' said Mitchell, 'and any ratty old shepherd or sundowner, that's gone mad of heat and loneliness, like the old codger we met back yonder, he could sit by the lagoon in the cool of the evening and fish to his heart's content with a string and a bent pin, and dream he's playing truant from school and fishing in the brook near his native village in England about fifty years ago. It would seem more real than fishing in the dust, as some mad old bushmen do.'

'But you'd draw the line somewhere?' I asked.

'No,' said Mitchell, 'not even at poets. I'd try to cure them, too, with good wholesome food and plenty of physical exercise. The Lost Souls' Hotel would be a refuge for men who'd been gaolbirds once, as well as men who were gentlemen once, and for physical wrecks and ruined drunkards as well as healthy honest shearers. I'd sit down and talk to the boozer or felon just as if I thought he was as good a man as me, and he might be for that matter, God knows.

'The sick man would be kept till he recovered or died and the boozer, suffering from a recovery, I'd keep him till he was on his legs again.'

'Then you'd have to have a doctor,' I said.

'Yes,' said Mitchell, 'I'd fix all that up all right. I wouldn't bother much about a respectable medical practitioner from the city. I'd get a medical wreck who had a brilliant career before him once in England and got into disgrace, and cleared out to the colonies, a man who knows what the DTs is, a man who's been through it all and knows it all.'

'Then you'd want a manager, or a clerk or secretary,' I suggested.

'I suppose I would,' said Mitchell. 'I've got no head for figures. I suppose I'd have to advertise for him. If an applicant came with the highest testimonials of character, and especially if one was signed by a parson, I'd tell him to call again next week; and if a young man could prove that he came of a good Christian family, and went to church regularly, and sang in the choir, and taught Sunday school, I'd tell him that he needn't come again, that the vacancy was filled, for I couldn't trust him. The man who's been extra religious and honest and hardworking in his young days is most likely to go wrong afterwards. I'd sooner trust some poor old devil of a clerk who'd got into the hands of a woman or racing men when he was young, and went wrong, and served his time for embezzlement; anyway, I'd take him out and give him another chance.'

'And what about woman's influence?' I asked.

'Oh, I suppose there'd have to be a woman, if only to keep the doctor on the line. I'd get a woman with a past, one that hadn't been any better than she should have been, they're generally the most kind-hearted in the end. Say an actress who'd come down in the world, or an old opera singer who'd lost her voice but could still sing a little. A woman who knows what trouble is. And I'd get a girl to keep her company, a sort of housemaid. I'd get hold of some poor girl who'd been deceived and deserted: and a baby or two wouldn't be an objection, the kids would amuse the chaps and help humanise the place.'

'And what if the manageress fell in love with the doctor?' I asked.

'Well, I couldn't provide against love,' said Mitchell. 'I fell in love myself more than once, and I don't suppose I'd have been any worse off if I'd have stayed in love. Ah, well! But suppose she did fall in love with the doctor and marry him, or suppose the girl fell in love with the secretary? There wouldn't be any harm done; it would only make them more contented with the home and bind them to it. They'd be a happy family, and the Lost Souls' Hotel would be more cheerful and homelike than ever.'

'But supposing they all fell in love with each other and cleared out,' I said.

'I don't see what they'd have to clear out for,' said Mitchell. 'But suppose they did. There's more than one medical wreck in Australia, and more than one woman with a past, and more than one broken old clerk who went wrong and was found out, and who steadied down in gaol, and there's more than one poor girl that's been deceived. I could easily replace 'em. And the Lost Souls' Hotel might be the means of patching up many wrecked lives in that way—giving people with pasts the chance of another future, so to speak.'

'I suppose you'd have music and books and pictures?' I said.

'Oh, yes,' said Mitchell. 'But I wouldn't have any bitter or sex problem books. They do no good. Problems have been the curse of the world ever since it started. I think one noble, kindly, cheerful character in a book does more good than all the clever villains or romantic adventurers ever invented. And I think a man ought to get rid of his maudlin sentiment in private, or when he's drunk. It's a pity that every writer couldn't put all his bitterness into one book and then burn it.

'No! I'd have good cheerful books of the best and brightest sides of human nature—Charles Dickens, and Mark Twain, and Bret Harte, and those men. And I'd have all Australian pictures—showing the brightest and best side of Australian life. And I'd have all Australian songs. I wouldn't have 'Swannie Ribber', or 'Home, Sweet Home', or 'Annie Laurie', or any of those old songs sung at the Lost Souls' Hotel—they're the cause of more heart-breaks and drink and suicide in the Bush than anything else. And if a jackeroo got up to sing 'Just before the battle, mother', or 'Mother bit me in me sleep', he'd find it was just before the battle all right. He'd have to go out and sleep in the scrub, where the mosquitoes and bulldog ants would bite him out of his sleep. I hate the man who's always whining about his mother through his nose, because, as a rule, he never cared a rap for his old mother, nor for anyone else, except his own paltry, selfish little self.

'I'd have intellectual and elevating conversation for those that . . .'

'Who'd take charge of that department?' I inquired hurriedly.

'Well,' reflected Mitchell, 'I did have an idea of taking it on myself for a while anyway; but, come to think of it, the doctor or the woman with the past would have more experience, and I could look after that part of the business at a pinch. Of course you're not in a position to judge as to my ability in the intellectual line; you see, I've had no one to practise on since I've been with you. But no matter, there'd be intellectual conversation for the benefit of black-sheep new chums. And any broken-down actors that came along could get up a play if they liked, it would brighten up things and help elevate the bullock drivers and sundowners. I'd have a stage fixed up and a bit of scenery. I'd do all I could to attract shearers to the place after shearing, and keep them from rushing to the next shanty with their cheques, or down to Sydney, to be cleaned out by barmaids.

'And I'd have the hero squashed in the last act for a selfish sneak, and marry the girl to the villain. He'd be more likely to make her happy in the end.'

'And what about the farm?' I asked. 'I suppose you'd get some expert from the agricultural college to manage that?'

'No,' said Mitchell. 'I'd get some poor drought-ruined selector and put him in charge of the vegetation. Only, the worst of it is,' he reflected, 'if you take a selector who has bullocked all his life to raise crops on dusty, stony patches in the scrubs, and put him on land where there's plenty of water and manure, and where he's only got to throw the seed on the ground and then light his pipe and watch it grow, he's apt to get disheartened. But that's human nature.

'And, of course, I'd have to have a "character" about the place, a sort of identity and joker to brighten up things. I wouldn't get a man who'd been happy and comfortable all his life; I'd get hold of some old codger whose wife had nagged him till she died, and who'd been sold off many times, and run in for drowning his sorrows, and who started as an undertaker and failed at that, and finally got a job pottering round, gardener, or gatekeeper, or something—in a lunatic asylum. I'd get him. He'd most likely be a humorist and a philosopher, and he'd help cheer up the Lost Souls' Hotel. I reckon the lost souls would get very fond of him.'

'And would you have drink at Lost Souls?' I asked.

'Yes,' said Mitchell. 'I'd have the best beer and spirits and wine to be had. After tea I'd let every man have just enough to make him feel comfortable and happy, and as good and clever, and innocent and honest as any other man, but no more. But if a poor devil came along in the horrors, with every inch of him jumping, and snakes, and green-eyed yahoos, and flaming-nosed bunyips chasing him, we'd take him in and give him soothing draughts, and nurse him, and watch him, and clear him out with purgatives, and keep giving him nips of good whisky, and, above all, we'd sympathise with him, and tell him that we were worse than he was many a time. We wouldn't tell him what a weak, selfish man he really was. It's remorse that hurries most men to hell, especially in the Bush. When a man firmly believes he is a hopeless case, then there's no hope for him: but let him have doubts and there's a chance. Make him believe that there are far worse cases than his. We wouldn't preach the sin of dissipation to him, no, but we'd try to show him the *folly* of a wasted life. I ought to be able to preach that, God knows.

'And, above all, we'd try to drive out of his head the cursed old popular idea that it's hard to reform—that a man's got to fight a hard battle with himself to get away from drink, pity drunkards can't believe how easy it is. And we'd put it to him straight whether his few hours' enjoyment were worth the days he had to suffer hell for it.'

'And, likely as not,' I said, 'when you'd put him on his feet he'd take the nearest track to the next shanty, and go on a howling spree, and come back to Lost Souls' in a week, raving and worse than ever. What would you do then?'

'We'd take him in again, and build him up some more; and a third or fourth time if necessary. I believe in going right on with a thing once I take it in hand. And if he didn't turn up after the last spree we'd look for him up the scrub and bring him in and let him die on a bed, and make his death as comfortable as possible. I've seen one man die on the ground, and found one dead in the Bush. We'd bury him under a gum and put 'Sacred to the Memory of a Man who Died. Let Him R.I.P.' over him. I'd have a nice little graveyard with gums for tombstones, and I'd have some original epitaphs, I promise you.'

'And how much gratitude would you expect to get out of the Lost Souls' Hotel?' I asked.

'None,' said Mitchell, promptly. 'It wouldn't be a Gratitude Discovery Syndicate. People might say that the Lost Souls' Hotel was a den for kidnapping women and girls to be used as decoys for the purpose of hocussing and robbing bushmen, and the law and retribution might come after me—but I'd fight the thing out. Or they might want to make a KCMG or a god of me, and worship me before they hanged me. I reckon a philanthropist or reformer is lucky if he escapes with a whole skin in the end, let alone his character. But there! Talking of gratitude: it's the fear of ingratitude that keeps thousands from doing good. It's just as paltry and selfish and cowardly as any other fear that curses the world; it's rather more selfish than most fears, in fact, take the fear of being thought a coward, or being considered eccentric, or conceited, or affected, or too good, or too bad, for instance. The man that's always canting about the world's ingratitude has no gratitude owing to him as a rule. Generally the reverse, he ought to be grateful to the world for being let live. He broods over the world's ingratitude until he gets to be a cynic. He sees moonlight shining on it and he passes on with a sour face, whereas, if he took the trouble to step inside he'd most likely find a room full of ruddy firelight, and sympathy and cheerfulness, and kindness, and love, and gratitude. Sometimes, when he's right down on his uppers, and forced to go amongst people and hustle for bread, he gets a lot of surprises at the amount of kindness he keeps running against in the world, and in places where he'd never have expected to find it. But, ah, well! I'm getting maudlin.'

'And you've forgot all about the Lost Souls' Hotel,' I said.

'No, I haven't,' said Mitchell; 'I'd fix that up all right. As soon as I'd got things going smoothly under a man I could trust, I'd tie up every penny I had for the benefit of the concern; get some "white men" for trustees, and take the track again. I'm getting too old to stay long in one place—I'm a lost soul that always got along better in another place. I'm so used to the track that if I was shut up in a house I'd get walking up and down in my room of nights and disturb the folk; and, besides, I'd feel lost and light-shouldered without the swag.'

'So you'd put all your money in the concern?'

'Yes, except a pound or two to go on the track with, for, who knows, I might come along there, dusty and tired, and ragged and hard-up and old, some day, and be very glad of a night's rest at the Lost Souls' Hotel. But I wouldn't let on that I was old Mitchell, the millionaire who founded Lost Souls. They might be too officious, and I hate fuss . . . But it's time to take the track, Harry.'

There came a cool breeze with sunset; we stood up stiffly, shouldered our swags and tucker bags, and pushed on, for we had to make the next water before we camped. We were out of tobacco, so we borrowed some from one of the bullock drivers.

'QUESTION NOT'

ADAM LINDSAY GORDON
(EXCERPT FROM 'YE WEARIE WAYFARER')

Question not, but live and labour till yon goal be won,
Helping every feeble neighbour, seeking help from none;
Life is mostly froth and bubble, two things stand like stone,
Kindness in another's trouble, courage in your own.
Courage, comrades, this is certain, all is for the best—
There are lights behind the curtain—Gentles, let us rest.